LISA M. BITEL is a visiting assistant professor at
the University of Kansas.

Isle of the Saints

Isle of the Saints

Monastic Settlement and Christian Community in Early Ireland

LISA M. BITEL

Cornell University Press

ITHACA AND LONDON

Copyright © 1990 by Cornell University

All rights reserved. Except for brief quotations in a review, this book, or parts thereof, must not be reproduced in any form without permission in writing from the publisher. For information, address Cornell University Press, 124 Roberts Place, Ithaca, New York 14850.

First published 1990 by Cornell University Press.

International Standard Book Number 0-8014-2471-2
Library of Congress Catalog Card Number 90-55118
Printed in the United States of America
*Librarians: Library of Congress cataloging information
appears on the last page of the book.*

♾ The paper in this book meets the minimum requirements
of the American National Standard for Information Sciences—
Permanence of Paper for Printed Library Materials, ANSI Z39.48-1984.

To Peter and Sophie

On the western edge of the world is a certain island called Ireland. . . . From the first, the converted natives of this island were firm in faith, and toward the church of God—but especially to the Roman *curia*—passionate in their devotion. . . . On this island there have been so many men of extreme holiness that it is appropriate to call it "isle of the saints."

—*Life of St. Abbán*

Contents

Contents

Figures

Preface

I BEGAN THIS BOOK WITH ONE QUESTION: WHY DID THE CHRISTIANS of early Ireland support a class of religious professionals devoted to the veneration of dead holy men and women? Many historians have asked similar questions of other medieval societies. Their answers, while pointing the way for my own inquiries, were not fully satisfying to me. Impersonal factors such as political circumstances, kinship ties, the economics of donations, and descriptions of spirituality—the standard rationales for such behavior—helped me to explain medieval institutions and ideals, but did not make the ordinary interactions among the early Irish any more accessible or meaningful.

Historians of monastic communities in Ireland and elsewhere have not fully realized the fundamental religious meaning of the nonreligious ties among medieval people, their spiritual leaders, and their saints. Observers of modern religious communities of any denomination know that a successful congregation consists of far more than a group that meets for formal services. A church or a temple is not just the sum of clergy, congregation, and dogma; many more ties bind members of a lively congregation to one another. This is the case even today, when religion has lost the primacy it once held in Western culture. How much more complex was a Christian community thoroughly infiltrated by saints?

This book is my own solution to the mystery of saints, monks, and their lay neighbors. It combines two traditionally discrete fields, early Irish history and medieval European history. The book also uses the methodologies of several disciplines, including history, anthropology, and archaeology, but never relies on one alone. I have tried to examine both textual representation and historical reality, to tell stories and to present convincing social analysis. Above all, I have tried to transcend the polarity of worldliness and withdrawal that characterizes much of the historiography of Christian monasticism.

This book uses Irish hagiography to explain the monastic world, focusing on the major monasteries that produced the *vitae*. It examines the relationships among saints, monks, and lay people, and the monastic interpretations of those relationships. If it sometimes mixes historical reality with monastic perceptions, then it successfully straddles the most forbidding boundary of all: the great chasm between our world and that of the early Middle Ages.

Many people and organizations contributed to this book, supplying advice, criticism, or resources for my research. I thank the Dublin Institute for Advanced Studies, the Royal Society of the Antiquaries of Ireland, the Library of the Society of the Antiquaries of London, the late James Carney, Vincent Hurley, Charles Thomas, Caroline Bynum, Arthur Kleinman, Peter Brown, Lester Little, John Ackerman, Patrick Geary, Joseph Nagy, Kathleen Kete, Felicity Devlin of the National Museum of Ireland, and Barbara Shortridge and David Brower of the University of Kansas Cartographic Service, who supplied the maps. I am particularly grateful to David Herlihy and John Kelleher. To Peter Cooper Mancall I owe thanks for many ideas, some felicitous prose, several fine photographs in this book, and his cheerful company while trudging around the monastic ruins of Ireland.

LISA M. BITEL

Lawrence, Kansas

Abbreviations

Adomnán: A. O. and M. O. Anderson, eds. *Adomnán's Life of Columba.* London, 1961.

ALI: W. N. Hancock, et al., eds. *The Ancient Laws of Ireland.* 6 vols. Dublin and London, 1865–1901.

AU: Seán mac Airt and Gearóid Mac Niocaill, eds. *The Annals of Ulster to A.D. 1131.* Dublin, 1983.

Bede, HBE: Bede. *The History of the English Church and People (Historia Ecclesiastica gentis Anglorum),* trans. Leo Sherley-Price. London, 1955, rpt. 1982.

CIH: D. A. Binchy, ed. *Corpus Iuris Hibernici.* 6 vols. Dublin, 1978.

DIL: E. G. Quin, gen. ed. *Dictionary of the Irish Language,* compact ed. Dublin, 1983.

FM: John O'Donovan, ed. *The Annals of the Kingdom of Ireland by the Four Masters.* Dublin, 1848–1851.

FO: Whitley Stokes, ed. *Félire Óengusso Céli Dé.* London, 1905.

Gwynn and Purton, "Monastery of Tallaght": E. J. Gwynn and W. J. Purton, eds. "The Monastery of Tallaght." PRIA 29 C (1911), 115–79.

HF: Michael Herren, ed. *Hisperica famina I. The A-Text.* Toronto, 1974.

HVSH: W. W. Heist, ed. *Vitae sanctorum Hiberniae.* Subsidia Hagiographica 28. Brussels, 1965.

IER: *Irish Ecclesiastical Record.*

JCHAS: *Journal of the Cork Historical and Archaeological Society.*

JRSAI: *Journal of the Royal Society of the Antiquaries of Ireland.*

Kenney, *Sources:* J. F. Kenney. *Sources for the Early History of Ireland.* Vol. 1, *Ecclesiastical.* New York, 1929; rpt. Dublin, 1979.

MGH: *Monumenta Germaniae historica,* SS Scriptores. 32 vols. Hanover, 1826–1934.

Migne, PL: J. Migne, ed. *Patrologia Latina.* 221 vols. Paris, 1844–1864.

PBNE: Charles Plummer, ed. *Bethada Náem nÉrenn.* 2 vols. Oxford, 1922

[xiii]

Plummer, *Misc. hag.:* Charles Plummer, ed. *Miscellanea hagiographica Hibernica.* Brussels, 1925.

PRIA: *Proceedings of the Royal Irish Academy.*

PVSH: Charles Plummer, ed. *Vitae sanctorum Hiberniae.* 2 vols. Oxford, 1910.

Stokes, *Lismore:* Whitley Stokes, ed. *Lives of the Saints from the Book of Lismore.* Oxford, 1890.

UJA: *Ulster Journal of Archaeology.*

USMLS, Conchubranus: Ulster Society for Medieval Latin Studies, ed. "The Life of Saint Monenna by Conchubranus," I, *Seanchas Ard Mhacha* 9 (1979), 250–73; II, 10 (1980–81), 117–40; III, 10 (1982), 426–53.

Wasserschleben, *Collectio:* H. Wasserschleben, ed. *Die irische Kanonensammlung.* Leipzig, 1885.

VT: Whitely Stokes, ed. *The Tripartite Life of Patrick and Other Documents Relating to the Saint.* London, 1887.

ZCP: *Zeitschrift für celtische Philologie.*

Isle of the Saints

Rathlin

Doire

Bennchor

Mag Bile
Nóendruimm

Inis Muiredaig

Ard Macha

Dún Lethglas

Cluain Eois

Cell Sléibe

Dub Ileán

Fochard

Fidnach

Achad Fobuir

Mainistir Buite

Cluain Brónaig

Cenannas

Slemain

Mag Eo

Ard Breccáin

Daim
Liac

Ard Ileán

Fobar

Lusca

Cluain Iraird

Cluain Moccu Nóis

Durmag

Rathan

Ára

Cluain Ferta
Brénainn

Lann Ela

Tamlachta

Lothra

Birra

Tempul Crónáin

Cenn Éitag

Glenn Dá Locha

Tír Dá Glas

Inis Cheltra

Ros Cré

Achad Bó

Cell Dara

Cell Da Lua

Achad Úr

Ferna Mór

Inis Chathaig

Liath Mór

Tech Moling

Imlech

Ard Ferta

Cell Íte

Ard Pátraic

Riasc

Lis Mór

Ard Mór

Corcach

Sceleç
Mhichil

0   50 Kilometers

0   50 Miles

1. Monastic communities

[xvi]

INTRODUCTION

The Saints and the Sources

THIS BOOK IS ABOUT MONKS IN IRELAND BETWEEN A.D. 800 AND
1200. Nowhere in barbarian Europe did monks and their saints so
thoroughly dominate the social and spiritual life of the population as in
Ireland. Although the monks' theology taught them to withdraw from
society, they actually lived and worked in the midst of farms and kingly
forts. Their purpose was at once grand and mundane, selfless and self-
serving. The monks helped other people gain access to God through the
mediation of the saints. As keepers of saintly shrines, they controlled
physical and spiritual access to the saints. Since many of the monks were
also priests or bishops, they also blessed people, taught them Christian
doctrine and practice, and performed rituals for them. Monks directed the
powers of the saints to the personal good of their secular neighbors and
allies, even praying for what now seem decidedly secular ends: good harvests, victory in battle, recovery from illness. For all of these services the
monks expected and received land, gifts, and military protection. More
important, they also expected everyone to join together in a Christian
community led by themselves, working to obey God's commandments
and to take his word to heart. The monks wanted nothing less than to
impose a divinely approved agenda on Christians in this life, and to open
for them a route to the next life in paradise.

When Christian proselytizers arrived in Ireland in the fourth or fifth
century, they brought a religion of Roman sensibilities to a remote island
that had never endured Roman invasions and an urban ecclesiastical ideal
to a thoroughly rural milieu. Caesar's generals had gazed longingly across
the sea from Britain, but they never found the opportunity for another

[1]

Celtic conquest. Ireland, unlike Britain, had no Roman governor, no urban centers, no stone-paved roads for troops, no established trade routes into the heart of the Empire.

Ireland instead had between a quarter and a half million people settled along its coasts, rivers, lakeshores, and low uplands. They lived in fortified homesteads or small clusters of huts, and to survive they farmed and herded. Even their warrior leaders were farmers. The sagas, which describe this late Iron Age society, praise the fearless, sword-wielding aristocrats who battled constantly with their neighbors for status and booty. The *Táin Bó Cuailnge*, Ireland's best-known saga, for example, tells of the Connachtmen's great cattle raid on the people of Ulster. Yet once warriors had rustled cattle, they herded them home, where they distributed some to faithful clients; the rest they pastured for themselves, setting their children and slaves to tend them.

Hundreds of such warriors called themselves kings and ruled Ireland in the age of the first Christian missions. Originally leaders of tribes (*túatha*), by the early Middle Ages these men had become kings of territories with geographical boundaries (figure 2). Kingdoms, called by the tribal names of their leaders despite the diverse kin-groups they included, ranged in population during the pre-Norman period from 500 souls to as many as 12,000.[1] Irish kings were not yet the lawgivers who governed other barbarian societies in early Europe; as a later chapter will show, for a long time they remained primarily war leaders and political representatives of their territories, still casting shadows of pagan semidivinity well into the Christian Middle Ages.

As early as the seventh century, however, certain aristocratic dynasties began to force other tribes into submission as client kingdoms, creating more politically unified territories. Some kin-groups soon ruled entire provinces. In particular, several branches of the Uí Néill dynasty of Connacht and Ulster, as well as the Eoganacht tribes of Munster, sought to establish political hegemony over large parts of the island.[2] But everywhere, constantly, one king fought another in order to impose tribute and service on the vanquished. The genealogies of early Ireland tell a thousand stories of vanished princes and lost kingdoms. Entire noble dynasties disappeared as others flourished. And it is no coincidence that the successful dynasts allied themselves with powerful saints and prosperous monastic communities.

1. A. P. Smyth, *Celtic Leinster* (Blackrock, 1982), 4–5.
2. F. J. Byrne, *Irish Kings and High-Kings* (London, 1973), esp. 40–47, 87–105, 165–201.

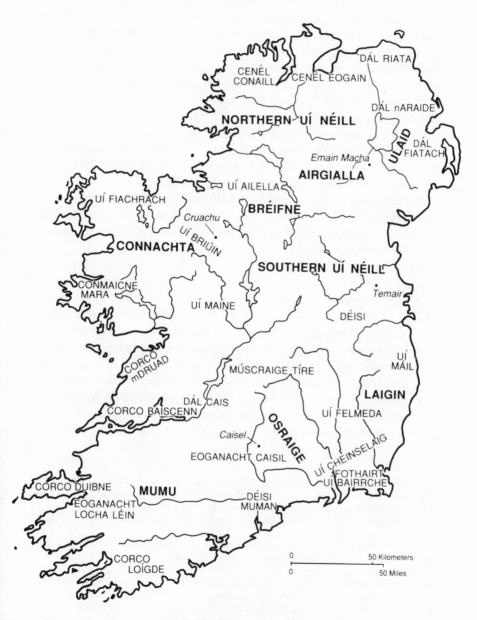

2. Tribal and population groups

[3]

Between the fifth century and the arrival of the Vikings, around 800, Irish society converted, and not only to Christianity. While monk-bishops and monk-priests pursued their missions, the island underwent constant political, social, and demographic change. This was first evident among a flourishing class of native intellectuals—jurists, poets, musicians, and craftsmen—who chose to accept Christian practices and ideas. Until recently, historians and Celticists have insisted that Christian and "native" literati were discrete groups, one producing theology, hagiography, and other Continental-style texts, and the other maintaining a body of ancient oral *senchas* or traditional learning. As proof of the existence of these two groups, scholars point to the thinly disguised gods who roam Irish literature, and the secular laws that conflict with Christian canons.[3]

But missionaries and converts quickly found a place for themselves within the shifting social hierarchy, and intellectuals soon began to combine the *senchas* with imported ideas and scholarship. When, at the end of the sixth century, a monk wrote a Christian prayer called the "Amra Columcille," he chose to preserve it in the Irish language.[4] Within a hundred years or so of the new religion's arrival, Irish monks were already recording the native language on precious vellum. They copied down traditional poetry and prose and laws, as well as more orthodox ecclesiastical texts. Poets became priests and monks became lawyers.[5] They incorporated native laws into Christian canons, and Christian world history into native cosmologies. No Irish scholar, no matter how staunchly Christian, would reject the pagan *senchas*. The scribe of the twelfth-century manuscript of the *Táin* wrote in a famous colophon, "A blessing on everyone who will memorize the Táin faithfully in this form, and who will not put any other form on it."[6] The society soon contained only one

---

3. Myles Dillon, *Early Irish Literature* (Chicago, 1948), xi–3, 51–53; Proinsias Mac Cana, "The Sinless Otherworld of *Immram Brain*," *Ériu* 27 (1976), 95–115; Pádraig Ó Riain, "Traces of Lug in Early Irish Hagiographical Tradition," ZCP 36 (1977), 138–56.

4. P. Grosjean, "L'hymne d'Adamnán à Colum Cille," *Rev. des études indo-europ.* 1 (1938), 8 pp.

5. Donnchadh Ó Corráin, Liam Breatnach, and Aidan Breen, "The Laws of the Irish," *Peritia* 3 (1984), 382–438; Liam Breatnach, "Canon Law and Secular Law in Early Christian Ireland," *Peritia* 3 (1984), 439–59.

6. R. I. Best and M. A. O'Brien, eds., *The Book of Leinster*, vol. 2 (Dublin, 1956), 399. But see the other colophon to the *Táin*, ibid.: "Sed ego qui scripsi hanc historiam aut uerius fabulam quibusdam fidem in hac historia aut fabula non accommodo. Quaedam enim ibi sunt praestrigia demonum. quaedam autem figmenta poetica. quaedam simila uero. quaedam non. Quaedam ad delectationem stultorum."

varied group of scholars that was responsible for keeping all elite traditions.[7]

Although the sixth- and seventh-century Christian penitentials describe Christian communities that tried to live apart from their pagan neighbors, by the eighth century Christian clerics enjoyed high status in the larger society; in fact, a bishop could claim the same social status as a king.[8] Some historians believe that Christian ideas posed a threat to the social hierarchy, since people of low status could become clergy and thus attain positions of power within Christian communities.[9] But when the nobility adopted Christianity and coopted its offices, slaves soon lost the chance to rule as bishops.

The new class of Christian clerics, almost all of them monks, fit well into a society that was already remodeling itself. For centuries, the Irish had organized themselves into a complex hierarchy that included slaves and hostages at the bottom, peasants and fighters in between, and kings at the top; women and children derived their status exclusively from male guardians. But in the three centuries after 432, when Saint Pátraic supposedly brought Christianity to Ireland, this traditional structure changed, in two distinct and related ways. First, as in other barbarian societies, Irish inheritance customs had allowed for multiple male heirs to any piece of property or position of power, including the office of the king. As a result, brothers, uncles, and cousins who could not secure positions of leadership or enough property and clients drifted down through the status hierarchy, displacing those below them.[10] Second, some territorial kings interfered with the tribes of others. Powerful dynasts sometimes imposed their kinsmen as rulers of smaller neighbor kingdoms, or set them up as abbots of prosperous monastic communities. The families that had formerly held these positions of power then displaced weaker kin-groups, and so on.[11] Thus, by the eighth century, the number of the ruling elite was probably shrinking proportionately to the increasing number of their clients and laborers.

---

7. Donnchadh Ó Corráin, "Legend as Critic," in *The Writer as Witness,* ed. Tom Dunne, *Historical Studies* 16 (Cork, 1987), 23–38.

8. D. A. Binchy, ed., *Críth Gablach* (Dublin, 1941), 24.

9. John V. Kelleher, "Early Irish History and Pseudo-History," *Studia Hibernica* 3 (1963), 118.

10. Donnchadh Ó Corráin, *Ireland before the Normans* (Dublin, 1972), 44–45.

11. Donnchadh Ó Corráin, "The Early Irish Churches: Some Aspects of Organisation," in Ó Corráin, ed., *Irish Antiquity* (Cork, 1980), 238–31; Ó Corráin, "Dál Cais—Church and Dynasty," *Ériu* 24 (1973), 52–63.

Although these changes were important, they involved primarily the elite. To people of every class, hearth and family remained the most important social focus. Indeed, the network of relationships that linked one family to another formed the building blocks of Irish society. The family was the basic landholding unit, producing the multiple heirs who caused so much trouble at elite levels. A person's identity derived entirely from his or her kin. Kinless men were landless outlaws. Family—whether the nuclear unit or the great Christian family of all believers—was the model for all social organization.[12] Yet family, too, was changing; for example, under monastic influence, laws regarding family control of property became progressively less restrictive during the early Middle Ages.[13]

The arrival of the Scandinavians around 800 only added momentum to the changes already taking place in this dynamic society. The Vikings came when population growth and dynastic struggles were already causing more conflict than ever before.[14] Despite the protests of monastic annalists, the Viking invasions did not devastate the farms, forts, and monasteries of Ireland. Although the Vikings' initial raids came as a shock, the invaders destroyed no more churches than the unruly Irish themselves, and were not responsible for any permanent disruption of learning or craftsmanship in the monasteries. They merely took part in the already fierce and endless struggle between kingdoms, playing the side that profited them best. The saints' lives hardly even mention the arrival or presence of the Vikings. By counterattack and negotiation, the Irish managed to limit Scandinavian settlement to a series of coastal trading posts. From these fortified ports, the Vikings expanded Irish horizons to include the other islands and shores of the North Sea, helping to open up the economy of Ireland. In the meantime, many of them engaged in trade with the Irish, converted to Christianity, and married Irish women.[15]

Around 900, after the worst of the Viking attacks was over, a combination of causes brought population growth. Kings began to gain enough strength to impose order on their clients, limiting somewhat the destruction of life and property resulting from a lack of centralized authority. The

12. D. A. Binchy, "Secular Institutions," in Myles Dillon, ed., *Early Irish Society* (Dublin, 1954), 58–59.

13. L. Bitel, "Women's Donations to the Churches in Early Ireland," JRSAI 114 (1984), 9–10; Ó Corráin, *Ireland before the Normans*, 44; Jack Goody, *The Development of the Family and Marriage in Europe* (Cambridge, 1983).

14. Liam de Paor, *The Peoples of Ireland* (South Bend, Ind., 1986), 77–80.

15. A. T. Lucas, "Irish-Norse Relations: Time for a Reappraisal?" JCHAS 71 (1966), 62–75; D. A. Binchy, "The Passing of the Old Order," *Proceedings of the International Congress of Celtic Studies* (Dublin, 1962), 127–28.

weather also improved slightly. The little climatic optimum gradually raised the temperature on the average about 1° C higher than today, thus expanding the bounds of arable and lengthening the season by several weeks.[16] A well-fed population produced more babies. Most important, no great plagues attacked Ireland between 700 and 1300.[17] In short, mortality at prosperous population centers, such as king's forts and monasteries, must have decreased. Bad years still left people hungry, aristocratic raiders still murdered each other, people all around collapsed from mysterious ailments. But the changes, taken together over a long period of time, most likely allowed for increase in the size of population islands.

This society of fighters, poets, monks, and farmers remained apart from, yet a part of, the rest of medieval Christendom. While the Irish had been ignorant of the capital of the Caesars, they looked to the pope's Rome as the center of the Christian world. Even before the Vikings reminded them of the lands beyond their shores, the Irish had sent traders, evangelists, and pilgrims to Britain and the Continent. Some, such as Columbán, Johannes Scottus, and Eriugena, went to stay; others returned, such as less famous scholars with their heads full of foreign ideas and the merchants who brought Gaulish coins and wines. One import the travelers never brought home was Benedict's *Rule;* the Irish continued to interpret monastic ideals in an independent way that earned both the respect and the distrust of their Continental brothers and sisters.[18]

Despite its peculiar position on the fringe of barbarian Europe, Ireland is the perfect subject for a study of societies struggling with the lengthy process of Christianization. Not many historians have considered the monks of early Ireland. Although excellent books have documented monastic spirituality, organization, and property, as well as social and political relationships between monks and laics, these works have tended to treat the better-known communities of France and Germany.[19] A few Irish

16. David Herlihy, "Ecological Conditions and Demographic Change," in Richard De Molen, ed., *One Thousand Years* (Boston, 1974), 13.
17. J. C. Russell, "That Earlier Medieval Plague in the British Isles," *Viator* 7 (1976), 65–78; William P. MacArthur, "The Identification of Some Pestilences Recorded in the Irish Annals," *Irish Historical Studies* 7 (1951), 199–200.
18. For a selection of recent studies on this topic, see the many articles by Schäferdick, Prinz, et al. in Heinz Löwe, ed., *Die Iren und Europa im früheren Mittelalter* (Stuttgart, 1982), 1:171–422.
19. On the social and political relations between religious and secular communities see these classic works: F. Graus, *Volk, Herrscher und Heiliger im Reich der Merowinger: Studien zur Hagiographie der Merowingerzeit* (Prague, 1965); Friedrich Prinz, *Frühes Mönchtum im Frankenreich: Kultur und Gesellschaft in Gallien, den Rheinlanden und Bayern am Beispiel der monastischen Entwicklung (4. bis. 8. Jahrhundert)* (Munich and Vienna, 1965). For more recent

historians have studied the monasteries of pre-Norman Ireland, but they have not focused on the social context of monastic communities.[20]

Yet the Irish texts have much to contribute to our understanding of monasticism and of the early Middle Ages in general. Thanks to the early Christianization of the learned classes, an extensive collection of saints' lives, secular laws, secular tales and sagas, poetry, genealogies, ecclesiastical canons, martyrologies, and monastic annals all exist for the period, although Irish scribes produced none of the *diploma* so common in Continental libraries.[21] Monks composed or recorded almost all of these texts beginning in the seventh and eighth centuries and frequently revised or glossed them in succeeding years; only ten of Ireland's earliest manuscripts predate the year 1000.[22] Besides the plentiful written sources,

---

examples, see Barbara H. Rosenwein, *Rhinoceros Bound: Cluny in the Tenth Century* (Philadelphia, 1982), including a detailed review of Cluniac historiography, 3–29; Penelope Johnson, *Prayer, Patronage, and Power: The Abbey of La Trinité, Vendôme, 1032–1187* (New York, 1981); Constance Bouchard, *Sword, Miter, and Cloister: Nobility and the Church in Burgundy, 980–1198* (Ithaca, N.Y., 1987). A few works have begun to probe the spiritual meaning of clerical social networks; see Lester K. Little, *Religious Poverty and the Profit Economy in Medieval Europe* (Ithaca, N.Y., 1978); André Vauchez, *La spiritualité du Moyen Age occidental, VIIIᵉ–XIIᵉ siècles* (Vendôme, 1975).

20. The two major monographs on Irish monasteries are John Ryan, *Irish Monasticism: Origins and Early Development* (Dublin, 1931); and Kathleen Hughes, *The Church in Early Irish Society* (London, 1966).

On monastic culture and learning, see Bernhard Bischoff, "Il monachesimo Irlandese nei suoi rapporti col continente," in Bischoff, *Mittelalterliche Studien: Ausgewählte Aufsätze zur Schriftkunde und Literaturgeschichte*, vol. 1 (Stuttgart, 1966), 195–205; also the articles in Löwe, *Die Iren und Europa*, 1:425–548, 2:549–732.

On the material context of Irish monasticism, see, for example, M. J. O'Kelly, "Church Island near Valencia, Co. Kerry," PRIA 57 C (1958), 159–94; Michael Herity, "The Building and Layout of Early Irish Monasteries before the Year 1000," *Monastic Studies* 14 (1983), 247–84; Vincent Hurley, "Additions to the Map of Monastic Ireland," JCHAS 85 (1980), 52–65. See also the series of county archaeological surveys currently being produced in Ireland, such as Brian Lacy et al., eds., *Archaeological Survey of County Donegal* (Lifford, 1983).

For recent analyses of hagiographic material see Máire Herbert, *Iona, Kells and Derry: The History and Hagiography of the Monastic Familia of Columba* (Oxford, 1988); Richard Sharpe, "Vitae S. Brigidae: The Oldest Texts," *Peritia* 1 (1982), 81–106; Kim McCone, "Brigit in the Seventh Century: A Saint with Three Lives?" *Peritia* 1 (1982), 107–45. Charles Doherty has made use of the economic and social evidence: Doherty, "Some Aspects of Hagiography as a Source for Irish Economic History," *Peritia* 1 (1982), 300–328.

21. Kenney, *Sources*, is the definitive bibliography of ecclesiastical sources. See also Kathleen Hughes, *Early Christian Ireland: An Introduction to the Sources* (Ithaca, N.Y., 1972); F. J. Byrne, "Seventh-Century Documents," IER 108 (1967), 164–82; Donnchadh Ó Corráin, "A Handlist of Publications on Early Irish Society," *Historical Studies* 10 (1976), 172–203. On *diploma*: Wendy Davies, "The Latin Charter-Tradition in West Britain, Brittany, and Ireland," in D. Whitelock, D. Dumville, and R. McKitterick, eds., *Ireland in Early Medieval Europe* (Cambridge, 1982), 258–80.

22. Kenney, *Sources*, 9.

archaeological evidence adds to the picture of the monks' world. Many early medieval sites remain visible and accessible in Ireland, where industrial development has not yet erased all traces of earlier centuries (see Appendix A for corresponding Irish and English place names).

Hagiography, written by and for monks, provides more evidence for the study of Irish monasticism than any other type of source, written or material.[23] Although monks produced many kinds of texts, they wrote more saints' lives than anything else. Over the course of six centuries, monastic hagiographers composed the *vitae* of hundreds of saints. Almost all of them are anonymous; almost none are securely datable to a specific century. Most of the lives, written in both Latin and Irish, date from 800 to 1200, the period after the first Viking raids and before the arrival of the Normans (see Appendix B for variant names of saints).[24] The majority survive in three great codices: the Salamanca codex, containing the oldest recensions of many lives; the Kilkenny codex; and the Codex Insulensis. Other *vitae* are scattered among late medieval manuscripts in Ireland and elsewhere. Almost all of the saints' lives have been edited and published.[25]

The saints' lives form a coherent canon, bound by common characters, themes, style, and purpose. Saints, kings, and their contemporaries in one *vita* crop up in another; similar episodes are repeated in different forms in different lives. Hagiographers drew from native saga, Continental *vitae*, the Bible, and anything else they had handy, including other Irish saints' lives.[26] They filled the lives with details designed to convince listeners and

---

23. The major bibliographies of *vitae* are Kenney, *Sources*, 288–521; Hughes, *Early Christian Ireland*, 129–47; R. I. Best, *Bibliography of Irish Philology and Manuscript Literature: Publications, 1913–1941* (Dublin, 1969), 152–62; Rolf Baumgarten, *Bibliography of Irish Linguistics and Literature, 1942–71* (Dublin, 1986), 387–600; Plummer, *Misc. hag.*, 171–271; Michael Lapidge and Richard Sharpe, *A Bibliography of Celtic-Latin Literature, 400–1200* (Dublin, 1985), 83–87, 101–30.

24. Close analysis of the political detail in each *vita* may help to date various recensions, as in Charles Doherty, "The Historical Value of the Medieval Lives of Máedóc of Ferns," 2 vol., unpublished master's thesis (University College, Dublin, 1971); also Herbert, *Iona, Kells and Derry*. The dating of the canon of *vitae* is a matter of great debate. See Kenney, *Sources*, 294–95; Pádraig Ó Riain, "Towards a Methodology in Early Irish Hagiography," *Peritia* 1 (1982), 146–59; Kim McCone, "An Introduction to Early Irish Saints' Lives," *Maynooth Review* 11 (1984), 26–59; Doherty, "Some Aspects of Hagiography"; also Richard Sharpe's forthcoming book on the Codex Salmanticensis, *An Introduction to "Vitae Sanctorum Hiberniae."*

25. The major collections of Irish saints' lives are HVSH, PBNE, PVSH, and Stokes, *Lismore*; important lives edited singly include Cogitosus' life of Brigit in Migne, PL 72; Adomnán; the lives of Pátraic by Tírechán and Muirchú included in Ludwig Bieler, ed., *Patrician Texts in the Book of Armagh* (Dublin, 1979); Whitely Stokes, ed., *The Tripartite Life of Patrick and Other Documents Relating to the Saint* (London, 1887).

26. Baudouin de Gaiffier, "Hagiographie et historie: Quelques aspects du problème," in *La Storiografia altomedievale*, vol. 1 (Centro Italiano di studi sull'alto medioevo, April 10–16, 1969), 139–66; Ludwig Bieler, "Hagiography and Romance in Medieval Ireland," *Medievalia*

readers of the authenticity of their tales. Although the *vitae* treat fifth-, sixth-, and seventh-century saints, the stories are set in later contexts more familiar to the hagiographers and their readers. The hagiographers' efforts thus provide dense incidental information for the historian, interpreted from a specifically monastic view of the early medieval world. Other sources may explain development and change in early Ireland; but only the saints' lives, covering roughly four hundred years, shed light on the *longue durée*. The traditional daily occupations, the institutions, the material environment, and the mentalities of the early Irish all leap to life in the *vitae*.

The saints preside over the *vitae* as they presided over the spiritual consciousness of the medieval monks, and indeed, over the chapters of this book. They provide symbols, guidance, and objects of devotion. However, the hagiographers never sought to hold up their saints as models of attainable behavior; they clearly believed that no one, not even a highly virtuous monk, could actually become a saint. Saints were born, not made; sanctity, like nobility, was evident from birth.[27] Men and women were saints in their lifetimes, performing miracles by the hundred and freely using their powers to benefit their allies and devotees. The saints, through their monks, did more than provide spiritual satisfaction. They also guided their followers to settlement sites, economic prosperity, social order, good health, and the afterlife. The saints penetrated every aspect of a Christian's conscious and unconscious life, from the desperate hope for a good harvest to the rents paid an ecclesiastical landlord, from the prayer mumbled in a moment of panic to the social constraints on warfare.

The heroes of hagiography were identifiable by their standard virtues and holy powers. They were missionaries and confessors, not the vulnerable martyrs of the Continent. "Now there are three kinds of martyrdom," wrote a seventh-century Irish scholar, "white martyrdom, and green [*glas*] martyrdom, and red martyrdom."[28] By this he meant renunciation

---

et Humanistica n.s. 6 (1975), 13–24; W. W. Heist, "Irish Saints' Lives, Romance, and Cultural History," *Medievalia et Humanistica* n.s. 6 (1975), 25–40; Felim Ó Briain, "Saga Themes in Irish Hagiography," in Séamus Pender, ed., *Féilsgríbhinn Torna* (Cork, 1947), 33–42.

27. De Gaiffier has suggested the opposite of Continental saints ("Hagiographie et historie," 141); however, J.-C. Poulin has shown that the saints of the early medieval Continent, while providing virtuous models for the clergy, were primarily protectors and miracle workers to be admired, not imitated, by the laity: *L'idéal de sainteté dans l'Aquitaine Carolingienne d'après les sources hagiographiques (750–950)* (Quebec, 1975), esp. 99–131.

28. Whitely Stokes and John Strachan, eds., *Thesaurus Paleohibernicus*, vol. 2 (London, 1903), 246–47; Clare Stancliffe, "Red, White and Blue Martyrdom," in Whitelock et al., *Ireland in Early Medieval Europe*, 21–46.

of the secular world, penance and self-mortification, and death. While the Irish saints never achieved red martyrdom, they excelled at the other two. Many were missionaries to the pagan interior of the island and were renowned for their extreme asceticism. Most of them lived and worked during the sixth and seventh centuries, when there were still converts to be won and room for new churches. All of them built ecclesiastical settlements, and all were bishops, abbots, or abbesses; some, such as Pátraic, were responsible for the creation of scores of churches and the recruitment of hundreds of monks and nuns. This is what made an Irish saint: He or she was a pioneer on the early Christian frontier.

The Irish saints did not betray the idiosyncrasies that made a late medieval Continental saint such as Francis so attractive. Some Irish saints emerged as distinct personalities, such as forgetful Cainnech and irritable Munnu; but these characteristics were symbolic and literary rather than genuine. Many saints shared traits. Most holy men and women were aristocrats, educated people, political leaders, child prodigies. In some cases, originally distinct saints may even have been conflated into the same miracle worker of hagiography.[29] A hagiographer's purpose was not to construct an accurate biography, but to overwhelm the reader or listener with the saint's abundant virtues and talents.

Saintly perfection in the *vitae* had a purpose. Virtue manifested power, specifically a saint's power to intercede with God for his or her allies. Monastic writers demonstrated clearly that saintly perfection made miracles possible.[30] Fintan of Dún Bleisce performed so many wonders that his hagiographer did not even bother to narrate them. "What was the wonder?" the writer asked, since Fintan followed Christ's humble example of washing the feet of his brothers and displayed such great virtue that "he seemed beyond the nature of a man." The manifestation of the saint's perfection on earth was his temporal rule of monasteries and lay congregations; his rule ultimately enabled him to command God to protect "these and all whom you have engaged in worship via us."[31]

Hagiographers taught two vital lessons. The first was the power of the saints and their value to surrounding society; they described this lesson through the saints' miracles and superhuman traits. The second was that the monks inherited the saints' powers and functions and became equally

---

29. Pádraig Ó Riain, "Cainnech alias Columcille, Patron of Ossory," in Pádraig de Brun et al., eds., *Folia Gadelica* (Cork, 1983), 20–35; Ó Riain, "St. Findbarr: A Study in a Cult," JCHAS 72 (1976), 63–82.

30. Poulin, *L'idéal de sainteté*, 108–15; Clare Stancliffe, *St. Martin and His Hagiographer: History and Miracle in Sulpicius Severus* (Oxford, 1983), 232–47.

31. HVSH, 117, 353.

indispensable to their allies. The monks promoted the saints and their powers because they had the job of extending that fifth-, sixth-, and seventh-century influence into the years beyond. The propagandists of the saints made it clear that their heroes were mighty men and women who became the patrons of certain dynasties, territories, and, most important, monasteries.

The saints were deputies to God. The monks were heirs, spiritually, materially, and sometimes even by blood, of the saints. If secular folk would be Christians, they had little choice but to accept the roles of pilgrim to the monastic enclosure and ally or client of the monks. By doing so, lay people became part of the family of the saint, creating a formal connection with a supernatural protector that was at once social, economic, political, and profoundly religious. The connections between God, the saints, the monks, and the laics were so sophisticated and complex that they often caused crossed loyalties and conflicting responsibilities. But at their source was the special link between the saints and their disciples, the monks.

This book begins its examination of saints and monks with a look at the natural and supernatural environment that surrounded monastic settlements. The early medieval world was hostile to human survival; as a result, the monks learned to seek out places on the landscape that offered natural resources, but that were also inherently holy and protective. They depended on the saints and the traditional methods of their pre-Christian ancestors to guide them in choosing settlement sites and coaxing the land to feed them. Monks also relied on their neighbors, intentionally building their monasteries near other settlements; only the rare hermit lived in wild isolation. The monks yearned not to escape, but to reorganize the settled landscape with themselves and their shrines at its center.

Monks built sacred enclosures that looked inward upon the relics of the patron saint, but also outward to the lay people they served. Safe within their walls, the monks extended the protection of the saint to secular allies outside. Monasteries attracted visitors, temporary and permanent, and became one of the demographic focuses of a society that lacked towns. Traders, pilgrims, political leaders, poets, and all kinds of wanderers passed through the monk's gates.

Monks created social architecture that mimicked the concentric walls around their enclosures. They bound themselves to secular folk with a network of social relationships aimed at mutual support of both a material and a spiritual nature: the kin-style ties of the religious elite; ties between monks and their clients and tenants; alliances with local political leaders;

relationships with pilgrims and patients who visited the monastery; and contact between the monastic settlements spread over the island.

All of the many kinds of relationships described throughout this book had spiritual dimensions. The job of the monks was not merely to pray and perform parish duties, but to act as saints and thus protect and heal, provide refuge, dispense divine justice; in effect, to approach God, through the saints, for the benefit of all. Theirs was an admirable and critical mission; to assure peasants and warriors alike of the divine plan behind the failed crops, the demons, the plagues, the constant petty warfare. The responsibility of lay people was not just to placate the saints and to support the monks while they prayed, blessed, and healed. By participating in complex social relationships with the monks, they acted out their faith in the powers of God and his saints and in a specifically Christian world to come. For as everyone—monk, laic, and saint—realized, the most trivial of interactions made a spiritual statement that reverberated throughout the entire network.

PART ONE

SETTLEMENT

CHAPTER ONE

Monastic Settlement

WHEN THE IRISH SAINTS DECIDED WHERE TO BUILD THEIR MON-
astic settlements, they took account of both practical and spiritual
priorities. They chose places with ample natural resources where people
were already living or had lived before. When the saints chose their *loca*, as
the hagiographers called them, they also searched for holy places. Practical
considerations of soil type, access, inheritance, and land tenure were no
more important than the visibly and inherently holy quality of certain
places.

The settlement process was complicated and lengthy. It began with
Pátraic and other early missionaries and continued throughout the Middle
Ages whenever monks built or rebuilt monasteries. The hagiographers
told it as a simpler story: They described how, long ago, the saints had
chosen ecclesiastical sites according to God's arbitrary will, expressed by
angelic messengers or other miraculous signs. The hagiographers used
their stories to explain to their monastic brothers and sisters why they
lived where they did. The saints reorganized the landscape to suit Christian perceptions and then the monks reinterpreted the settlement process,
as the *vitae* of the ninth century and later show. The saints' lives reflect not
the concerns of settlers on the sixth-century Christian frontier, but those
of monks who lived between 800 and 1200.

For example, the twelfth-century life of Déclán described how a fifth-
century saint solved the problem of selecting a site that was spiritually
appropriate and that could efficiently support a community of monks.
Déclán, divinely guided, decided to settle on an island called Ard Mór.
When the saint and his troop of disciples reached the mainland beach,

they found that the local inhabitants had stolen all the available boats. The frightened monks wanted to move elsewhere. They knew that they needed to be able to travel back and forth to the mainland to survive, especially after Déclán had died and was no longer there to protect them in person. They made a tactful suggestion to their leader:

> We implore you with heart and voice to desert that island, or to ask the Father in the name of the Son through unity with the Holy Spirit . . . that this channel should be thrust out of its place in the sea, and in its place before your settlement should be level ground. Anyway, the place cannot be well or easily inhabited because of that channel. Therefore, there cannot be a settlement there; on the contrary, there could scarcely be a church there.

Déclán, reluctant to yield his holy site, testily suggested that God must know whether or not Ard Mór could support a community. Still, they all prayed and Déclán, with Moses-like aplomb, struck the ground with his staff, whereupon the waters receded. Déclán turned Ard Mór from desolate island to habitable and accessible peninsula.[1]

Déclán's hagiographer noted two beneficial ecological effects of the miracle. First, the land formerly beneath the sea channel became the best land of the peninsula. Second, a freshwater river that had cut the island in two now flowed out to sea, creating an estuary perfect for settlement and agriculture. Although the hagiographer did not note it explicitly, his tale also demonstrated the monks' desire to dwell near other settlements; the once remote island became linked to the previously existing secular community and inhospitable neighbors became ardent supporters of Ard Mór. The monastery flourished, as its extensive remains show. Monks there understood how to resolve conflicts between their need for natural resources and available tenure and their saintly patron's quest for a holy site.

Not every community was lucky enough to find such a favorable site. It was not always obvious to the monks whether a place would support them materially and spiritually. One of the clearest signs of a suitable site was previous or contemporary settlement, including earlier religious use. Where generations had farmed and worshipped, monks knew that they too could survive. Monastic settlers who founded successful communities learned how to spot these signs and how to exploit the chosen site with agriculture, settlement, and ritual. Later monks benefited from their acute reading of the landscape and continued to apply the same techniques

1. PVSH 2:43–44.

when acquiring new property. With all the resources of a regular settlement plus the special protection offered by a recognized holy site, successful monastic settlements became important focuses of social, economic, political, cultural, and spiritual life in early Ireland.

Natural Environment

The unique natural environment of Ireland limited the monks' choice of settlement sites, as it had the choice of their pre-Christian ancestors. No monastic writers set out to categorize climate, soils, flora, and fauna, or to consider how the environment affected their lives and their settlement. Scribes penned couplets in the margins of manuscripts praising the songs of birds, the sound of the wind among the elms, the bounty of fruits and nuts outside the hermit's hut. But this was merely the edge of nature, close to monastic settlements, saluted in romantic formulae. Monks also prayed for protection against the bitterness of the wind, the thunder, and fog-shrouded demons.[2] The monks were too familiar with the land's beauties and its hostilities. They took it for granted that skies were cloudy, that trees were bent by the wind, that people had to live in huts with drains around the walls so that the rainwater dripping through the roof would not make a bog of the floor.[3]

Foreigners pointed out the island's most influential environmental features to Anglo-Saxon and Norman readers. The potential bounty of the Irish landscape seemed almost limitless to Bede, who wrote enthusiastically of Ireland's position and climate. "Snow rarely lies longer than three days," he explained, "so that there is no need to store hay in summer for winter use or to build stables for beasts." Besides fodder for domestic animals, the land "abounds in milk and honey, and there is no lack of vines, fish, and birds, while red deer and roe are widely hunted."[4] Bede had never visited Ireland, and probably got his information from a homesick Irish monk.

Four hundred years later, Gerald of Wales also acknowledged the fertility of green Ireland but complained that "this country more than any other suffers from storms of wind and rain." Rainstorms made soils soft

2. Gerard Murphy, *Early Irish Lyrics* (Oxford, 1956), 4, 6, 66–68, 10–18, 24, 26.
3. M. J. O'Kelly, "Monastic Sites in the West of Ireland," *Scottish Archaeological Forum* 5 (1973), 7. See also Murphy, *Early Irish Lyrics,* 20–21, for a ninth-century poem in which a monk speaks of gazing longingly "dochum nime nél," "toward cloudy heaven."
4. Bede, HBE 1:2.

and soggy in Ireland, limited the size of grain kernels, crushed trees to the ground, and raised tempests on the seas. Writing from the driest coast of the island, he moaned that "you will scarcely see even in the summer three consecutive days of really fine weather."[5]

Gerald was right about the rain. Because of its position at the "edge of the world," as St. Columbán put it, Ireland enjoys mild temperatures but suffers heavy winds and rains. On some parts of the island the rain falls steadily for more than two hundred days each year, and the sun averages only an hour's appearance each winter day. Hills and mountains ring the coast and contain the water that constantly washes down the eskers and drumlins, collecting in every gully and plain (Fig. 3).[6] Water is always in the air and on the ground, bringing the damp into bodies, clothing, crops, housing. Things that absorb moisture flourish; those that do not erode or rot.

As a result, early Ireland was no breadbasket. When Gerald toured the countryside he saw more pasturage than crops, partly because of the lack of agricultural technology, but largely because of the character of the soil itself. Only a third of the modern Republic's land is suitable for a wide range of uses, including agriculture and pasturage. One-fifth consists of mountains or hills useful only for rough grazing; almost a third is of limited use because of poor drainage. Bogs have spread over some of the uplands as well as the central lowlands, accounting for about 7 percent of the surface (Fig. 4).[7]

Conditions in the pre-Norman period were different in several ways. Forest covered much more of the arable included in today's wide-use range soils, but plant cover also probably reduced the amount of present-day shallow and eroded soil. Also, premodern tillage, with its constant, labor-intensive attention to artificial drainage, allowed for more extended use of wetter soils than is possible with modern methods. However, in general, less arable probably existed in the Middle Ages than today.[8] As the eighth-century legal text *Tír Cumaile* recognized, even good land needed to be cleared and manured; the rest of the island was uncultivable because of marsh, mountain, or bog.[9]

5. Gerald of Wales, *The History and Topography of Ireland* (London, 1982), 33–35, 53–54, 58 (chaps. 2, 3, 26, 34).

6. P. K. Rohan, *The Climate of Ireland* (Dublin, 1975); E. E. Evans, *The Personality of Ireland: Habitat, Heritage, and History* (Cambridge, 1973), 18–25, 29, 38, 114n.

7. M. J. Gardiner and P. Ryan, "A New Generalised Soil Map of Ireland and Its Land-Use Interpretation," *Irish Journal of Agricultural Research* 9 (1969), 95–109.

8. Ibid., 108.

9. Gearóid Mac Niocaill, "Tír cumaile," *Ériu* 22 (1971), 81–86.

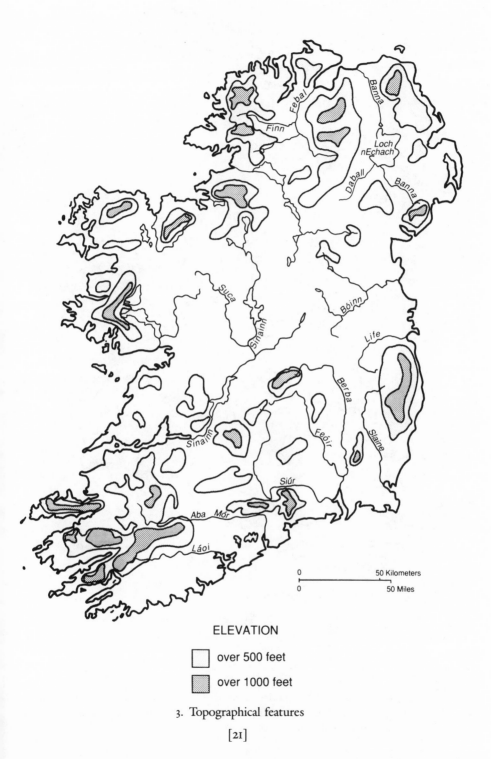

ELEVATION

☐ over 500 feet

▨ over 1000 feet

3. Topographical features

[21]

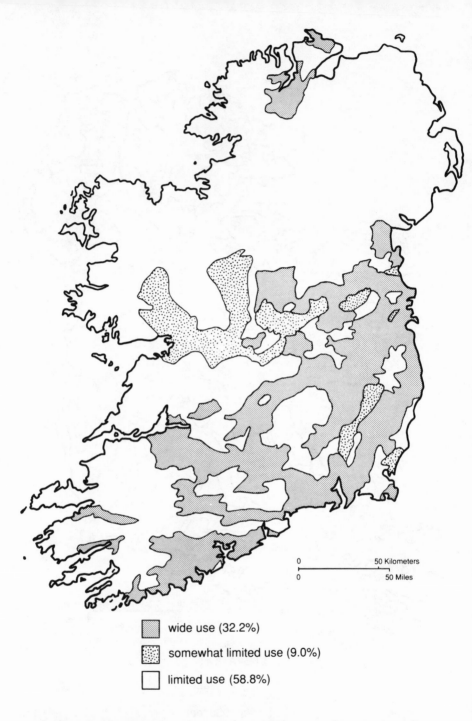

wide use (32.2%)

somewhat limited use (9.0%)

limited use (58.8%)

4. Agricultural use of soil in modern Ireland. After M. J. Gardiner and P. Ryan, "A New Generalised Soil Map of Ireland and Its Land-Use Interpretation," *Irish Journal of Agricultural Research* 9 (1969), 95–109.

Pace Bede, the Irish had never enjoyed the land's gifts without working for them. Nature allowed them little innovation or variation in land use and settlement, which were characterized above all by continuity. Over some four thousand years, they developed agricultural techniques with which to wrest a living from fields and pastures. The practices of neolithic and Bronze Age farmers had gradually drained the light hillside soils of nutrients and allowed the spread of blanket bog on the uplands, sending some settlers of later periods down toward the valleys. There they repeatedly cleared the land, but never successfully prevented the readvance of trees and scrub until about the fourth century. Shortly before Pátraic's arrival, in the mid-fifth century, farmers began once more to hack woods and scrub out of the fertile soil. This time a continuous occupation by a fairly stable population finally prevented forest regeneration in many small areas.[10]

By the eighth century, people had established farms on rolling arable, around estuaries, and along the shores of rivers, lakes, and sea. Elsewhere those with isolated estates and those in tiny rural communities struggled to snatch patches of ground from the encroaching wilderness. Especially in the east and south, the land was dotted with enclosed fields of wheat, rye, barley, and oats; wherever occupation stopped, even briefly, the trees returned.[11] Cattle roamed everywhere grain would not grow; sheep also grazed on the scrubby hillsides. Pigs were left to root in the woods. In fact, animal husbandry probably supported the majority of early Irish farmers.[12] Wherever people kept domestic animals they also hopefully planted small vegetable gardens, set up fenced enclosures for their stock, and built shelter for themselves. Permanent settlement had spread over enough land by the seventh century that certain trees were growing scarce, warranting laws that reserved their cutting to the owners of the land on which they grew.[13]

10. Archaeologists have suggested that monks were responsible for the expansion of agriculture and clearance of forest. See F. H. A. Aalen, "Perspectives on the Irish Landscape in Prehistory and History," in Terence Reeves-Smyth and Fred Hamond, eds., *Landscape Archaeology in Ireland* (Oxford, 1983), 365–67; de Paor, *Peoples of Ireland*, 75. But compare the evidence of pollen analysis: M. O'Connell, "The Developmental History of Scragh Bog, Co. Westmeath, and the Vegetational History of Its Hinterland," *New Phytologist* 85 (1980), 301–19, esp. 316.

11. Aalen, "Perspectives on the Irish Landscape," 362–65.

12. PVSH 1:205. See also Michael Ó Sé, "Old Irish Cheese and Other Milk Products," JCHAS 53 (1948), 82–87; Finbar McCormick, "Dairying and Beef Production in Early Christian Ireland: The Faunal Evidence," in Reeves-Smyth and Hamond, *Landscape Archaeology*, 253–62; J. O'Loan, "Livestock in the Brehon laws," *Agricultural History Review* 7 (1959), 65–74; A. T. Lucas, "Cattle in Ancient and Medieval Irish Society," *O'Connell School Union Record 1938–58* (Dublin, 1958).

13. CIH 1:202–203; ALI 4:148–49.

The poor and often hilly or soggy quality of soil demanded agricultural equipment adapted to the terrain. In many areas the spade and the foot remained the favored tools from neolithic times through the nineteenth century. The spade was suitable for small communities and isolated farmsteads that could not afford a plow and team. Many farmers used a light, wheelless plow. Even a light plow was useless on many hilly fields or small wet patches where the turf had to be cut deeply and turned over to drain properly.

A heavy, wheelless plow had been in use in Ireland since about the fourth century; in the sixth century it acquired a moldboard to turn the sticky soil as it created furrows. But the heavy plow was difficult to use except where the combination of human and animal resources and soil type was appropriate. The community had to have enough cooperating members to make available large patches of arable, since the plow required long strips of land for its cumbersome team of oxen to work most efficiently. The soil had to be fairly flat and neither too light and dry nor too heavy and wet. Most farmers could not afford the expensive plow or the oxen to pull it.[14] In several places the saints' lives mention ironclad plows, suggesting that some wealthy monastic communities had both the right type of soil and the right equipment to make the most of it. But episodes in the lives also show poorer farmers attempting to borrow from the monks the animals and equipment that they themselves could not afford. The secular laws also assume that individual families were unable to get plowing equipment.[15]

Limited by weather, natural resources, and inadequate equipment even on the best of sites, monks and their secular neighbors frequently failed to coax sufficient food from the land. The *Annals of Inisfallen* called 919 "a year of scarcity and hunger," a description that applied to many a year.[16] The hagiographers recorded chronic food shortages among monastic communities. Ciarán and Cóemgen, according to their hagiographers, both lived in settlements that could not feed themselves and had to disperse. Cóemgen later moved to Glenn Dá Locha, where he lived on a hermit's diet of water and herbs; when an angel came to suggest that he

14. Evans, *Personality of Ireland*, 38–40; D. A. Binchy, ed., *Críth Gablach* (Dublin, 1941), 4, 5, 6.

15. HVSH, 169, 240–41; Binchy, *Críth Gablach*, 4. The value of a hoe to a farming community is made clear by the heavy penalties imposed upon a monk who damaged one: Ludwig Bieler, ed., *The Irish Penitentials* (Dublin, 1975), 64.

16. Seán Mac Airt, ed., *The Annals of Inisfallen* (Dublin, 1951), 146–47; see also 176–77, 186–87.

5. View of Glenn Dá Locha showing valley location. The church, called St. Kevin's Kitchen, was probably built in the eleventh or twelfth century; its tower was added later.

form a cenobitic community down the valley, Cóemgen refused on the grounds that the valley could never support one (Fig. 5).[17]

Farmers and herders were as adept as Cóemgen at estimating how many the land could feed and how many would tax its undependable yields. When Saint Monenna led a group of nuns to live in the woods at the future Cell Sléibe, the local swineherd was amazed that they had brought no supplies with them. He feared that the women would eat the nuts and bark they found in the woods and deprive his pigs of their feed. Monenna's community hovered at the edge of starvation for many years, even though the nuns learned to till the fields and keep cows.[18]

17. PVSH 1:246.
18. USMLS, Conchubranus 1:256–67, 260–63; 3:428–33; see also HVSH, 115, 211, 277; PBNE 1:217–18.

The desperation of the monks in the *vitae* might be dismissed as hagiographic exaggeration, but the annals corroborate the hungry image of early Ireland. Certainly, many hagiographic episodes mention the wealth of monastic communities, their herds of cattle, lush gardens and fields, woodland property, frequent feasts, and provisions for beggars. But if some prospered, others starved. At least prominent ecclesiastical communities could fall back on donations and dues from their clients and allies in times of general want. Secular families found no such relief. Berach's hagiographer told how in a season of *dochma mór* (great scarcity) a landholder and his wife lived on an island farm. When the man left in search of food he ordered his wife to kill their new baby because they could not hope to feed it.[19]

Hunger had many causes in early Ireland. Normal climatic conditions were beneficial to crops but were deadly when extreme. A serious downpour could destroy rye, wheat, or even hardy oats in the fields. Showers at harvest time damaged food supplies in 858, when a rainy autumn was "destructive to the fruits of the earth."[20] One of the most practical miracles of the saints was to prevent rain from falling on reapers. Even in dry conditions, farmers needed special equipment, a drying kiln, to burn the moisture out of the grain before it could be ground into flour.[21] When the rains cooled into snow, they killed again if the crops were already planted and growing. The *Annals of Ulster* noted for the year 670: "A great snowfall occurred. A great famine." Snow brought hunger again in 760, 764, and 895.[22]

Any of these setbacks might have meant one bad harvest, one hungry season. But production was so delicately balanced between weather, soil, and spade that a single failed crop often meant years of famine. In 1012, for example, one great downpour destroyed the grain crop and farmers had to choose between planting or eating what was left. In assuaging hunger that year, they had nothing to sow for the next. Several bad seasons followed 1012, as the 1015 reference to famine in Munster indicates.[23] In 1092 and 1093 heavy frost and snow occurred in the early spring; fierce winds later in the growing season blew the already weakened grain to the ground. A pestilence, possibly famine related, also struck in 1093. Hunger was ram-

---

19. PBNE 1:40.
20. Mac Airt, *Annals of Inisfallen,* 182–83; AU, 316–17.
21. HVSH, 170, 191; A. Gailey, "Irish Corn-drying Kilns," *Ulster Folklife* 15/16 (1970), 52–71; Evans, *Personality of Ireland,* 38.
22. AU, 138–39, 214, 216, 348, 550.
23. Mac Airt, *Annals of Inisfallen,* 182–83.

pant for several years, for in 1095 another bad winter killed off many cattle.[24]

Because famine was familiar, the seeds and stock with which to control food production and help ward off hungry seasons became signs of prosperity and thus also objects of conflict. Cattle raiding was one of the nobility's most popular pursuits, to judge from annals and other literature; the soil itself was less worth fighting for. Monastic writers complained constantly of theft and poaching. In time of war, destroying an enemy's crop or burning his storehouse was a familiar and effective tactic. On the other hand, sharing resources was one of the greatest signs of trust and friendship. In the saga *Táin Bó Cuailnge,* the hero Cú Chulainn proved his affection and respect for Fergus mac Roig by offering, "If the salmon were swimming in the rivers or river-mouths, I'd give you one and share another. If a flock of wild birds were to alight on the plain I'd give you one and share another; with a handful of cress or sea-herb and a handful of marshwort; and a drink out of the sand."[25] Because the focus of the tale is cattle rustling, the poem is all the more touching. The monks demonstrated similar friendship by feeding the hungry poor. In a land where food was rarely abundant, conflict was the norm and sharing the pious exception.

The Geography of the Wasteland

A historian can capture the landscape of early Ireland in a comprehensive map: Patches of arable and pasture, which supported monastic settlements and secular farms, are scattered among the forests, mountains, bogs, and waters. When a monk of the early Middle Ages left his settlement to go to another, he ventured into a world that could be charming when the sun shone and the air smelled of flowers and spring, but was more often dreary with drizzle, wind, and distant blue hills. Natural hindrances and bad weather took their toll, and travel was never easy. But forbidding or welcoming, the landscape lured a monk with an arsenal of wonders and dangers, natural, supernatural, and human.

Paddling down a river in the rain or trudging along a soggy path at the edge of a bog, a monk was aware, above all, of being *between* places rather

24. Ibid., 246–49.
25. Thomas Kinsella, trans., *The Tain* (Oxford, 1977), 118; R. I. Best and M. A. O'Brien, eds., *The Book of Leinster,* vol. 2 (Dublin, 1956), 305.

than *at* a place. He saw woods and mountains, rivers and plains, beasts, birds, spirits, visions; he heard strange noises and even met the occasional fellow traveler, who might well turn out to be an enemy. The monk's understanding of each new episode in his journey and each new view of the landscape helped him decide where to stop or settle and when to move on. But the monk formed his understanding not just from a glance at the immediately visible environment; his view of the tangible world was weighted with the social and cultural baggage that he carried with him.

Old roads and extensively linked waterways enabled the monks of early Ireland to journey from one point to another. Five main roadways (*sligeda*, literally "cuttings" or "clearings"), all originating in the east near Dublin, radiated westward. Slige Midlúachra ran from Drogheda to the north Antrim coast; Slige Assail to Ráth Cruacháin; int Slige Mór, the "Great Road," ran from Dublin to Galway; Slige Dála to Limerick; and Slige Cualann to Waterford.[26] Four of the roads corresponded to the ancient division of Ireland into the five provinces of Leinster, Munster, Ulster, Connacht, and Mide. One of the roads went to the heart of each province except Mide, which was cut by Slige Assail en route to Connacht. Int Slige Mór bisected the island into the old division of Leth Cuinn (Conn's half, the northern half) and Leth Moga (Mug's half, the southern half). Smaller tracks led from these main arteries to settlements and other gathering places. The heroes of the *Táin Bó Cuailnge* raced these roads in chariots; the saints and their monastic retinues paced them more slowly and sedately.

Human occupation determined the beginning and end of roads and sometimes modified their courses in relation to natural features of the landscape. The land itself often determined the exact course of a trail between two places; roads snaked through mountain passes and fords, avoiding forests, bogs, and marshes, often running across the tops of eskers.[27] No roads led out of a habitation without going to another, or to a place where humans gathered. No one ever moved randomly in the wilderness. Roads never ended at cities either, because Ireland had none, in the Continental style. As one Norman hagiographer put it, "The people of Ireland, being ignorant, simple-minded and unenlightened, did not yet know of coastal cities, coastal markets ready for merchandise,

26. Colm Ó Lochlainn, "Roadways in Ancient Ireland," in John Ryan, ed., *Féil-sgríbhinn Eóin mhic Néill* (Dublin, 1940), 465–73; HVSH, 178.
27. Ó Lochlainn, "Roadways," 466. The plains of Leinster, for example, were only accessible to large parties at a few strategic points; see Alfred P. Smyth, *Celtic Leinster* (Blackrock, 1982), 10–11.

municipal towns, or even foreign shores.[28] But this writer exaggerated, for the Irish had developed ports from which they conducted maritime trade as early as the neolithic period and had constructed roads inland from their harbors. The Vikings also created important trading towns at Dublin, Cork, Limerick, and a few other sites.[29] Several seaports were traditional points of departure for monks and others on pilgrimage.[30]

Besides leading to ports and settlements, tracks and trails led past tombs and assembly points (*óenaig*) and to ritual and regnal sites such as Temair and Ailech. The difficult path to Ailech, an Iron Age trivallate enclosure perched on top of a large hill, had no other function except access to the fort.[31] People continued to create new roads to sacred sites in the early Christian period, such as the pilgrims' way to Glenn Dá Locha. This old Bronze Age traders' track from the coast to the Leinster plains had followed a natural route along the river valleys and around a forest. However, soon after Glenn Dá Locha was founded, in the sixth century, pilgrims stubbornly forced a more arduous track through the woods and over the mountains in order to follow a purported penitential route based on Saint Cóemgen's original journey to the site.[32] Easy access and the forms of the landscape were not always prime considerations in creating roads; whenever humans moved to new places, they made new paths.

The early Irish recognized the need to keep roads passable. Not even Cú Chulainn and the Ulster heroes of the sagas could have driven their chariots over the great *sligeda* in rainy winters had the roads been untended. Excavations at the bog of Allen have shown that the Bronze Age Irish had kept tracks open through boggy areas in the fifth century B.C. by laying down numerous layers of stout planks and covering them with gravel, birch rods, and finally sod, creating a *tóchar,* or causeway.[33] Eleven hundred years later, Cogitosus described how overlords forced communities to keep their stretch of the local road clear by building and rebuilding similar causeways of wood and stone.[34] When trees and rocks blocked

28. HVSH, 285.

29. Liam Price, "Glendalough: St. Kevin's Road," in Ryan, *Féil-sgríbhinn Eóin mhic Néill,* 249–51; Ann Lynch, *Man and Environment in Southwest Ireland 4000 B.C.–A.D. 800* (Oxford, 1981), 123–24; National Museum of Ireland, *Viking and Medieval Dublin* (Dublin, 1973; rpt. 1982); Donnchadh Ó Corráin, *Ireland before the Normans* (Dublin, 1972), 104–10.

30. PVSH 2:83.

31. Brian Lacy et al., *Archaeological Survey of County Donegal* (Lifford, 1983), 110–11.

32. Price, "Glendalough: St. Kevin's Road," 149–63.

33. R. A. S. MacAlister, "An Ancient Road in the Bog of Allen," JRSAI 62 (1932), 137–41.

34. Migne, PL 72:786–87; see also PBNE 1:172. Cf. HVSH, 3: "familia cum bobus et plaustris trans fretum perrexit."

untended roads, saints single-handedly lifted such obstructions, miraculous solutions to common problems; ordinary people tried, not always so successfully, to remove the many natural obstacles to easy movement across the island.[35]

Any distance was long to a traveler, even when the road was free of rocks and trees and the waters calm. Rapid journeys were literally miraculous; only the saints moved speedily, sometimes avoiding twisting, overgrown paths by flying in their chariots over bogs.[36] As Máedóc's twelfth-century biographer wrote of that saint's overnight trip to Rome, "However, no man in the world knows, but only the god of the elements, how this journey was made, for God can make of difficult roads and rough paths by sea and land a direct way and short path for his saints of strong devotion in a single night, [as easily] as if they had a long time in which to traverse it."[37] But other monks hastened on their journeys in vain. Monks from Cluain Moccu Nóis went to Cell Íte for water blessed by Íte, which they hoped would heal their abbot, Óengus. When they arrived at Cell Íte, its abbess had already died, but prescient Íte had left the holy water behind. But by the time the monks of Cluain got home, their abbot had also died.[38] Munnu had a similar experience, arriving at Í to visit Columcille after the saint had left for a better world.[39]

Rivers, streams, and lakes often provided a safer, less difficult access to interior settlements during the early Middle Ages than overland routes. Even in the twelfth century, Gerald of Wales's understanding of Irish topography was dependent on his travels along the eastern and southern coasts and his short trips inland from major Viking ports.[40] Before the permanent drainage of some lands in the past century or two, more bodies of water were linked together. The water level of the large rivers was fairly regular all year long, making them highly navigable.[41] A journey by foot from Cluain Moccu Nóis to the shore opposite Inis Chathaig was "a long and rough and difficult way over the borders of many territories"; by water, from the head of the Shannon to its source, the trip was far less taxing.[42] The Shannon twists and turns for two hundred miles from its

35. HVSH, 279, 354; PVSH 1:194. Cf. HVSH, 394, where Daig solves the problem of crossing water.
36. PVSH 1:177, 180; PBNE 1:184, 187–88, 327.
37. PBNE 1:229; 2:222–23.
38. PVSH 2:129–30.
39. HVSH, 199–200.
40. Gerald of Wales, *Topography and History*, 14.
41. R. Lloyd Praeger, *The Irish Landscape* (Cork, 1953), 10; R. A. S. MacAlister, *Ancient Ireland* (London, 1935), 4–5.
42. PVSH, 1:212.

source before flowing out to sea; settlements at accessible sites along the dips and turns of its length provided hospitable stops for the river traveler.[43] Intrepid monks and others had little hesitation about taking a hide-covered coracle onto such a wide river or even into the ocean to visit island communities.[44]

The monks were well aware of the dangers involved in any kind of travel. Wind and rain plagued them on the road and on the waterways. Accidental drowning due to storms and their effects on rivers or seas was so common that the hagiographers recorded it almost casually. Although Adomnán wrote from Scotland, his experience was in keeping with that of his Irish brothers when he described how Columcille and his community were at constant war with the sky and sea in order to travel back and forth from Í to the mainland.[45] Saint Columcille was a practical sailor, and knew how to bail out a boat in bad weather; but his true métier was the performance of miracles, as his boatmen reminded him during a storm when they begged him to quit bailing and start blessing.[46] Brénainn and his monks encountered snow at sea, leading the monks to wonder forlornly whether hell was as cold as their place on the ocean.[47] The saints often brought their monks through storms at sea successfully, but the frequency of such episodes in the *vitae* points to a genuine fear of the rough waters on the monks' part. (On the other hand, calm seas left sailors waiting in port for winds to move their boats.[48]) All sea travel was so perilous that even Brénainn, the intrepid maritime adventurer, blessed the ports he entered to express his thanks at safely finishing his journey.[49]

Inland waters presented dangers to travelers in both good and bad weather. Mochuda's hagiographer told the gruesome story of a shipwreck victim who swam the Shannon to the nearest boat, there to have his head struck off by the sword of one of the sailors.[50] Only strong swimmers could cross some raging rivers.[51] Small boys living in monastic communities found it difficult to ford deep rivers, as adult monks did, and easily slipped and drowned.[52] Even small streams swallowed up gospels and

---

43. MacAlister, *Ancient Ireland*, 4–5.

44. Seamus O'Neill, "Irish Maritime History: Early Period to Norse Invasions," *Studies* 34 (1945), 404–11; E. G. Bowen, *Saints, Seaways, and Settlements in the Celtic Lands* (Cardiff, 1969).

45. Adomnán, 348–50; HVSH, 187, 356–58, 367–68, 442, 452–54, 538.

46. Adomnán, 350–55.

47. PVSH 1:147.

48. Adomnán, 454.

49. PVSH 1:109, 119.

50. PBNE 1:307.

51. PVSH 1:386–89; 2:196–97.

52. HVSH, 235–36, 267, 391–92.

treasures dropped by incautious pilgrims.[53] Some travelers could not even attempt to cross water by themselves, and were at the mercy of those living nearby; they stood on the shore and clamored to be carried or ferried to the other side.[54] Worst of all perceived perils of the waters were the monsters that lived in rivers, lakes, and seas. While Saint Brénainn passed by many beasts of the sea unharmed, others were not so fortunate. Monsters often surprised monks and nuns, and swallowed them up before they could escape.[55]

Storms were a lesser threat to overland travelers, who could seek shelter, but cold and bad weather remained a problem for those spending a night on the road. Camped out near Temair, the warmth of his sanctity kept Molaise's bivouac free of snow, but the rest of those in the area shivered through the night.[56] Monks and other travelers tried to plan journeys to reach a known settlement by nightfall, but sometimes the darkness caught them on the road.[57] Máedóc got lost on Slíab Betha one night and would have had to sleep under a bush except that angels carried him to a vacant fort nearby.[58] Saint Féichíne even arranged miraculously to lengthen the daylight so that he and his disciples could return safely to the monastic enclosure and avoid a long night by the dark road.[59]

But weather and darkness were not the worst of a journey. A monk in transit watched the woods before and behind him, and kept a sharp eye on the bend of the road or the river for attackers. The denizens of the wilderness were animals or demons, never fully human even when they seemed to take human form. They inhabited the wild for one purpose only: to prey upon those foolish enough to leave the safety of home.

Wild animals inhabited the wastes, some indifferent to travelers, some hungry for them. Deer, rabbits, and small rodents grazed on the edges of clearings, where edible shoots and grasses were plentiful. But deep in the woods or on lonely plains lurked terrible beasts. Columcille, searching the woods on the Isle of Skye for a solitary spot in which to pray, found himself confronting a wild boar. The animal was dashing furiously away from pursuing hounds and hunters. The saint saved himself by raising his

53. HVSH, 356; USMLS, Conchubranus, 1:130–31.
54. PVSH 2:254; Adomnán, 258, 260, 270, 300, etc.
55. Adomnán, 244–49, 386–89; HVSH, 213–14, 359, 367–68; PVSH 1:122; PBNE 1:61, 72–73, 76–78; Plummer, *Misc. hag.*, 7–96.
56. PVSH 2:138; 1:89.
57. HF, 82, 87; VT, 176.
58. PBNE 1:184.
59. HVSH, 99; PVSH 1:212; 2:14. See also HVSH, 130–31, 259–60; PVSH 1:9–10, 107–8.

hand and telling the animal to drop dead, and it did so.[60] But the boar was an impressive enemy, not so easily bested by others; its meat was the most prestigious a warrior could eat, and heroes fought dreadful duels over the best joints of its semidomesticated cousin, the pig.[61]

Wolves also roamed the woods and hills, coming close enough to settlements to steal cattle and sheep. The hagiographers repeatedly wrote of saintly youths guarding flocks and dealing with ferocious wolves as if they were the meekest of lambs, giving them calves to eat, or taming them as pets.[62] Less pious and more practical shepherds periodically hunted them to protect flocks that were their families' livelihood.[63]

Even seemingly harmless or domestic animals presented a threat when encountered outside a transient's own domestic context. Farmers set their vicious dogs upon strangers. Columcille journeyed to meet Cainnech and Cóemgen at the fort of Uisnech but was attacked by dogs before the three could enter the enclosure.[64] Brigands even kept dogs in the wild to unleash upon travelers.[65] Semidomesticated pigs turned on their owners, too; set loose to root in the woods, carnivorous pigs gobbled up children.[66] No animal was completely harmless or trustworthy: even mice and birds came from the wild to attack crops.[67]

In fact, along with his pack and staff, every traveler carried a headful of suspicions and fears of animals that conditioned his understanding of the landscape. Beasts were incomprehensible and therefore dangerous; the wilderness, not the farmyard, was their natural habitat. In folk tradition, the mildest and dumbest of beasts often behaved in completely mysterious ways; the relationship of people to animals often suddenly altered for no apparent reason. Sagas and legends often centered on a semidivine animal, a beast that behaved uncommonly. The *Táin Bó Cuailnge* recounts battles between two magical bulls. Birds figured as omens of otherworldly activity. Gods of the old days went through many transformations from animal to human, human to animal, as did many residents of the otherworld. Characters in the tales put on and took off bird suits as they did

60. Adomnán, 384.
61. R. Thurneysen, ed., *Scéla Mucce Meic Dathó* (Dublin, 1935; rpt. 1975), esp. 7–16; see also references to boars in PVSH 1:219; 2:170.
62. HVSH, 230, 258; PVSH 1:219, 238–39; PBNE 1:183–84, 195, 213, 216.
63. HVSH, 130.
64. Ibid., 364; PVSH 1:248.
65. PVSH 1:202; Richard Sharpe, "Hiberno-Latin *Laicus,* Irish *Láech* and the Devil's Men," *Ériu* 30 (1979), 81.
66. VT, 198.
67. HVSH, 130.

cloaks.[68] Heroes assumed attributes of animals, such as Cú Chulainn, the Hound of Cualann, whose battle frenzy turned him into a thing unrecognizable as human.[69]

The saints alone controlled animals that others feared. Saints sucked on wolves' teats and were nurtured with the milk of hinds and miraculous red-eared white cows.[70] Sheep leaped from wells when saints were baptized; whole flocks of sheep, herds of pigs, cattle, and horses appeared and disappeared at a prayer or command.[71] Animals were creatures of the border between settlements and the wilderness, and thus appeared in several *vitae* as magical boundary makers for the saints; for instance, Saint Ciarán sent a cow to wander between Birra and Achad Bó, fixing their borders.[72] Other wild animals took on human attributes and served the saints as slaves and disciples. Brigit was mistress of foxes and other forest creatures, while Ciarán's first disciple at his desert retreat was a fox.[73]

Travelers feared the animal inhabitants of the wild because the line between humans and beasts was, like the border between civilized settlement and the uninhabited wastes, too tenuous and easily crossed. Some Christian writers tried to make the boundary more orthodox and solid. Brénainn's hagiographer described how his foster mother, Íte, lectured him because he had built a hide-covered curragh, tainted by animals, in which to sail to the Isle of the Blessed. He would never reach his destination, she explained, except in a proper wooden boat.[74] The same recension showed the saint preaching a sermon on the coexistence of man and beast, with man as the Genesis-style master of nature. Some iconoclasts tried to erase the traditional mystical links between animals and people. But the monks and their lay brothers and sisters already knew how to coexist with animals; many of them slept in the same cottages as their dogs and cows.[75]

It was exactly this proximity to their animals that caused the early Irish

---

68. Eleanor Knott, ed., *Togail Bruidne Da Derga* (Dublin, 1936; rpt. 1975), 3. For the Celtic reverence of animals and animal gods, see Anne Ross, *Pagan Celtic Britain* (London and New York, 1967), 297–353.

69. John Strachan and J. G. O'Keeffe, eds., *Táin Bó Cuailnge* (Dublin, rpt. 1967), 69–70; Kinsella, *The Tain*, 150–52.

70. HVSH, 118, 361; PVSH 1:250–51; PBNE 1:12, 164.

71. HVSH, 175–76; PVSH 1:221–22; PBNE 1:45, 110.

72. PBNE 1:114.

73. PVSH 1:219–20; 2:199–200, 201, 202–3; see also PBNE 1:127, 162. See Mary Donatus MacNickle, *Beasts and Birds in the Lives of the Early Irish Saints* (Philadelphia, 1934).

74. PVSH 1:136.

75. E. E. Evans, *Irish Folk-Ways* (London and Boston, 1957; rpt. 1976), 39–43.

anxiety when they dealt with the beasts. Animals were not yet the familiars and evil spirits of the late Middle Ages, nor the objects of exploitation that they became in the early modern period, nor the bourgeois pets of the nineteenth century.[76] They and their occasional masters were residents of the same untamed environment, enjoying more kinship than some monks wanted to admit. At home on the farm or in the holy enclosure, among family, friends, and clients, a monk might ignore the kinship between himself and the barnyard animals. But trudging along a footpath, that monk was never quite certain which he encountered, man, beast, or man-beast. This was the ultimate threat of the space between settlements: the wasteland reminded monks that an animal lurked within all humans.

Bandits who were cast out of settlements lived in the wild by rejecting the customs of men and assuming the habits of animals. They sheltered in caves or constructed rude huts for themselves, hunting and foraging for fruits and nuts. They waited, like wolves and boars, to fall upon unwary monks and other travelers.[77] Cainnech, for example, was courting trouble when he ventured out by himself one day. Three "extremely cruel laymen" came upon him and decided to murder him for his high-class linen garments. The robbers mocked Cainnech's naiveté in wandering alone: "This is a puny little cleric's staff [*baculus*]," they said, "which strays into these many places." Cainnech foiled the bandits' murderous attempt, but it is unclear whether the innocent saint learned a lesson about safety on the highways.[78] More canny transients recognized brigands by their eerie songs of triumph, like the howls of hungry wolves, over decapitated victims.[79] Hagiographers dreaded the robbers roaming mountain passes and skulking about the edges of European villages; these marauders made the trip to Rome seem almost impossible for pilgrims.[80]

Bandits were creatures outside of living society, like beasts, like the dead; for beasts had no soul and no community, and without these there was no life. Colmán Ela heard the voice of a "son of life" ("audio vocem filii vite") among those raised in a triumphant howl over murdered victims. He went to save the young warrior from a death-in-life among the

76. Kathleen Kete, "Pet-Keeping Culture in 19th-Century Paris: Representations of Modern Life" (Ph.D. diss., Harvard University, 1989); Keith Thomas, *Man and the Natural World* (New York, 1983), 36–37. See PVSH 2:175, in which Mochóemóc banished demons to the cliffs of Caisel where they could bother only animals; Mochóemóc and his hagiographer clearly distinguished between beasts and demons.

77. HVSH, 219; Sharpe, "Hiberno-Latin *Laicus,* Irish *Láech,*" 80.

78. HVSH, 193–94.

79. Ibid., 149, 211.

80. Ibid. 183–84, 400; PBNE 1:211.

brigands. But before the youth could join Colmán's band of monks he had to die and be revived by the saint, crossing a clearly symbolic threshold from banditry into a Christian social existence.[81] The social death of outlaws and their ghostly existence outside of Christian society suggests that the wilderness was not just inhuman but otherworldly. Beyond settled society, not only human laws but even the boundaries between life and death lost force.

Natural Resources and Neighbors

Life was precarious even for those safely settled. The weather, the soil, and the lack of equipment all hindered food production, and a community's survival depended upon finding a relatively hospitable corner of the landscape. Like their fathers and grandfathers, monks were farmers, and like them preferred sites that offered such basic resources as fresh water, well-drained, clayey soil, and timber.

Communities needed access to water sources, as the hagiographers acknowledged. For example, monks in Colmán Ela's *vita* built a monastery at the confluence of two rivers; Máedóc's house of Ros Inber sat where angels chanted and sang and also where a lough met two rivers.[82] Others settled at springs or, like Mochóemóc's comrade Lachtaín, where the moisture of rivers flowing through the land created an *ager viridus*, a verdant plain.[83] Hundreds of settlements with *inis* or *cluain* in their names grew up on island or shoreline sites in the midst of usually moist and fertile land.[84] Waterside or bog-side settlements also provided convenient travel routes and afforded protection, especially to island or peninsular sites. Some farmers and monks actually heaped up mud and debris into islands, called *crannogs*, on which to live.[85]

Elevation and soil type also influenced settlement patterns. The first wave of monastic settlers around the sixth and seventh centuries spread

---

81. HVSH, 211.

82. Ibid. 218; PBNE 1:235; see also PBNE 1:103–4, PVSH 1:87.

83. PVSH 2:168.

84. E. I. Hogan, ed., *Onomasticon Goedelicum locorcem et tribum Hiberniae et Scotiae* (Dublin, 1910), 253–70, 460–70.

85. Smyth, *Celtic Leinster,* 30–31; Kathleen Hughes and Ann Hamlin, *Celtic Monasticism: The Modern Traveller to the Early Irish Church* (New York, 1977), 23–25; O. Davies, "Contributions to the Study of Crannogs," UJA 8 (1945), 14–30. For examples of religious settlements on islands, lakeshores, or river shores, see HVSH, 97, 99, 125, 156, 183, 195, 197, et passim; VT, 84, 168, 212. For secular habitations in such locations, see HVSH, 99, 169, 175, 190.

onto some unoccupied sites in the lower hills and valleys, but they also continued to use already inhabited upland and coastal sites. Secular settlers of the period followed the same pattern.[86] Those without the iron equipment required for heavy soils preferred such well-drained land. In Leinster, as A. P. Smyth has shown, monastic settlements regularly sat just below the 500-foot contour.[87] The *vitae* confirmed the monks' interest in upland sites. Often an island site was also an elevated site, on a cliff or an esker surrounded by wetlands. To some, an upland position was even more important than water or other resources. Fintan's monastery of Cluain Eidnech, for example, on the lower slopes of Slíab Bladma, had no convenient water supply.[88]

No monastic settlement could exist far from the woods. Many monasteries retained references to trees in their names, such as Cell Dara, "church of the oakwood." Episodes of the *vitae* commonly took place just beyond the monastic gates in the forest, where the monks found fuel, wild game, and a food supply for their pigs. They could have burned turf to keep warm and subsisted on a vegetarian diet, but they still would have needed the forest in order to build and rebuild their elaborate churches and the houses and huts of their communities.

Although the monks preferred to live on the low, wooded hills of an island, they often had to accept less ideal sites. They were not pilgrims to a new world, but colonizers of an already settled landscape. Hagiographers may have praised the saints who fled human society, but the reality of monastic withdrawal is clear from a map of monastic foundations.[89] The *dísert* (wasteland) of the saints was rarely far from clustered settlements, called *clachans*, or the ring-forts of single families, called *ráths*. Even the stone cells of the western shores, once thought to be the solitary retreats of hermits, were actually quite close to farms. They seem isolated today only because they were built on the seacliffs, and the wattled huts of their neighbors have now disappeared.[90]

With a few exceptions, such as the rocky sea island of Scelec Mhichíl, the monks sought accessible sites and even strove to make their settle-

---

86. Vincent Hurley, "The Early Church in the Southwest of Ireland: Settlement and Organization," in S. M. Pearce, ed., *The Early Church in Western Britain and Ireland* (Oxford, 1982), 297–332, esp. 307–10.

87. Smyth, *Celtic Leinster,* 28–29, 152–57.

88. HVSH, 146–47; PVSH 2:97–98.

89. HVSH, 200, 203, 362; USMLS, Conchubranus 1:258.

90. Hurley, "The Early Church in the Southwest of Ireland," 310. See also Hurley, "Additions to the Map of Monastic Ireland: The Southwest," JCHAS 85 (1980), 52–65.

ments more easily approachable. Their monasteries had to be convenient for client laborers and for traders bringing animals laden with goods to their gates; their shrines had to be accessible to pilgrims. The monks themselves traveled to other communities, and wanted a good road home. Monks cleared new paths and maintained harbors; Bennchor, for example, sat near the sea and had its own welcoming harbor of Inber Beg.[91] The monks also built causeways on marshy sites and ferried visitors to island monasteries.[92] They even complained about less considerate brethren who withdrew to remote hermitages. Saint Mochuda, according to his hagiographer, denounced Saint Crónán: "To a man who avoids guests and builds his church in a wild bog, away from the level road, I will not go; but let him have beasts of the wilderness for his guests."[93]

Human geography influenced monastic settlement in other ways. Ecclesiastics sought places where people lived, or had lived, in order to settle there themselves. Previous generations of Irishmen and women had found and farmed the best places; good land was too scarce for choice sites to remain uninhabited. The hagiographers described monks building monasteries in the abandoned ring-forts of the Iron Age, sometimes with peasant families still living in or near them. Abbán and his monks occupied the fort (*oppidum*) at Camross, where they were attacked by Cormac mac Diarmata, who wanted the site for himself. But after the saint miraculously subdued Cormac, the king "offered not just the church but indeed the whole fort to God and the saint."[94] Abbán must have shared ownership and occupation of the fort with others before Cormac granted the entire site to him.

Monks usually acquired abandoned forts and enclosures either at the invitation of the owner or because the fort had long stood empty of inhabitants. When the nobles of Munster offended Saint Brénainn, for example, he forced them to abandon their fifty forts, presumably so that monks could move in.[95] Whether the hagiographer was right in blaming Brénainn for the abandonment of the forts is unimportant. Some of the empty forts taken by monks may have been former habitation sites that had lost their owners in the demographic shifts of the fourth or fifth century. But the references to deserted forts in the *vitae* suggest that many

91. PVSH 2:7, 14; see also B. J. Graham, "Urban Genesis in Early Medieval Ireland," *Journal of Historical Geography* 13 (1987), 8.
92. HVSH, 183; PBNE 1:172; Adomnán, 258, 270–72, 296–98.
93. PVSH 1:194.
94. HVSH, 268–69.
95. PVSH 1:140; see also HVSH, 97; PBNE 1:35.

of the sites given over to monastic use may never have been permanently inhabited. These may have been inaugural enclosures used exclusively for rites of kingship and for assemblies. Thus the monks not only acquired property and a settlement site when some layman endowed them with an old fort; in many cases, they also received a ritual site, the purposes and connotations of which were entirely familiar to them.

The monks acquired neighbors both by settling near other communities and by attracting people to live around their own prosperous farms. Although the remains of stone buildings help to locate monasteries, the less durable homes of secular folk have disappeared. Excavations of early medieval monastic sites rarely extend to the fields surrounding enclosures, in order to recreate the entire mixed monastic and secular community. There are, however, a few exceptions. At the monastery of Riasc, in Kerry, a nucleated settlement related to the monastic enclosure may have existed contemporaneously 200 meters to the south, along with an attached field system. It seems that Riasc began as a Christian cemetery, possibly with resident clergy who had parish functions; later it developed into a monastic site with an adjacent secular cluster.[96] At another site, Ard Pátraic in county Limerick, aerial photography has revealed the faint traces of many small fields, suggesting that the land directly surrounding the enclosure was intensely cultivated for many centuries, possibly going back to the settlement's earliest days.[97] Archaeologists have uncovered evidence of secular settlement at other ecclesiastical sites, including Cenannas, Daim Liac, Domnach Sechnaill, Sord, Lusca, and Cell Deilge.[98] Many of these farming communities developed within or around the circular boundaries of monastic enclosures; that is, secular settlement may have grown up after the monastery had been founded on the site. But it is impossible in most cases to develop a chronology of settlement sophisticated enough to determine who appeared first at most sites, monks or secular residents.

Neighbors not only guided but limited the monks' choice of sites. Since the great arable expansion preceded the monks by a century or two, little inhabitable wilderness was left on an island where arable was scarce. Elab-

96. Thomas Fanning, "Excavation of an Early Christian Cemetery and Settlement at Reask, Co. Kerry," PRIA 81 C (1981), 67–172; see also Hurley, "The Early Church in Southwest Ireland," 297–332; M. J. O'Kelly, "Church Island near Valencia, Co. Kerry," PRIA 59 C (1958), 57–136.

97. E. R. Norman and J. K. S. St. Joseph, *The Early Development of Irish Society* (Cambridge, 1969), 107–108.

98. Leo Swan, "Enclosed Ecclesiastical Sites and Their Relevance to Settlement Patterns of the First Millennium, A.D.," in Reeves-Smyth and Hammond, *Landscape Archaeology*, 269–94.

orate laws of trespass protected the arable of Ireland as early as 700.[99] Those with rights to good land fought to maintain possession, legally and often violently. Pátraic, for example, interrupted two brothers who were about to hew each other with swords in a quarrel over division of their father's land. According to Tírechán, Pátraic persuaded them to donate the land for an ecclesiastical site.[100]

The best site for a monastic settlement often was offered by a pious Christian. Not everyone was willing to yield his family's fields to monks, however. The secular laws restricted alienation in order to protect the heirs of pious donors.[101] Monks who could not wheedle some choice parcel of ground from zealous converts or their kin were left with the wasteland that was too soggy or rocky or wooded to be farmed without considerable extra effort. Successful monastic communities campaigned actively for land, offering their ritual services in exchange. Some communities even extorted endowments and donations by threatening to withhold their services, or to turn monastic rituals against reluctant donors. Hagiography records the advertisement of services and the threats that monks made to neighbors and clients.

According to the saints' lives, many landowners gave gladly to ecclesiastics. When Columcille told Áed Sláine to donate a site to Colmán Ela, the king graciously responded, "He may choose wherever he would like."[102] Others gave land in exchange for healing services, for example, the king who bestowed a *civitas* upon Ruadán after the saint cured him. This hagiographic motif sent an obvious message to monks and prospective donors.[103] As we shall see, wealthy families frequently allowed members to set up religious communities on one of their properties as a means of providing for them and simultaneously gaining spiritual benefits. The monks also claimed that donated property was exempt from the rents and dues normally paid on it to the owner's overlord, establishing the early Irish equivalent of a tax deduction.[104]

99. Donnchadh Ó Corráin, "Some Legal References to Fences and Fencing in Early Historic Ireland," in Ó Corráin, ed., *Irish Antiquity*. Irish arable may have been enclosed more than four thousand years ago: H. J. Case et al., "Land Use in Goodland Townland, Co. Antrim, from Neolithic Times until Today," JRSAI 99 (1969), 39–54; Michael Herity, "Prehistoric Fields in Ireland," *Irish University Review* 1 (1971), 258–65; Seamus Caulfield, "Neolithic Fields: The Irish Evidence," in H. C. Bowen and P. J. Fowler, eds., *Early Land Allotment in the British Isles* (Oxford, 1978), 137–44.
100. VT, 148–49.
101. CIH 1:214, 224–29 (esp. 224–25), 244–45, 247.
102. HVSH, 214.
103. Ibid., 161; see also 128, 165, 393; PVSH 1:69, 228; PBNE 1:14, 27, 35, 216–17.
104. HVSH, III, 228; PVSH 2:51; Wasserschleben, *Collectio*, 79.

More often, monks faced resistance from landowners and had to fight for a plot on which to build a monastery or a field to add to their estates. Hagiographers understood such conflicts as confrontations between the saints, who demanded the holy places to which God had led them, and landholders, who were unwilling to alienate precious arable and grazing land. The *vitae* characteristically reduced the disagreement to a formulaic encounter between saint and *tyrannus,* the hagiographers' name for a selfish landlord. The saint always emerged victorious. One of the most elaborate episodes concerned Pátraic's efforts to obtain two sites, Ráith Dáiri and Ferta, from their owner and namesake, Dáire mac Findchada. Pátraic settled nearby without clarifying grazing rights in an adjacent outfield. Dáire left his horses in the pasture as a legal means of claiming the land. Pátraic miraculously smote the horses dead. Dáire retaliated by trying to evict Pátraic, but the saint struck the landholder with illness. The episode ended with Dáire healed, penitent, and generously offering to Pátraic the hill upon which would one day stand Ard Macha.[105]

The hagiographers recorded how the saints routinely caused unwilling donors to sicken or even die, often extending the punishment to the landholders' families. When landowners relented, the saints usually restored all to life and health. But if the owners steadfastly refused to relinquish land, the saints punished them mercilessly. Ruadán wanted to build a church in a certain field but the owner would not allow it; Ruadán caused the sea to swallow the field.[106] Property-owning Christians were caught between laws against alienation and ecclesiastics who, after the example of their saints, demanded endowments. To these people the saints taught a harsh lesson.

When the dramatic warnings of the *vitae* failed to bring them land, the monks tried other methods. Prestigious communities, such as Ard Macha, attracted property-owning noblemen and women into their ranks. Some of these wealthy converts brought family and property with them to the monastic settlement.[107] Ard Macha and other powerful communities, such as Cluain Moccu Nóis and Cell Dara, also drew donations from a wider and more geographically dispersed pool of donors than some tiny, local community; by collecting dependent churches and farms in many different areas of the island, these communities avoided exhausting the

105. VT, 228.
106. HVSH, 161; see also 345–46.
107. Tomas Ó Fiaich, "The Church of Armagh under Lay Control," *Seanchus Ard Mhacha* 5 (1969), 75–127.

generosity of local donors.[108] Less successful communities paid rent for their sites. St. Finnian found that he owed the king of the Fothairt an ounce of gold for building a church on the monarch's fields; the story represents dues paid to local rulers by Finnian's community.[109]

The hagiographers' stories of gifts and endowments reflected the monks' hunger for property, but not necessarily their acquisition of it. Whether they were given property, inherited it, rented it, or extorted it, few monks between the ninth and twelfth centuries founded new communities. The wild days of the Christian frontier were long gone; no habitable wilderness lurked beyond pagan settlements to lure ambitious monastic dynasts. Donations of the period generally included only grazing rights, extra arable, and small properties attached to existing foundations.[110] Monks also refounded communities on previously donated and abandoned sites. The author of Pátraic's ninth-century *Vita tripartita* described deserted ecclesiastical and secular settlement sites, indicating his own monastery's interest in acquiring the properties.[111] The annalists often mentioned one monastic administration governing two houses, one of which had declined in population and property, perhaps as the result of Viking raids.[112] In such political mergers some properties must also have changed hands.

The hagiographers' tales of *tyranni* also helped explain to the monks why they lived where they did. The saints' struggles to extract property from local landholders revealed why monasteries were not always ideally situated.

The Sacral Landscape

One last, fundamental concern helped the monks justify their choice of settlement sites. Like their ancestors, they surveyed two landscapes. Trees, rocks, animals, and human improvements spread across one. The other was a sacral landscape of good and evil places and things. The monks and their contemporaries moved among openings to the otherworld, helpful

108. Kathleen Hughes, *The Church in Early Irish Society* (London, 1966), 157–72; Smyth, *Celtic Leinster,* 27–28.

109. HVSH, 100.

110. See, e.g., donations recorded in Gearóid Mac Niocaill, *Notitiae As Leabhar Cheanannais: 1033–1161* (Cló Morainn, 1961).

111. VT, 194, 198, 204.

112. For a few of numerous examples, see AU, 226, 237, 242, 374, 408.

ancestors and spirits, and dens of demons and other malign beings. On the Romanized Continent, Peter Brown has written, Christians broke the barriers of a thousand years when they joined these two landscapes of the living and the dead at the graves of the saints.[113] In the barbarian hinterland, Christians had long accepted the conjunction of worlds at certain familiar points on the landscape. Indeed, the Irish monks sought out places where heaven met earth, so that they might inhabit them and draw on their spiritual aura.

Such points on the landscape were not always immediately apparent. Tradition taught of markers of the sacred, such as particular trees, wells, and man-made tumuli, that helped people find holy places and determine whether they were protective or dangerous. The monks also relied on the efforts of long-dead men and women who had already discovered the openings to the otherworld. Many of the same places remained sacred to the Irish before and after the coming of Pátraic, although their use and interpretation changed profoundly. The monks raised Christianized monuments where their ancestors had worshipped, died, or been buried; they allowed pagan monuments to guard the sites of churches and saints' shrines.

Holy places had hazards as well as advantages. People moving across the landscape sometimes disturbed the spiritual forces that lay hidden around them. If they were up to no good, the land could become an enemy. In saga, for instance, Queen Medb's army of Connachtmen marched through Cuailnge to cross the river Cronn in their attempt to steal the Ulstermen's bull, but the waters rose up against them. The army was forced to seek the headwaters of the Cronn and skirt the river altogether.[114] Similarly, thieves fleeing Saint Monenna's settlement of Cell Sléibe were caught by a roiling river that prevented their escape.[115] At other times, the powers of the sacred places delivered bizarre and incomprehensible omens. The annals noted in 866, for example, that Loch Léibinn in Westmeath became a lake of blood with clots like tiny lungs washing up on its shores. The annalist did not attempt to interpret the message.[116]

The Irish created several ways of alerting themselves to the presence of the numinous powers, so that they might exploit the volatile landscape and settle safely at holy places. Natural features sometimes marked sacral

113. Peter Brown, *The Cult of the Saints: Its Rise and Function in Latin Christianity* (Chicago, 1981), 1–12.
114. Kinsella, *The Táin*, 101–2; Best and O'Brien, *Book of Leinster*, 288–89.
115. USMLS, Conchubranus 1:256.
116. AU, 322; Joan Radner, ed., *Fragmentary Annals of Ireland* (Dublin, 1978), 126.

sites. People approached them warily testing for holiness, just as they poked the ground with a long stick when crossing a bog. For example, certain mountains associated with the old gods became sites of Christian churches and pilgrimage, climbed by penitents on the seasonal pagan festivals of Lugnasad or Beltaine.[117] Medieval texts described monastic islands with strange natural properties hinting that they had been holy before any monk set foot on them; there was one island where no female animal could survive, and another where people never died.[118] On the flat plains of what came to be Cell Dara were certain areas sacred to the fertility goddess Bríg, where her priestesses kept an eternal fire. The plains were left untilled even though fertile, a sign that the goddess owned them. Bríg's fields looked like any other wilderness but for her priestesses' fire and the settlement that grew up around it. Saint Brigit replaced Bríg and the abbess of Cell Dara and her nuns assumed the priestesses' duties, but the fire continued to burn.[119]

Certain trees identified sacred places where people gathered for important rituals and political assemblies; many of these sites attracted permanent settlement.[120] Trees called *bili* stood at kingly forts and other places where kings were inaugurated. A *bile* could belong to a variety of species, although oak and hazel were thought to be especially otherworldly. Some monks built their communities near *bili,* such as *Bile Torten,* where Pátraic founded the community of Ard Breccáin, mentioned in the eighth-century Book of Armagh.[121] Annal entries for 995 referred to a *fidnemedh,* which may have been a sacred grove, attached to Ard Macha. The grove may even have attracted Pátraic to build a church there.[122] Many church names included elements denoting woods, possibly sacred woods, such as Finnian's church of Mag Bile, "plain of the *bile.*" A few texts mention *bile*

---

117. Máire Mac Néill, *The Festival of Lughnasa: A Study of the Survival of the Celtic Festival of the Beginning of Harvest* (London, 1962).

118. See, e.g., Carl Selmer, ed., *Navigatio Sancti Brendani Abbatis* (South Bend, Ind., 1959).

119. Gerald of Wales, *History and Topography,* 60–61, 66; de Paor, *Peoples of Ireland,* 55–56; Fergus Kelly, *A Guide to Early Irish Law* (Dublin, 1988), 77.

120. For the value, supernatural and economic, of various trees, see Fergus Kelly, "The Old Irish Tree List," *Celtica* 11 (1976), 107–24; George Calder, ed., *Auraicept na n-Éces* (Edinburgh, 1917), 89–93.

121. See the description of *Bile Torten* in Edward Gwynn, *The Metrical Dindshenchas,* Todd Lecture 11 (Dublin, 1924), 240–42.

122. A. T. Lucas, "The Sacred Trees of Ireland," JCHAS 68 (1963), 16–54, esp. 17, 27; note Mac Airt's translation of *fidnemed,* however, in AU, 426–27. See also A. Watson, "The King, Post, and Sacred Tree," *Études Celtiques* 18 (1981), 165–81.

na cille, "the sacred tree of the church," as if every ecclesiastical settlement had its own.[123]

Springs were naturally sacred sites that attracted settlement by monks for both spiritual and practical reasons. In the seventh century, Tírechán wrote of a spring or well of Findmag in Corcu Theimne, called Slán or "good health," which later became a shrine to Pátraic. Local druids had enclosed the well of Slán with stones. Tírechán explained the capped well as a place where "the infidels said that some wise man had made for himself a shrine in the water under the stone to bleach his bones perpetually because he feared the burning by fire; and they worshipped the well as a god."[124] Despite Tírechán's very Christian interpretation of the well's pagan significance, he and his informant understood the spring to be a site of worship for the community. Devotees gathered at the well to throw trinkets into it as offerings.

The seventh-century stories of Tírechán often involved Pátraic arriving at a well to find druids there or nearby. Although Tírechán might simply have devised such scenes for literary purposes, he rarely described Pátraic meeting his priestly rivals except at wells or other sacred sites, indicating at least his belief that wells existed as markers on the sacral landscape.[125] The wells continued to attract worshippers throughout the Middle Ages; Gerald of Wales was repelled by the number and variety of magical wells in twelfth-century Ireland.[126] Those that became saints' shrines still draw pilgrims today.

Bili and wells were boundaries of a sort, marking the points where the natural world met the otherworld. Other boundaries marked holy places that attracted monastic settlement from the earliest times through the Norman occupation. Such major monasteries as Saigir sat on important territorial boundaries.[127] Fords, places that were traditionally quite busy

---

123. Lucas, "Sacred Trees," 30, 32; FO, lxxxiv; J. G. O'Keeffe, ed., *Buile Suibhne* (London, 1910), 17.

124. Ludwig Bieler, ed., *Patrician Texts from the Book of Armagh* (Dublin, 1979), 152–55; VT, 122–23.

125. See also Adomnán, 348–50.

126. Gerald of Wales, *History and Topography*, 62–64 (chaps. 40–41); Gerald Logan, *The Holy Wells of Ireland* (Gerrards Cross, 1980); C. Ó Danachair, "The Holy Wells of Co. Limerick," JRSAI 85 (1955), 193–217; "The Holy Wells of North Co. Kerry," JRSAI 88 (1958), 153–64; "The Holy Wells of Corkaguiney, Co. Kerry," JRSAI 90 (1960), 67–78.

127. Pádraig Ó Riain, "Boundary Association in Early Irish Society," *Studia Celtica* 7 (1972), 12–29, esp. 17–19. See also John Carey, "The Location of the Otherworld in Irish Tradition," *Éigse* 19 (1982), 36–43.

with otherworldly activity, also drew the monks, and later the Normans.[128] The crossing place over flowing water was dangerous because it was a boundary between two banks of dry land, often between territories, and even between worlds. Saga heroes and historical armies customarily fought at the "ford of battle," often a political boundary but also the neutral border between life and death. Later, local inhabitants marked such sites with stone pillars scratched with the names of fallen warriors of ancient times; at least, this is how scribes explained such places in etymological poems and stories.[129]

Finally, places of human burial topped by grassy tumuli and stone cairns were sacred and attracted settlement. Tombs littered the Irish landscape in the Middle Ages as they do today. They date from different periods of three thousand years of Irish prehistory. Court cairns are possibly the oldest, built during the early neolithic period. Passage graves are of about the same age; near Newgrange, in the Brug na Bóinne area of Meath, passage graves cover the low hills almost densely. Gallery graves and portal tombs, with entrances and skeletal structures of massive stones hidden under earthen tumuli, continued to be built after 2000 B.C. (Fig. 6). By the Bronze Age, about 1750 to 500 B.C., people marked the place of their dead with humbler forms of these giant tombs, or with standing stones or stone circles. After that, bodies went into holes underground or, in the case of some saints, into aboveground shrines set inside or near the oratory of a church.[130] After the change in burial techniques, and because of their ubiquity, the older monuments became almost natural features of the landscape, like *bili* or springs, and held the same mysterious meaning.

Their builders intended the tombs to dominate the local landscape, shouting out the presence of something sacred. They placed most of the tombs on upland sites, not inaccessible heights but prominent positions close to settlements. People built tombs on the most desirable arable of the slopes. Tombs often followed upon settlement at the same site; some sites reveal earlier postholes of dwelling places beneath the tombs. At Brug na

128. B. J. Graham, "Anglo-Norman Settlement in County Meath," PRIA 75 C (1975), 223–51.

129. Alwyn Rees and Brinley Rees, *Celtic Heritage* (London, 1961), 94. See also AU, 46, 69, 190, 214, 222, 246, 250, 274, 376, 386, 514, for battles at sites with names containing the element *áth* or *snám* (both = *vadum*).

130. Michael Herity and George Eogan, *Ireland in Prehistory* (London, 1977), 228; E. E. Evans, *Personality of Ireland*, 48; de Paor, *Peoples of Ireland*, 21–25; Peter Harbison, *Guide to the National Monuments of Ireland* (Dublin, 1970), 5–8; T. W. Moody, F. X. Martin, and F. J. Byrne, eds., *The New History of Ireland* (Oxford, 1976–), vol. 9, *Maps, Genealogies, Lists*, 13–15.

6. Portal dolmen (reconstructed) at Ballynageeragh, county Waterford

Bóinne, habitation and smaller passage graves also appeared long after the great tombs of Newgrange, Knowth, and Dowth.[131]

By occupying the center of the community, the tombs expressed a bond between the farmers, their ancestors, and their land. The megalithic burial chambers held others besides chiefs and leaders. The community had labored together to build the tombs, and worked to maintain the dwelling places of the dead; many members of the community found their resting place there, perched on the hillside where they could watch over their

131. George Eogan, *Excavations at Knowth* (Dublin, 1984); Gabriel Cooney, "Megalithic Tombs in Their Environmental Setting: A Settlement Perspective," in Reeves-Smyth and Hamond, *Landscape Archaeology,* 179–94; Seamus Caulfield, "The Neolithic Settlement of Northern Connaught," in Reeves-Smyth and Hamond, *Landscape Archaeology,* 195–217.

farms and children. The living and the dead worked together to protect and make fruitful the community's territory.[132]

The living and the dead continued to meet at the tombs during the Iron Age and Christian period. The tombs of past millennia remained visible but often from a greater distance as settlement shifted slightly downhill, away from the increasingly eroded upland soils to the valleys and plains. No one tended the tombs any longer. Grasses grew silently over the stone portals, curbstones lurched to the ground. In the medieval literature the tombs appeared as *sídi*, a tradition possibly developed in the Iron Age. The *síd* became a doorway to the otherworld, a place to be avoided even by the bravest of warriors unless he sought the land of the dead.

The mounds retained their function of marking holy places near or among settlements, even if popular understanding of their functions changed. Roads still passed the cairns and passage graves that had lent their names to the land. Iron Age Irish built hill-forts intentionally within view of older monuments, and often kingly forts sat upon earlier burial sites. Monks also built in the shadow of the ancestors' tombs. Over three thousand years at Fidnacha (Fenagh), in Leitrim, the site hosted a portal tomb, a court tomb, two or three passage tombs, standing stones, mounds, a ring-fort, an early Christian and medieval monastery, and associated secular settlement.[133] Some thirty miles to the northwest, on the coast of Donegal, Saint Columcille raised his little community of Druim Cliab at the foot of Ben Bulben. Across Sligo Bay, dominating the sky and assaulting the vision of the monks, was Knocknarea, the hilltop cairn of the great goddess-queen Medb. A few miles from the monastery were vast neolithic necropolises. Columcille and his brothers did not worship Medb and the pagan dead, but the monks used the tombs to find a holy place: a place where the dead of four thousand years watched over the living, where the living could reach the realm of the dead, and where the monks could build a church to the Christian Savior.

The Christian Reorganization of the Landscape

As the population slowly absorbed Christian teaching over several centuries, they gave new meaning to the many sacred places of their an-

---

132. Cooney, "Megalithic Tombs"; see also Colin Renfrew, *Approaches to Social Archaeology* (Southampton, 1984).

133. Cooney, "Megalithic Tombs"; Herity and Eogan, *Ireland in Prehistory*, 228. See also F. Henry, "Remains of the Early Christian Period on Inishkea North, Co. Mayo," JRSAI 95 (1945), 128–55.

cestors. The hagiographers and their brothers not only reorganized the landscape to suit Christian perceptions, but reinterpreted the settlement process itself. By the twelfth century, Gerald of Wales thought that surely *bili* outside church doors were merely ornamental; the Irish never told him that the ancient meaning of the trees endured.[134] Hagiographers revealed the slow process of reinterpretation. When Tírechán described the druids' covered well of Slán, he went on to explain how Pátraic demystified the pagan spring. The saint first gathered the local farmers and suggested that they uncover the well to see if a god's bones really rested inside, but they were unable to lift the cover. With characteristic showmanship, Pátraic made the crowd stand back, blessed the well, and single-handedly shoved the cover to one side, where it continued to lie in Tírechán's time. The well held nothing but water. Tírechán's account suggests that the place became a Christian pilgrimage site because of Pátraic's miracle.[135]

The monks also reinterpreted ritual sites such as royal forts. The prologue to the ninth-century martyrology *Félire Óenguso* boasted of the fall of Temair, Cruachu, Aillenn, Emain Macha, and Ráith Béicce meic Eogain and the consequent rise of adjacent monastic houses: "The great settlement of Tara has died with the loss of its princes; great Armagh lives on with its choirs of scholars. . . . The fortress of Cruachain has vanished with Ailill, victory's child; a fair dignity greater than kingdoms is in the city of Clonmacnois."[136] Yet the very proximity of Ard Macha to Emain Macha, Cluain Moccu Nóis to Cruachu, and other pairings of ancient royal sites with monastic settlements proves the importance of the older holy places to monks and to other people who lived near them.

Temair, for example, a complex site of passage graves, habitation, and earthworks, dominates the secular literature as the sacral and political symbol of Irish kingship. Its ditches and banks were built backward so that, although any human attacker could easily gain entry, the place was hedged with defenses against the forces of the otherworld.[137] Among the mounds and rings, kings had once celebrated the land's fertility and the prosperity of their own reigns in the *feis Temra*, literally the "sleeping with

---

134. Gerald of Wales, *History and Topography*, 77–78 (Chap. 61).

135. Bieler, *Patrician Texts*, 152–55; see also 243.

136. FO, 24–26; David Greene and Frank O'Connor, eds., *A Golden Treasury of Irish Poetry, A.D. 600 to 1200* (London, 1967), 64–65.

137. B. Wailes, "Irish Royal Sites," CMCS 3 (1982), 1–29; D. L. Swan, "The Hill of Tara, Co. Meath," JRSAI 108 (1978), 51–66; see also E. E. Evans, *Prehistoric and Early Christian Ireland: A Guide* (London, 1966), 175; Michael Herity, "A Survey of the Royal Site of Cruachain in Connacht," JRSAI 113 (1983), 121–42; G. S. Olmsted, "A Contemporary View of Irish Hill-Top Enclosures," *Études Celtiques* 16 (1979), 171–86.

Temair." Patrician legends portrayed Temair as a pagan headquarters where druids battled the saint. But, also according to legend, Pátraic converted Temair's king, Lóegaire mac Néill, and the traditional fertility rites lapsed. However, ambitious dynasts continued to fight for the title of king of Temair, for the annals are full of battles over the ancient capital. And Temair gained new meaning on the sacral landscape when it became symbolic of the Christian kingship of Ireland.[138]

The saints also transformed burial mounds into shrines. Sometimes they just renamed the sites after Christians; other times they converted the pagan bones beneath the mounds. Tírechán recounts how Pátraic and his retinue came to "a huge grave of astounding breadth," presumably a neolithic or Bronze Age tomb. The mound extended 120 feet, leading Pátraic's monks to doubt that any man so long lay beneath it. Pátraic raised the giant body to life by striking a marker stone and making the sign of the cross. He baptized the pagan and laid him to rest again.[139] Tírechán and his readers understood the significance of the mounds as ancient burial sites, although their precise origins as community tombs seem to have been lost in a folktale of giants. The monks consciously reinterpreted the tombs' functions, however, converting them from markers of the dead, their territory, and their community into Christian graves and destinations of pilgrimage.

The conversion of tombs also raises the question of whether pre-Christian graveyards continued to be used by Christians, as has recently been shown of some Merovingian cemeteries.[140] Such a question would be interesting to raise at Riasc, where graves lay under the postholes of a later church; archaeologists have assumed that the cemetery was the first and most important element of such early Christian sites.[141] Tírechán described how Pátraic came upon two graves, only one of which was marked with a cross. The cross mistakenly stood at a pagan's grave, so Pátraic moved it to the adjacent Christian's grave. But when challenged by his charioteer as to why he left a pagan resting next to a Christian, Pátraic gave no answer. Tírechán had none either, only remarking: "I think he left the man (as he was) because God did not want to save him."[142] Other

---

138. F. J. Byrne, *Irish Kings and High Kings* (London, 1973).

139. Bieler, *Patrician Texts*, 154–55.

140. B. K. Young, "Exemple aristocratique et mode funéraire dans la Gaule mérovingienne," *Annales, E. S. C.* 41 (1986), 394.

141. Fanning, "Excavation of an Early Christian Cemetery and Settlement"; Charles Thomas, *The Early Christian Archaeology of North Britain* (Oxford, 1971), 48–90.

142. Bieler, *Patrician Texts*, 154–57.

saints performed alterations at burial mounds and wells, but all the saints together could not move or destroy every pagan grave.[143] Many remained among Christian settlements as monuments to previous beliefs and older spirits. Christian doctrine won only a partial victory when the population forgot the tombs' original functions.

The monks followed the saints' example when they, too, modified and reinterpreted pagan monuments. Saint Mochuda had imprisoned a demon in a standing stone and used the monolith as a boundary marker for his monastery.[144] The settlers at Lankill, county Mayo, probably did much the same. Their site contained a possible burial mound with decorated curbstones similar to those at Newgrange. When monks built a church or an oratory there, they dragged one curbstone to a site about a hundred yards away, where they stood it on end and attempted to carve a cross on it. The stone took on a new function as a Christian boundary marker.[145] A motley collection of Christian and pagan relics also remains at Mevagh, in county Donegal. The ruined church contains a stone cross over two meters tall, but also an unmarked standing stone a few feet high, and a recumbent slab marked with cup-shaped depressions, typical of pre-Christian sites.[146]

Monks made more ambiguous use of pagan monuments at other sites. At Templebryan, in Cork, a thin, unmarked pillar stone about eleven feet tall and a bullaun (a bowl-shaped stone used to hold holy water), possibly of later date, mark the center of an early Christian monastic settlement. A little to the south and downhill, within view of the enclosure, stands a modest stone circle of the pre-Christian period.[147] At Knockdrum, also in Cork, a defensive enclosure tops a hill with excellent views out to sea and inland over a valley. Archaeologists cannot decide whether the enclosure was meant for ecclesiastical or secular use. The foundations of a house remain, along with a souterrain, an attractive cross-carved standing stone, and two pre-Christian cup-marked slabs (Fig. 7).[148] Knockdrum may have undergone a transformation similar to that wrought by Máedóc on Slíab

143. HVSH, 185, 275.
144. PVSH I, 303.
145. Françoise Henry, "Megalithic and Early Christian Remains at Lankill, Co. Mayo," JRSAI 82 (1952), 68–71.
146. Brian Lacy et al., *Archaeological Survey of County Donegal* (Lifford, 1983), 256–57.
147. Vincent Hurley, "Additions to the Map of Monastic Ireland," JCHAS 85 (1980), 64.
148. For a whimsical treatment of the site see Boyle Somerville, "'The Fort' on Knock Drum, West Carbery, County Cork," JRSAI 61 (1931), 1–14. Somerville mentions a stone alignment 400 yards from Knockdrum which he considered to be related to the enclosure.

7. Cross-inscribed pillar at Knockdrum, county Cork

Betha, where the saint marked a deserted king-fort with a cross, turning it into a Christian holy place.[149]

Although the origins and uses of Lankill, Mevagh, Templebryan, and Knockdrum may have varied considerably, Christians at all of these sites altered earlier monuments for the same purpose: to transform existing markers of the sacred into Christian symbols, adding new significance to already holy places. Thus also the neolithic traders' tracks across the Wicklow hills turned into St. Cóemgen's Road; from a path marked by standing stones and burials, it became a pilgrimage route dotted with churches and crosses.[150]

Even today, some of the monuments at Christian sites make a mysterious statement to wondering pilgrims. In one corner of the medieval church at Aghowle, county Wicklow, leans a rather phallic stone about two and a half feet high. Its use and age are unclear. Nearby sits a bullaun that may possibly retain symbolic female connotations in its bowl shape and in its water-collecting function (Fig. 8). The juxtaposition is even less subtle at Temair, where a nineteenth-century statue of Saint Pátraic glowers down on an ancient symbol of Ireland and her kings' virility: the so-called Lía Fáil standing stone. The original pillar was used in inaugural rites to symbolize the union of Temair's king with the female earth. The present stone was given the name Lía Fáil only in the nineteenth century. The stone beneath Pátraic's disapproving gaze today also stood anciently at Temair, but was formerly called *bod Fergusso*, "Fergus's penis," after a mighty Ulster hero famous for, among other attributes, his sexual prowess. The penile stone and the modern statue at Temair demonstrate both the continuity of holy places and their continuous alteration. The monks' reinterpretation simply added another layer of meaning to already polysemous holy places.

To combat the ambiguity of holy places, monastic historians altered the collective memory of the process of site selection. Uncomfortable with the old markers, hagiographers never depicted the saints searching for the trees, wells, and tumuli of the gods, or even worrying about arable or neighbors. Instead, monastic writers showed the saints gazing heavenward for a sign from the Bible's one God. Only one location was suitable for the saint's proposed settlement, and only the saint could lead monks or nuns to the site. The hagiographers ignored the complex priorities involved in the process of site selection. Instead they propagandized the abilities of

149. PBNE 1:184.
150. Liam Price, "Glendalough: St. Kevin's Road," in Ryan, *Féil-sgríbhinn Eóin mhic Néill*, 249–51.

8. Bullauns: left, Kilkeeran, county Kilkenny; right, Glenn Dá Locha, county Wicklow

the saints to choose places of great spiritual power; not the old powers, but specifically Christian power.

For example, the saints frequently could not recognize good sites for themselves until angels showed the way. Ruadán built a monastery on the land of Ara moccu Néit, but God sent an angel to inform him that "the Lord does not grant to you that your resurrection should be in this place." So Ruadán tried settling at Lothra, in Ormond, where he received a sign that he had made the right choice: A wild boar, living in a hollow tree, left the site so that the saint might have it. The wilderness and its old spirits thus yielded to a new religious use of the place.[151]

When angels were not available to lead the way, other Christian signs told a saint where to settle. The mere presence of angels on a spot indicated its suitability as a monastic site. Mac Nise and Pátraic knew that some great saint's monastery would stand at Lann Ela because they saw above it a hole in the heavens and angels passing to and fro.[152] Other saints, avoiding the domineering influence of the Patrician tradition, used blessed bells. Ciarán traveled far, but he knew his choice of Saigir to be correct when the clapperless bell that he carried, which normally rang only when beaten with a mallet, began to sound on its own. No other place caused the bell to ring.[153] Ciarán's hagiographer may never have admitted it, but he seems to have been suggesting also that the inherently supernatural character of the site reverberated upon the holy bell.

Saints and monks, like their ancestors, believed that one settlement site was more holy than another. Only one door to heaven opened for a holy man or woman, and it had a precise location on the sacral landscape. Lonely saints wandered the land looking for the sites of their future resurrection. Once they had found and opened the door, monks hoped to gain by living on the site and one day passing through the door, too. The younger Ciarán set up a settlement at Ard Tiprait, later Cluain Moccu Nóis, solely because he knew that those buried in its blessed earth would pass up to heaven.[154] The previous name of the place, "the high place of the well," suggests a possible earlier religious use.

While the traditional signposts to holy places were distasteful to monastic propagandists of the saints, the evidence of archaeology and even the hagiographers' own texts betray the dependence of monastic settlers on

151. PBNE 1:317; 2:308; see also HVSH, 102, 115–16, 229, 230; PVSH 1:70–71, 245–48.
152. HVSH, 406; see also PBNE 1:193–94; USMLS, Conchubranus 1:258; VT, 192.
153. PVSH 1:217–18.
154. Ibid. 211–12.

the old markers. But the hagiographers' new interpretation, in which the saints relied on divine guidance to their *loca,* also derived from older ideas. Generations had looked for places on the landscape that offered both material support and supernatural protection, and had developed methods for marking such places and exploiting them. The monks claimed to use new Christian methods, but nonetheless closely followed their ancestors' use of the land just by searching for and occupying holy places.

The monks had "an intensified sense of place," as the historian Liam de Paor has put it. This, with their wariness of an often hostile natural world, persuaded them to read sacral dimensions into their landscape and then to exploit the landscape for religious purposes. Like an abundance of turf or wood or water, the spiritual aura of a place made it attractive to settlers. The monks seem to have had two choices: to resist ancient markers of the sacred by avoiding or eliminating them or to reinterpret and Christianize them. Mostly, they chose reinterpretation. In reality, the monks' choices were more than two, and were rarely permanent. But the hagiographers continued to insist that the saints alone could explain why the monks settled where they did.

CHAPTER TWO

The Monastic Enclosure

As the hagiographers tell it, a saint usually went grate-fully to death after a long life of wonder-working and Christian pioneering. Saints did not simply expire of age and illness like other Irishmen and women. They did not pass into the darkness of the earth, but climbed to a higher vantage point where they kept a protective eye on all who called upon them. Their spirits passed continuously between heaven and earth, returning to hover over their relics and the monasteries they had founded.

Monastic architecture, like hagiography, advertised the eternal presence of the saints in their relics. The monks organized their settlements around the display of the saints' bones or other remains. Not everyone was allowed to enter the holy place and approach the saint, for the monks jealously controlled access to the relics. Their most useful architectural tool was a wall, which both protected the monks and their relics from intruders and contained the saint's holy aura. Within the monastery, internal walls further isolated the sanctum sanctorum, where the saint presided, from the profane spaces of the monastery.

The monastery's walls and markers sent a message across the Christian landscape, which still echoes today among monastic ruins: The saint dwells here with the monks. Those who gazed at the distant walls of Cluain Moccu Nóis or caught a glimpse of Cell Da Lua's tower understood. The saint's designated disciples, living inside the walls of the saint's *locus*, tending and praying to the saint's bones, flourished in the constant presence of their holy patron. The personal relationship between monks and saints, emphasized in the *vitae*, derived from this close, physical contact and exclusive access.

The Enclosure

By the ninth century, when the hagiographers were writing and redacting the *vitae* we read today, some monasteries were prosperous and populous. Many that had begun as a crude collection of wattled cells had become large settlements with artistically crafted stone churches and well-appointed domestic buildings. While hagiographers used an indiscriminate profusion of terms for monasteries—*eclais, domnach, tempull, reiclés, ecclesia, cellula, oratorium, monasterium, civitas*—the monasteries of the *vitae* were routinely large and wealthy communities. Yet not every settlement resembled Ard Macha of Pátraic or Ard Mór of Déclán. The hagiographers wrote for and about the most successful monastic communities, and hardly admitted the existence of small hermitages, oratories, tiny shrines operated privately by family groups, and episcopal sites. By neglecting to describe other kinds of religious settlements, hagiographers suggested a false uniformity in the appearance and function of all monasteries.[1] In reality, monastic settlements differed according to location, available resources, size and status, and function.

Nonetheless, most monasteries, even small settlements, displayed similar features in the layout of their buildings and internal spaces. To begin with, the monks always defined a holy place clearly so that people knew where the saint could be found. Most monasteries were surrounded by an enclosing wall (*vallum*) of dirt, stone, or wattle, often built in conjunction with a ditch. Monastic walls served a variety of practical functions. They delimited monastic property for legal purposes.[2] They protected inhabitants of the community from the elements and helped prevent erosion.[3] Defense was probably not the walls' most important purpose; any amateur archaeologist knows how easy it is to climb most enclosing walls. But walls and boundaries also represented the wealth and social status of a community, as the concentric rings and deep ditches around some monasteries and royal forts show. Some enclosures were splendidly multivallate, as at

1. Vincent Hurley, "Additions to the Monastic Map of Ireland: The Southwest," JCHAS 85 (1980), 53; Hurley, "The Early Church in the South-west of Ireland: Settlement and Organisation," in Susan M. Pearce, ed., *The Early Church in Western Britain and Ireland* (Oxford, 1982), 298–301; T. W. Moody, F. X. Martin, and F. J. Byrne, eds., *The New History of Ireland* (Oxford, 1976–), 9:100–101.

2. CIH 1:195; ALI 4:113.

3. W. Groenman-van Waateringe, "Field Boundaries in Ireland," in Donnchadh Ó Corráin, ed., *Irish Antiquity* (Cork, 1980), 285–90.

Nóendruimm, where three ostentatious walls of stone ringed the settlement.[4]

The size and shape of the enclosing walls varied. The outer ring at Nóendruimm contained six acres; the tiny monastery at Church Island sat on hardly half an acre. The amount of ground enclosed by walls probably depended on the wealth of the community; large and populous settlements enclosed a larger area. Some walls were rectangular or irregular in shape, influenced by the surface and elevation of the local terrain. For instance, the community on Scelec Mhichíl was confined by walls that wandered seemingly aimlessly among the island's rocks. The seabound cliff had no horizontal plane large enough for a proper circular enclosure.[5]

Whenever possible, however, the monks chose to build a curvilinear (Fig. 9) enclosure. The only existing diagram of an early Irish monastery, in the colophon of the eighth- or ninth-century Book of Mulling, represented the enclosure with a double circle.[6] The *vitae* also describe the effort made by monks to impose a circular plan on their settlements. At Cell Áir, for example, an enormous boulder halted the professional construction workers who were digging the ditch and building the walls. The workers would have had to relocate the enclosure, but their employer was a saint, who easily shifted the rock with a miraculous gesture. The ditch-diggers did not consider detouring around the rock or reshaping the walls, which indicates a certain commitment to the site and a plan for an enclosure of a particular shape and size.[7]

The symbolism of the circle was familiar to the monks from the spirals of pagan metalwork and the shapes of the abandoned forts that they inhabited as monasteries. Enclosures circled all of the major king-forts in pre-Christian Ireland, such as Temair, Tailtiu, and Ailech. Round walls protected these sacred sites for the reasons later adopted by the monks: The circular enclosure functioned as a replica of the cosmos, an attempt to

4. H. C. Lawlor, *The Monastery of Saint Mochaoi of Nendrum* (Belfast, 1925), 95–101; Charles Thomas, *The Early Christian Archaeology of North Britain* (Oxford, 1971), 10–47; Philip Ratz, "Monasteries as Settlements," *Scottish Archaeological Forum* 5 (1973), 125–35; Hurley, "Additions to the Monastic Map of Ireland," 53.

5. Liam de Paor, "A Survey of Sceilg Mhichíl," JRSAI 85 (1955), 174–87; E. R. Norman and J. K. S. St. Joseph, *The Early Development of Irish Society* (Cambridge, 1969), 95; Paul Walsh, "The Monastic Settlement on Rathlin O'Birne Island, County Donegal," JRSAI 113 (1983), 63; Michael Herity, "The High Island Hermitage," *Irish University Review* 7 (1977), 65.

6. Kathleen Hughes, *The Church in Early Irish Society* (London, 1972), 149; Lawrence Nees, "The Colophon Drawing in the Book of Mulling," CMCS 5 (1983), 67–91.

7. HVSH, 175.

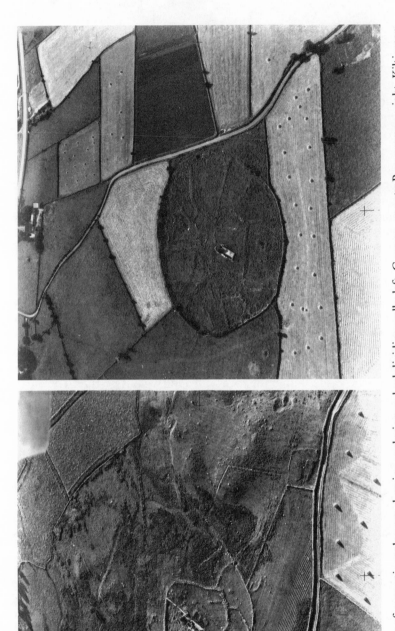

9. Aerial photographs of monastic enclosures showing enclosing and subdividing walls: left, Comeen, county Roscommon; right, Kiltiernan, county Galway. Courtesy of the Committee for Aerial Photography, University of Cambridge; copyright reserved.

create a place that existed simultaneously on this earthly plane and on the eternal plane.[8] The rejection of a circular plan was unimaginable, given the monks' adherence to earlier ideas of what was fitting and holy.

The monks developed a tradition of elaborate rituals for marking out the circular enclosure, to impress upon themselves and secular folk their exclusive prerogative to locate and inhabit holy places. They envisioned their saintly patrons acting out a three-part ritual in order to demarcate a sacred space. First, the saints marked the outer limits of the chosen *locus* with spades, or words of blessing, or both. In practice, a monastery's walls were sometimes constructed after its churches and cells, as at Riasc.[9] However, the monks themselves believed that the invisible boundaries of the sacred space came into existence as soon as the saint had claimed his or her *locus*. The second step was to locate the spiritual center of the space by marking out the walls of a church, an oratory, or a cemetery and consecrating it with relics. The third step was to divide and arrange the enclosure's inner spaces.[10]

The saints may well have performed a ritual to mark the boundaries of a community and the most holy areas within an enclosure. In later centuries, the monks probably ceremonially blessed newly acquired property to mark its conversion to Christian sacred space. The *Vita tripartita* of Pátraic pictured clerics proceeding as a group around the borders of a new community, sometimes accompanied by local political leaders, blessing its space and its limits.[11] At Druim Caili, Pátraic recruited more prestigious personnel to add extra sanctity to his foundation ritual: Here he measured the enclosure and buildings in procession with angels, elders of the community, his *muinter* (retinue), and his *bachall* (clerical staff). The saint specified measurements for the outer limits of the enclosure as well as for its major buildings, and instructed all of his communities to complete the ritual in the same fashion.[12]

Máedóc's hagiographer wrote that when the saint founded Druim Lethan, in the sixth century, he blessed the place, arranged its ramparts and

8. Charles Doherty, "Monastic Towns in Early Medieval Ireland," in A. B. Clarke and A. Simms, eds., *The Comparative History of Urban Origins in Non-Roman Europe* (Oxford, 1984), 45–49; Bernard Wailes, "Irish 'Royal Sites' in History and Archaeology," CMCS 3 (1982), 1–29; D. L. Swann, "The Hill of Tara, County Meath: The Evidence of Aerial Photography," JRSAI 108 (1978), 51–66.

9. Thomas, *Early Christian Archaeology*, 38.

10. PBNE 1:207, 300; 2:201, 291; VT, 192, 228, 236; Wasserschleben, *Collectio*, 174–78.

11. VT, 140, 230; cf. Wasserschleben, *Collectio*, 175: "Tres personae consecrant terminum loci sancti, rex, episcopus, populus."

12. VT, 236.

cemeteries, measured and marked out temples, churches, and round towers, and ordered its congregations and rituals.[13] Despite the anachronism
of round towers, which did not appear in Ireland until the tenth century,
Máedóc's hagiographer understood the ritual, as had the earlier hagiographer of Pátraic; the saint and his community publicized the exact
extent of the site and its function as a sacred space. The Irish verb used for
the act of marking boundaries and building foundations, *do-foirndea*, had
many related meanings. Its primary sense was "expresses, signifies" but it
also meant "marks out, delineates." In the latter sense, scribes used the
word in its various forms to express the idea of founding settlements, both
secular and holy.[14]

But the act was also a symbol of the saint's establishment on the site and
the site's existence on both the physical and sacral landscapes. The ritual
was potent even when performed on sites that were not especially holy. A
man living in the neighborhood of Ailbe's community of Imlech begged
the saint to imitate the religious ritual of foundation and mark the boundaries of his new house. Ailbe obliged. This service, he promised the man,
would protect the house from rain, wind, and abandonment. Ailbe imbued the limits of the new house with some of the sanctity of monastic
boundaries; his act would keep out hostile elements and keep the positive,
protective essence of the place.[15]

The monks invoked cosmic symbolism when they moved in a circular
procession around their foundations. When Máedóc founded Ros Inbir,
he blessed his chosen site aided by "a multitude of angels and high-saints
circling [*ina uirtimceall*] above."[16] Likewise, when the elders of I made a
clamor to their patron in time of drought, they redefined their boundaries,
reaffirming their relationship with the saint and the sanctity of the settlement. They circled (*circumirent*) their newly plowed fields, shaking relics
and calling on Columcille.[17] And when Máedóc sought to protect his lay
clients from Uí Cheinselaig raiders, he redrew the boundaries of his sanctuary around his people and their cattle; he described a circle (*timchell*)
with his staff.[18]

13. PBNE 1:207; 2:201.
14. Kuno Meyer, ed., *Sanas Cormaic: An Old-Irish Glossary*, Anecdota from Irish Manuscripts 4 (Dublin, 1912), 41–42 (Y 502).
15. HVSH, 128. *Depingeret* is the verb used in the Latin episode, the Latin past sub-
junctive equivalent of *do-foirndea*. See also HVSH, 191.
16. PBNE 1:235–36; 2:228–29.
17. Adomnán, 450–51.
18. PBNE 1:185; 2:179. See also R. I. Best, "An Early Monastic Grant from the Book of
Durrow," *Ériu* 10 (1926–28), 142.

The consecration of boundaries was only one sort of blessing in a busy schedule of benedictions and maledictions by which the monks lived. Yet the hagiographer's special concern for this ritual betrays its importance, for example, in the story of Saint Bairre's fosterers. These elder monks built churches in Leinster and began to sign them with the cross and to bless the buildings, but, recalling that they had a more powerful benediction at hand, asked their small pupil to bless the space, because every site that he consecrated "will be blessed and will be inhabited."[19] Throughout his *vita*, Bairre tried to give his *loca* the most effective blessings possible, to ensure their continued security and prosperity. At the settlement site of Corcach, the saint fasted and prayed before building in order to imbue the site with extra holiness.[20] Bairre's hagiographer made it clear that the monks of Corcach could sleep soundly at night, knowing that their enclosure had potent blessings to keep its borders.

The more holy the saint, the more powerful was his or her consecration. Brigit had supposedly confined Cell Dara with invisible limits that were just as effective as walls in keeping intruders out and holiness in. No solid walls marked the settlement's outer boundaries when Cogitosus described it in the late seventh century, but he thought none were needed, for at the boundaries "which Brigit laid at a certain limit, no human adversary nor advance of enemies is feared."[21] Such powerful sanctions served many of the same functions as stone walls or deep ditches. Other communities besides Cell Dara maintained their boundaries without walls. Some had more natural borders. Island monasteries, for instance, had no practical need for walls or ditches except to protect against rough sea winds. On Church Island monks did not bother to build the stone walls of the *caisel* (stone enclosure) until after they had replaced a wooden church and hut with stone buildings. It is unlikely that they needed the walls for defense, as the monastery was surrounded by the sea and had already survived possibly for centuries without walls.[22]

The secular literature hinted at a period when solid walls were not always the most common boundary markers.[23] A learned commentator on

---

19. PVSH 1:68.
20. Ibid., 70–71.
21. Migne, PL 72:790.
22. M. J. O'Kelly, "Monastic Sites in the West of Ireland," *Scottish Archaeological Forum* 5 (1973), 9.
23. Rudolf Thurneysen, *Zu irischen Handschriften und Litteraturdenkmälern*. Abhandlungen der koniglichenn Gesellschaft der Wissenschaften zu Göttingen. Philologisch-historische Klasse, NF 14, 2 (Berlin, 1912), 35.

the laws listed different types of boundary markers: "A flat mark, a stone mark, a tree mark, a deer mark, a stock mark, a mound mark, a division mark, and a water mark, an eye mark, a defect mark, a way mark."[24] The first of these, the "flat mark" or *clárblá*, was no marker at all, indicating "land which is not distinguished by any land mark, and which authorities cannot legally define."[25] Jurists accepted the concept of territory with invisible boundaries, but suggested that these unseen limits were impractical. Legal fines for trespass were much higher if the boundaries were properly marked with fences or ditches, while some sorts of trespass over unmarked borders brought no penalty at all.[26]

As a result, despite the proud claims of Cogitosus, the ecclesiastical establishment preferred properly enclosed communities as early as the eighth century, when many of the laws were first written down. As the ecclesiastical canons of this period put it, "The sanctuary of a sacred place must have markers around it."[27] Yet the monks were aware that stone crosses or cross-inscribed slabs could fill the same functions as walls; the sacred space need not be hidden, but merely marked out and enclosed. The famous carved crosses of early Ireland could set the limits of a settlement, just as they marked roads and the sacred places along them (Fig. 10). Michael Herity has shown that at the hermits' settlements of Dísert Bethech and Dísert Óengusa crosses provided the only protection against the surrounding wilderness. Sometimes, as at Castle Kieran and Ferna Mór, crosses circled the inside of the enclosure, doubling the security of physical walls.[28]

According to the hagiographers, crosses not only reinforced walls but also guarded breaks in the walls' defense. They agreed with canonists, who instructed Christians: "Wherever you find the mark of Christ's cross, do no damage."[29] Crosses guarded a monastery's entrances and exits. For instance, a cross protected the path to the southern chapel at Druim Moccu Blaí and guarded the door to a shed outside the enclosure at Í.[30] The monks also placed protective markers at internal thresholds, usually at the entrance to churches or church enclosures. A cross stood sentry at the

---

24. ALI 4:142; CIH 1:201.
25. ALI 4:143, modified translation; CIH 1:201.
26. CIH 1:68.
27. Wasserschleben, *Collectio,* 175.
28. Michael Herity, "The Buildings and Layout of Early Irish Monasteries before the Year 1000," *Monastic Studies* 14 (1983), 270–77.
29. Wasserschleben, *Collectio,* 175.
30. Adomnán, 306–307; HVSH, 203; VT, 240.

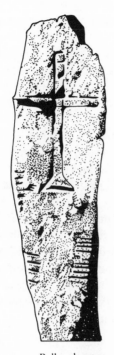

| Inishkea North | Ballynahunt | Knockdrum | Riasc |

10. Cross-inscribed pillars (scales vary)

door to Bairre's church at Corcach.[31] A giant millstone, which Brigit miraculously moved from a mountaintop to the plain below, later rested at the door to Cell Dara's inner enclosure, protecting the inner sanctum of the monastery. The stone remained untouched by a fire that damaged other monastic buildings. It also had the power to heal ailing pilgrims.[32]

The monks did not needlessly litter their enclosures with crosses and other monuments, but placed the symbol of Christ at gates invisible to unbelieving eyes. Crosses marked and protected exits that opened vertically, to heaven above. When Mochuda was expelled from Rathan, the dead of his community rose to accompany him; politely but firmly, the

31. PBNE 1:17; see also H. J. Lawlor, *Chapters on the Book of Mulling* (Edinburgh, 1897), 167–85; Nees, "Colophon Drawing," 67–91.
32. Migne, PL 72:787.

saint requested that they return to their graves, promising that the cross of Cusantin would be a rendezvous point for them all at Judgment Day, when they would pass together over the earthly boundary to heaven.[33] Crosses marked cosmic entrances as well as exits. Monenna returned two days after her death in a vision to her nun, Taunat, to complain that her community had already relaxed its rules. She chose the cross outside the sisters' dormitory for her entrance.[34]

The monks also drew on older traditions when they marked the entrances and exits to the otherworld. When Brénainn felt death approaching, he went to a place in the monastic enclosure that was highly symbolic of transition in many cultures: the threshold of a house. It was appropriate that Brénainn the wanderer should die, not in the arms of his disciples, as did Columcille, but on his way through the door.[35] As we have seen, grave mounds and markers also had functioned as gateways to the otherworld since the neolithic, and continued to do so in monastic settings. Saint Buite found a golden ladder standing conveniently in his cemetery, which he climbed to heaven.[36] The highways to heaven began inside the enclosure, and were apparently as familiar and as well signposted as any of the dirt tracks crossing the plains and hills.

Cemeteries, Shrines, and Churches

The monks perceived a difference in the quality of spaces inside and outside the enclosure. All space within the enclosures was sacred, but the monks located and marked the most holy areas, which were the centers of their settlements. Eighth-century canons decreed that monks should ritually divide their enclosures and designate the sanctum sanctorum, refusing lay people entry into it by means of "four boundaries around a sanctuary, the first into which laymen and women enter, the second into which only clerics come. The first is called holy, the second holier, the third most holy. Note that the name of the fourth is lacking."[37]

Bones or some other tangible token of the saint's days on earth rested in a grave or shrine in the most holy center of the settlement, either the

---

33. PVSH 1:192–93.
34. USMLS, Conchubranus 3:444.
35. PVSH 1:150.
36. Ibid., 95.
37. Wasserschleben, *Collectio*, 175. See note and variant, 176–77. Also cited in Hughes, *Church in Early Irish Society*, 148.

community's cemetery or its church. The saintly patron may have left clothing or sacred books with disciples, or brought the relics of another saint to bless and protect a monastic settlement. Lacking the body of their own founder, Pátraic, the monks of Ard Macha collected a battery of apostolic remains.[38] Prestigious Irish monasteries prized bits of Martin of Tours.[39] But most precious to a community was the body of its own patron, the one who founded the settlement and whose deeds and virtues the community's hagiographers commemorated in writing. The monks agreed with the canonists that the saint was the focus of every monastic settlement, extrapolating from the principle that "the blood of martyrs consecrates a place, the place does not make the blood holy."[40]

The clerics of every settlement demonstrated the importance of relics by spending as much wealth, space, and labor as they could spare to set apart a special place for the saints' remains. Cell Dara's main church held two tombs, according to Cogitosus. Brigit lay to the right and her bishop, Conláed, to the left of the main altar, which was separated from the congregation by a decorated partition. Craftsmen adorned the tombs with gold, silver, and gems. Two precious crowns were suspended above the resting saints.[41] In contrast, the monks of Tempul Crónáin placed their founder's tomb just outside their tiny church (Fig. 11). Crónán's remains lay in an unassuming shrine about the size and shape of a small doghouse, constructed of thin slate slabs. Crónán's church sat among the bleak rocks of the Burren, while Brigit and Conláed reposed on the rich plains of Kildare. The monks of both sites honored their patrons with shrines placed prominently in the sacred center of their communities, one in the church, the other outside in the graveyard.

Hagiographers insisted that the saints themselves left their bodies to their monastic heirs. Actually, the popularity of relics reached its height after the eighth century, when communities sought extra relics of their patrons or those of other important saints to reinforce the holiness of their settlements. Translations, the ritual removal of relics from one site to another, occurred throughout Europe more frequently after 800, when monks deposited holy bones in shrines of precious metals or in richly decorated altars.[42] Numerous translations in the Irish *vitae* betray the

38. Ludwig Bieler, ed., *Patrician Texts in the Book of Armagh* (Dublin, 1979), 186–88.
39. HVSH, 226–27; PBNE I:122, 124, 266. See also Kenney, *Sources,* 668.
40. Wasserschleben, *Collectio,* 178–79.
41. Migne, PL 72:788–89; Thomas, *Early Christian Archaeology,* 145–46, 207–12.
42. Patrick J. Geary, *Furta Sacra: Thefts of Relics in the Central Middle Ages* (Princeton, N.J., 1978), 45–49.

11. Crónán's shrine at Tempul Crónáin

attempt by many communities to supplement their relic collections.[43] According to one hagiographer, the nuns of Cell Eochaille begged their patron, Saint Senán, for the relics of a lowly monk, any lowly monk, to protect them and their church.[44] This episode probably referred to a translation of some relics of a minor saint from one of Senán's major settlements, such as Inis Chathaig, to a subsidiary community of nuns.

In fact, monks of different monasteries competed intensely and sometimes unscrupulously for the patronage of the saints. Almost as the holy man or women drew a last breath, disciples and clients began to wrangle over the bones. According to hagiographers, the saints resorted to illusion to prevent bloodshed in such situations; but the hagiographers were actually explaining how two communities might claim the presence of the same saint in each of their cemeteries or churches. The *Vita tripartita*, for example, describes the disposition of Pátraic's body: The Uí Néill and their ally, the monastery of Ard Macha, and the Airgialla, with their monastic community of Dún Lethglas, both believed that they had secured the relics. As it turned out, the Uí Néill accepted a false oxcart carrying an imaginary coffin, while Dún Lethglas got the genuine article.[45] Clearly, Dún Lethglas had already legitimated the tradition of Pátraic's burial in its cemetery, despite the envious claims of the more politically powerful community, as even Ard Macha's hagiographers had to admit.[46]

Monastic communities struggled, sometimes unsuccessfully, to prevent thefts of their sacred bones, teeth, tools, books, bits of cloth, and wood.[47] When Abbán lay dying the monks of two of his communities were in attendance, ready to take the body. One snatched the saint as soon as his soul had migrated. Although the saint performed a miracle reminiscent of Pátraic, in which two oxcarts appeared carrying two bodies, the results were different: Both communities claimed to have Abbán's bones, and shrines at both monasteries worked wonders in his name.[48] His hagiographer recounted the episode not only to remind Christians of where Abbán's body lay but to boast of the value of his relics, so powerful that

43. See, e.g., Bieler, *Patrician Texts*, 136.
44. Stokes, *Lismore*, 74, 221.
45. VT, 258.
46. HVSH, 144–45.
47. Geary, *Furta Sacra*, esp. 132–43; HVSH, 179–80; PBNE 1:124–73; Bieler, *Patrician Texts*, 120; H. S. Crawford, "A Descriptive List of Irish Shrines and Reliquaries," JRSAI 53 (1923), 74–93, 151–76.
48. HVSH, 272–74.

even the ersatz bones caused miracles, and so coveted by monks of other communities that the brothers cheerfully resorted to crime to obtain them. The potential benefits to their settlements were too overwhelming for monks to resist the furtive acquisition and competitive display of relics.

When the remains of the saintly dead were laid in the ground, the very soil of cemeteries became hallowed. The graves of the ancients had already been profoundly holy places to Irish monks, but now the resting places of blessed Christians became central to the religion and its rituals. The shrines drew Christians anxious to approach the saints, who they believed would intercede for them with God. Cogitosus described the needy, disabled, and awestruck pilgrims who mobbed Cell Dara. These people needed desperately to see and even touch the saints; Crónán's tomb at Tempul Crónáin and the mortuary house at Sabull had holes in their sides through which the faithful reached to fondle the saints' bones.[49]

But as mediators between God's dead saints and live lay folk, the monks carefully controlled access to their cemeteries. Even in death only certain Christians could penetrate the most holy space of the enclosure, the saint's resting place. Most often, monks reserved the enclosure's burial grounds for their brothers and for kings and nobility who could pay handsomely for the privilege.[50] One hagiographer mentioned the case of a mother and son; the boy, who became a cleric, was buried inside the enclosure in the community's cemetery, while his mother was buried near him but outside the graveyard's walls.[51] At Termon Cumainig (Carrickmore, county Tyrone) tradition and archaeological evidence both suggest that, in addition to the main cemetery of monks and their special friends, separate graveyards existed for women, children, and murder victims. From the Middle Ages until the nineteenth century unbaptized children were often buried in *cillíns*, located on the outer edges of consecrated ground or in more ancient holy places such as abandoned *ráths*.[52]

The monks chose the church as a second focus of their settlements. The church was the community's other important sacred center, because there

---

49. Migne, PL 72:790; Thomas, *Early Christian Archaeology*, 141–44; D. M. Waterman, "An Early Christian Mortuary House at Saul, Co. Down," UJA 23 (1960), 82–88; Herity, "High Island Hermitage," 68; Herity, "The Ornamented Tomb of the Saint at Ardoileán, Co. Galway," in Michael Ryan, ed., *Irish and Insular Art, A.D. 500–1200* (Dublin, 1985).

50. PVSH 1:245–48; PBNE 1:128, 160–61, 172–73, 174–75, 222–23.

51. VT, 204.

52. Ibid., 202; Ann Hamlin and Claire Foley, "A Women's Graveyard at Carrickmore, Co. Tyrone, and the Separate Burial of Women," UJA 46 (1983), 41–46; R. B. Aldridge, "Notes on Children's Burial Grounds in Mayo," JRSAI 99 (1969), 83–87.

the monks broke the barrier of silence between heaven and earth and, with the aid of their saintly mediator, spoke to God. Indeed, hagiographers often used the church as a metaphor for the entire enclosure; saints founded *ecclesiae* and *cellae*, only occasionally *monasteria* and *civitates*, and never *familiae* or *communitates*. The church or oratory was the only other feature common to most monastic settlements besides the cemetery and enclosing walls.[53] Like cemeteries, and situated near them, churches remained closed to most lay people. Monks built churches to house their formal and exclusive rituals; rituals involving lay people took place elsewhere. Even when lay folk attended mass, all but royalty probably stood outside the inner sanctum while the monks carried on their rites within the church. The tiny size of most early churches would have prevented a large attendance even if the laity had been invited.[54]

The church most popular in the early sources, the wooden *dairthech* or "oak-house," has disappeared with almost no trace. The annalists repeatedly reported the burning of such buildings.[55] Early documents, such as Cogitosus' life of Brigit and the *Hisperica famina*, described wood-beamed oratories in elaborate detail. "Do you hew the sacred oaks with axes, in order to fashion square chapels with thick beams?" asked the hisperic poet. He answered himself:

This wooden oratory is fashioned out of candle-shaped beams;
it has sides joined by four-fold fastenings;
the square foundations of the said temple give it stability,
from which springs a solid beamwork of massive enclosure;
it has a vaulted roof above;
square beams are placed in the ornamented roof.
It has a holy altar in the centre,
on which the assembled priests celebrate Mass.
It has a single entrance from the western boundary,
which is closed by a wooden door that seals the warmth.
An assembly of planks comprises the extensive portico;
there are four steeples at the top.
The chapel contains innumerable objects,
which I shall not struggle to unroll from my wheel of words.[56]

---

53. Kathleen Hughes and Ann Hamlin, *Celtic Monasticism* (New York, 1977), 56.

54. Françoise Henry, *Irish Art in the Early Christian Period* (London, 1965), chap. 2: "Early Monasteries."

55. Aidan MacDonald, "Notes on Monastic Archaeology and the Annals of Ulster, 650–1050," in Ó Corráin, *Irish Antiquity*, 305–6.

56. Migne, PL 72:789; HF, 68–69, 108–109.

The wooden churches of the Irish were also known to outsiders. In the eighth century, Bede wrote of wooden churches built in the Irish fashion; four hundred years later, Bernard of Clairvaux noted a wooden plank church at Bennchor.[57]

Only the postholes of wooden churches remain today at many sites, usually obscured by the ruins of later stone buildings. These, however, reveal something about the size, shape, and site orientation of early wooden structures. Wooden churches were sprinkled throughout Ireland, though less along the rocky west coast than inland and in the east. Because of the weight of their roofs they were generally small, rectangular, and built on a proportion of length to width of about three to two.[58] Hagiographers confirmed several of these architectural details and also referred to the rebuilding of wooden churches that had become too small for their expanding monastic communities.[59]

The hagiographers seemed unconcerned with the shapes of their churches, perhaps because the rectangle was so pervasive. The rectangular stone churches of the Continent had invaded Ireland and Britain as early as 600; like almost everything that came from closer to Rome, this shape appealed to Christians in the hinterland as something orthodox and therefore good.[60] Still, according to Tírechán, Pátraic founded rectangular churches in Conmaicne, which suggests that other, possibly earlier, shapes may have existed outside the Patrician sphere of influence.[61] A much later life describes Máedóc erecting "a fair-built quadrangular regular church" at Ros Inbir.[62] While the *Vita tripartita* recommends that every Patrician church should measure twenty-seven feet, it does not record whether that measurement was length, width, or both; some historians have even assumed it meant the diameter of a round church.[63]

Throughout Ireland wooden churches gave way to larger stone buildings as monastic communities gained wealth and power. By 700, many

57. Bede, HBE III.25; Bernard of Clairvaux, *The Life and Death of Saint Malachy the Irishman,* trans. Robert T. Meyer, Cistercian Fathers ser. 10 (Kalamazoo, Mich., 1978), 32; Hughes and Hamlin, *Celtic Monasticism,* 58.

58. Herity, "Building and Layout," 250; E. E. Evans, *Prehistoric and Early Christian Ireland* (London, 1966), 35.

59. USMLS, Conchubranus III, 446–49; PVSH 2:257; Migne, PL 72:788; PVSH 2:257–58.

60. Charles Thomas, *Christianity in Roman Britain to A.D. 500* (London, 1981; rpt. 1985), 143–47.

61. Bieler, *Patrician Texts,* 150–51.

62. PBNE 1:235–36; 2:228–29.

63. VT, 236; John Ryan, *Irish Monasticism: Origins and Early Development* (Dublin, 1931), 288.

western settlements had already arranged their enclosures as they would remain for centuries and had built churches that would last until the invasion of Norman architectural styles.[64] Prosperous, populous monastic communities, especially in the east and the midlands, undertook a program of expansion in the ensuing centuries.[65] The sacred buildings, monuments, and spaces of these larger settlements had to be made grand and beautiful to house the saint's relics and to accommodate lay visitors as well as the daily activities of the monks themselves. The monks rebuilt churches using techniques that they may have copied from the humble corbeled stone huts of the west coast; but the shape and style of these stone churches (*dom liacc, daimliac*) derived from their wooden predecessors. In fact, our knowledge of the earlier wooden churches is culled as much from the reconstruction of collapsed stone buildings as from the few remaining pictorial representations of wooden churches.[66]

Each monastic church was surrounded by a sanctuary called a *termonn* (from Latin *terminus*). At many settlements the inhabitants partitioned off the church to form a sanctum sanctorum, as at Riasc or Dub Ileán. At Nóendruimm the church sat within its own curvilinear enclosure. At Ard Ileán the rectangular church was enclosed by slightly larger rectangular walls, while the church on Inis Muiredaig was left in a large irregular space when monks there walled off other spaces.[67] The presence of the saints' relics lent special protection to this buffer zone between church and more profane spaces. Political refugees fled to the safety of the *termonn* and saints cursed those who violated the sanctuary with theft, assault, or murder.[68] In monastic eyes, no laws held force in the *termonn* but those of the saint who guarded it.[69]

Other especially holy areas besides churches and cemeteries existed within the monks' walled settlements. Wells inside their enclosures had the same spiritual aura as wells in the wilderness. Because the monks used them for baptism, the wells symbolized ritual cleaning and rebirth, and so were doubly holy. On the small island of Rathlin O'Birne, for example,

64. Herity, "Building and Layout," 268.

65. Doherty, "Monastic Town," 60.

66. Henry, *Irish Art*, Chap. 2; Máire de Paor and Liam de Paor, *Early Christian Ireland* (London, 1978), 58–60.

67. Herity, "Building and Layout," 247–84; Herity, "The Layout of Irish Early Christian Monasteries," in Michael Richter and Proinséas Ní Chatháin, eds., *Ireland and Europe: The Early Church* (Stuttgart, 1984), 105–16.

68. PBNE 1:185; 2:179; Adomnán, 178–83.

69. AU, 481; ALI 5:302; Wasserschleben, *Collectio*, 175–77; Hughes, *Church in Early Irish Society*, 148.

monks marked their well with not one but two cross-incised slabs, one on top of the well itself.[70] The space that surrounded wells, charged as it already was with the sacred, became the site of miracles.[71] Fire also invoked the protection of the saints, as at Cell Dara. The paschal fire at Saint Ciarán's Saigir consecrated both temporal and physical space; monks kept it burning for a year at a time, extinguishing and relighting it only at Easter. Like his relics, Ciarán's eternal flame symbolized the saint's presence, but the fire was also a sort of continuous prayer to God and his saints, possibly laden with Old Testament connotations.[72] Sacral markers subtler than fire or well water also dotted the enclosure. Columcille declared that angels frequented certain corners of Cluain Moccu Nóis, although he did not specify exactly where within the enclosure they alighted. Nor did Adomnán, his hagiographer, elaborate.[73] Sensitive as they were to things and places holy, determined as they were to mark and regulate holiness, the monks still were not able to map every important point on the sacral landscape.

Profane Spaces

Daily life took the monks back and forth over their boundaries. They constantly moved from the presence of the saint to other areas of their settlements. Mixed communities of monks, artisans, and their families, dependent agricultural laborers, and other workers needed living and working spaces within or near the enclosure. Monastic communities also housed guests and students, ideally in separate buildings. The monks had to construct sheds for equipment and animals and for storing grain, cheeses, and other foodstuffs. Larger enclosures probably had kitchen gardens or animal pens within their walls. The monks tried to arrange these spaces and buildings according to their spiritual importance within the settlement, although at times the application of ideals to architectural reality remained tenuous (Fig. 12).

No plan of St. Gall exists for early Ireland, and so the siting of most buildings within the enclosure is poorly documented. But both archaeological evidence and occasional literary references suggest that the

70. Paul Walsh, "The Monastic Settlement on Rathlin O'Birne Island, County Donegal," JRSAI 113 (1983), 61.
71. VT, 8; PBNE 1:122; 2:118; USMLS, Conchubranus II, 122–23.
72. PBNE 1:110–11.
73. Adomnán, 218, 219, 496–99; see also PVSH 1:150.

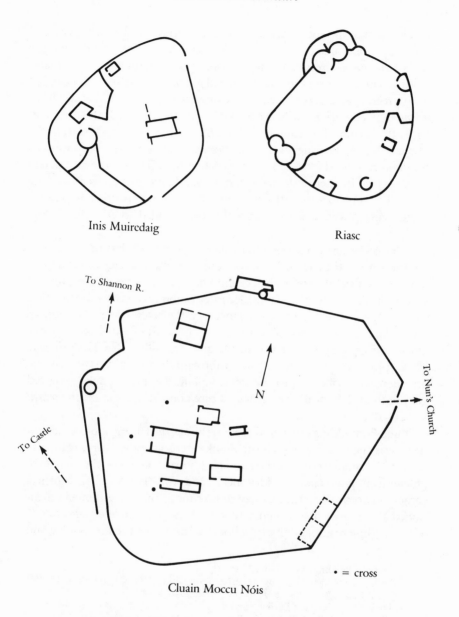

Inis Muiredaig

Riasc

To Shannon R.

N

To Castle

To Nun's Church

• = cross

Cluain Moccu Nóis

12. Layouts of monastic enclosures (enclosing wall modern). After Michael Herity, "The Building and Layout of Early Christian Monasteries before the Year 1000," *Monastic Studies* 14 (1983), 247–84; and E. E. Evans, *Prehistoric and Early Christian Ireland: A Guide* (London, 1966).

monks allotted specific spaces of their monasteries to different activities.[74] The transitional area between the most sacred space of the church and the rest of the enclosure was usually an open *platea,* a square or courtyard. Cormac's ninth-century glossary equated *platea* with the Irish *faithche,* the open green before a fort or church. Commentary on the legal tract *Bech-bretha* defined *faithche* as "the extent of a lawful green in Irish law . . . as far as the sound of a [church] bell or the crowing of a cock reaches."[75] Michael Herity has suggested that domestic buildings in early western communities stood farthest from the oratory, which was at the eastern end of the *platea.* In later settlements, monks set churches in the center of the *platea,* to emphasize the distance between church and other buildings; strategically placed crosses within the *platea* added to this effect (Fig. 13).[76]

Every community had open space around its church, but the *platea* was not the same as the *termonn,* nor was it just an empty stretch of ground. It was a site of carefully controlled, ceremonial contact between the saint and lay people. A variant of the eighth-century canon cited earlier decreed that while only clerics could enter the sanctuary, the second most holy area of the enclosure was a space "into the courts [*plateas*] of which we let enter crowds of country people not much given to villainy."[77] Here, in the *platea,* pious lay people took part in formal religious rituals such as the presentation of offerings to the saint. Columcille, for example, reviewed gifts of food that local Christians had ceremonially laid out on the *platea* of Cúil Rathain.[78]

Domestic buildings clustered around the *platea.* The most prominent of these was the house in which the monks ate, sometimes slept, read, and wrote. The monks called it the *tech mór* ("great house") or the *proindtech* (*proind* from *prandium,* "midday meal," and *tech,* "house"). The brothers gathered two or three times a day to take meals there.[79] Adomnán mentioned a variety of objects and activities in the *monasterium* or *proindtech* of Í, including reading, domestic chores, a large open fire for cooking and

74. Herity, "Buildings and Layout," 247–48.

75. Meyer, *Sanas Cormaic,* 52, 95: "a platea .i. on faithche" (Y 1073); Thomas Charles-Edwards and Fergus Kelly, eds., *Bechbretha* (Dublin, 1983), 82–83.

76. Herity, "Building and Layout," 277–79.

77. Cited and trans. by MacDonald, "Aspects of the Monastery and Monastic Life," 295–96.

78. Adomnán, 320; Aidan MacDonald, "Aspects of the Monastery and Monastic Life in Adomnán's Life of Columba," *Peritia* 3 (1984), 291–92; see also HVSH, 124; Migne, PL 72:787; see also PVSH 2:127.

79. Ryan, *Irish Monasticism,* 290.

13. Cross of the Scriptures at Cluain Moccu Nóis, county Offaly, seen through the west-facing entrance to the cathedral.

warmth, and large storage vessels of water.[80] According to the *Hisperica famina*, after meals monks went off to work, some in individual cells, some outside, and the rest in the main building itself.[81] The very name of the "great house" implies a structure larger than others in the enclosure. The *Vita tripartita* suggests that the *tech mór* of an enclosure ideally measured twenty-seven feet, presumably in length, just like its church, while its separate kitchens (*chuli*) measured seventeen.[82]

The saints' lives mention small huts (*cellula, domunculus, tegoriolum, both, cró*) that served as the personal quarters of individual monks or small groups. The abbot or abbess lived in a house apart from his or her charges in most settlements.[83] Columcille had his own *tegoriolum* at Í, a place where he read, wrote, and entertained visitors.[84] When he visited other communities under his direction, Columcille also stayed in separate quarters. On Hinba, for example, he barred himself in a house for three days while communing with the Holy Spirit.[85] Cainnech also seems to have had his own little house, which he was always forgetting to lock up properly.[86] The abbot's house was private, as an episode from Comgall's life illustrated. The saint's attendant tucked him into his bed in his *habitaculum* one night, but made the mistake of checking on him later. He witnessed the private visions of his master, a joyous and terrifying experience during which the saint's house filled with splendid light and his faced glowed with extraordinary beauty. Comgall scolded his monk and ordered him to do penance for his intrusion.[87] The annals also often mentioned the *tech abaid* (abbot's house) of a community. At Ard Macha, for example, the abbot's house stood in its own enclosure or *les*.[88] Some danger lay in identifying the abbot's house so clearly; the abbot of Nóendruimm met disaster when in 975 he was burned "in his own house" by enemies.[89] Yet the Irish monks, like the Benedictines of the Continent, continued to use the distribution of private space to indicate the abbot's prestige within the community.

80. Adomnán, 256–60; MacDonald, "Aspects of the Monastery and Monastic Life," 285; MacDonald, "Notes on Monastic Archaeology and the Annals of Ulster," 310–11.

81. HF, 80–81.

82. VT, 176.

83. MacDonald, "Aspects of the Monastery and Monastic Life," 285–88; Ryan, *Irish Monasticism*, 290–91.

84. Adomnán, 358–60, 494.

85. Ibid., 502–4; MacDonald, "Aspects of the Monastery and Monastic Life," 286.

86. HVSH, 187–88, 190–91.

87. PVSH 2:5–6.

88. AU, 365; MacDonald, "Notes on Monastic Archaeology in the Annals of Ulster," 310.

89. AU, 413; cited by Hughes and Hamlin, *Celtic Monasticism*, 74.

Individual monks also had personal sleeping quarters in some communities, although other settlements contained dormitories.[90] These cells brought not prestige but withdrawal, according to the hagiographers. Mochuda built *cellulas contemplationi aptas* at Lis Mór.[91] While Ciarán was still a pupil of Finnian at Mag Bile, he not only slept but took his meals in his own cell (*cella*).[92] In the western settlements, the best evidence of private quarters for monks remains in stone. At Scelec Mhichíl, Baile Muirne, Church Island, and Riasc, several little huts appear to have been the dwelling place of one or two monks. Ruins at other sites show that frequently a cluster of huts lined the walls of stone enclosures.[93] The hagiographers noted huts where two or three, seven, or more brothers slept.[94] But the stone cells at Scelec and other western sites seem a bit small for cohabitation.

The solitude of private cells was unknown outside ecclesiastical settlements. No one in early Ireland slept alone unless he or she had to, since it was colder and more dangerous and a waste of precious space and fuel. Nor did the spiritual rewards of solitude always outweigh its physical discomforts. The seventh-century *Hisperica famina* compared an ideally tidy monastic hut with a less pleasant alternative that must have been more familiar to many monks:

> This hollow hall surrounds a clean chamber
> which is continually swept with switches of birch,
> nor does any kindling pile up there.
> ⟨Here⟩ there is a foul-smelling room
> that contains hardened grains of dirt,
> nor do the leafy brooms sweep the aforesaid chamber.[95]

The monks also used architecture to separate subgroups of the monastic community from each other and from the monks. Within larger settlements, students, nuns, lepers, ascetics, and guests often had their own quarters. The only architectural feature common to all monastic enclosures was their focus on the saint.

---

90. HVSH, 226; PVSH 2:9–10; PBNE 1:189; USMLS, Conchubranus III, 436–37.
91. HVSH, 339.
92. PVSH 1:206.
93. O'Kelly, "Monastic Sites in the West of Ireland," 1–16; O'Kelly, "St. Gobnet's House, Ballyvourney, Co. Cork," JCHAS 57 (1952), 18–40; O'Kelly, "Church Island, near Valencia, Co. Kerry," PRIA 59 C (1958), 57–136.
94. Hughes and Hamlin, *Celtic Monasticism*, 74–75.
95. HF, 80–81.

The Human Community

No single hagiographer or annalist conveyed the complexity of monastic layouts, or the bustle of the more prosperous settlements. Cogitosus came the closest; he evoked all the pilgrims, hawkers, traders, and supplicants who crowded Brigit's community. "Who can count," he demanded, "the different crowds and numberless peoples flocking in from all the provinces—some for the abundant feasting, others for the healing of their afflictions, others to watch the pageant of the crowds, others with great gifts and offerings."[96]

The later *vitae,* taken together, also reveal a colorful and chaotic collection of visitors to the monastery. Many of these came to stay, drawn to the saint and the holy place. Kings, queens, and nobles visited or retired inside the enclosure. Lepers roamed the roads, stopping at monasteries long enough to demand food, clothing, or blessings and sometimes moving in permanently. Paupers also appeared in monastic communities and angels came for extended visits. Despite the low opinion of them held by some clerics, merchants, poets, and players arrived to ply their wares and talents. Some monks kept their own families in the enclosure. There were also the smiths and shoemakers, the farmers and laborers, the shepherds and serfs, the men who cleaned monastic stables and the women who washed the brothers' clothes. All of these different kinds of people—the *populus,* as opposed to the *clerus*—lived among or near the monks, some on a daily basis, some for a few days at a time. Not every monastic community harbored such a cross section of society, but even tiny monasteries included some lay inhabitants and visitors.

As early as the seventh century some monastic settlements had grown into considerable population centers. Certain settlements increased in size during the eighth and ninth centuries, while population was slowly increasing throughout Ireland, and probably maintained relatively high levels throughout the pre-Norman period. However, the population expanded within the limits of its previous settlements, focusing on islands of prosperity and security such as the larger monasteries.[97] Cóemgen's hagiographer, for example, observed a spurt of demographic growth at

---

96. Migne, PL 72:790; S. Connolly and J.-M. Picard, trans., "Cogitosus: Life of Saint Brigit," JRSAI 117 (1987), 27.

97. Ann Lynch, *Man and Environment in Southwest Ireland,* 4000 B.C.–A.D. 800 (Oxford, 1981), 5.

Glenn Dá Locha when the community needed more churches ("illec cresceret cellas").[98] More churches also meant a larger nonmonastic population. The construction reflected not only a need to accommodate more people within the enclosure but a demand for building materials and skilled labor from those living near it. In turn, a growing number of people laboring either directly or indirectly in the service of the monks brought a significant surplus of monastic wealth, which allowed for costly rebuilding and expansion. The prosperity of monastic settlements made possible natural population increase, but internal migration to monasteries must also have contributed.

Whatever the causes, hagiographers and annalists insisted that monastic populations reached highly inflated numbers. Rathan supposedly housed 847 clerics, not to mention its attached lay community.[99] The annals usually suggest only slightly more conservative figures in the several hundreds, except Ard Macha, which claimed a population of several thousand in the eleventh century, with quarters and streets for the various subgroups.[100]

The presence of growing numbers of lay people in the monastic settlement affected the monks' architectural plans only indirectly. The monks simply decreed that their secular and semisecular dependents were to stay out of the sacred space; the porter of the settlement determined who might enter the enclosure, distinguishing between the worthy and the unworthy.[101] In Ard Macha, according to the ninth-century *Liber angeli*, monks and nuns lived next to married people with semiclerical status, but the community had separate churches for separate orders of Patrician devotees.[102] In most settlements, the huts of lay dependents clustered near monastic enclosures, but outside their walls. The archaeological evidence of enclosures with related hut and field systems suggests that living within sight of the monastic enclosure was useful to farmers and herders, doubtless economically as well as spiritually.

Beyond the houses of dependents were lands under monastic jurisdiction: fields plowed by monastic tenants and clients; woods where the community let its pigs root and where people chopped trees for fuel;

98. HVSH, 363.
99. PBNE 1:306. The hagiographer may be referring to the population of the entire *paruchia*.
100. AU, 481, 527, 553.
101. Wasserschleben, *Collectio*, 25.
102. Bieler, *Patrician Texts*, 186.

streams and lakes that provided water and fish and routes of travel away from the enclosure. As later chapters will show, the monks extended their influence outward in all directions from their walled sanctuaries. People of the surrounding territory looked to the monastery, to its walls and churches, for economic support, political alliance, and above all spiritual fulfillment. Once the lay community had accepted the saint's presence behind the enclosure, the monks could begin to extend the saint's protection to those living near the holy place.

The sacral geography of the enclosure excited the imagination of those who lived both inside and outside monastic walls. For those outside, the walls announced the distance between them and the religious professionals who made daily contact with the divine. At the boundary, the rules of nature gave way to the power of magic; generally the Christian magic of the saints but sometimes an older magic inherited by them. To the monks inside consecrated walls, shrines, graves, churches, *termoinn,* wells, and fires defined many boundaries simultaneously: the lines between monks and laics, between Christian settlement and demon-haunted wilderness, between visible and invisible worlds, and between physical human space and the boundless space of the saints.[103]

Of course modern archaeologists have described the monastic enclosure from a different perspective. To many eyes, the boundaries dividing the enclosure into subspaces were merely low walls made of dirt and stone. The living area inside the enclosure was often meager by modern standards. The monks' huts were leaky and their churches dim and chilly; their shrines were often primitive, like Crónán's doghouse-shaped tomb. The holiness of the ground around the monks did not relieve these discomforts.

But to the monks, none of the rude details of daily movement between sacred and profane spaces, or other sordid conditions of life, detracted from the spiritual aura of their surroundings. They took comfort in the warmth of the saint while they lay in their cold, lonely cells. The saint refreshed them as they stumbled through the mud to matins in the predawn dark. And when they tired of the earthly struggle, the saint who lived among them was waiting to conduct them to the heavenly Jerusalem.

103. On boundaries, see Alwyn Rees and Brinley Rees, *Celtic Heritage* (London, 1961), 94.

PART TWO

THE COMMUNITY

CHAPTER THREE

The Monastic Family

THE SAINT'S ENCLOSURE, ISOLATED BY CONCENTRIC WALLS AND ditches, is a useful metaphor for communities of monks in early Ireland. Each community built networks of protection and support around itself, which radiated outward from the religious elite like the walls that circled Nóendruimm and other settlements. At the center was the monastic family, composed of abbot and monks or abbess and nuns. From its privileged place within the enclosure, the family chose its friends, clients, and allies on the outside. The monks' near neighbors became their tenants and clients, bringing them food and other supplies in return for religious services: blessings, baptisms and burials, magical cures. The leaders of the monastic family formed political alliances with local noblemen, providing warriors and ladies with the same rituals as farmers and peasants, receiving in exchange military protection and considerable donations. Less familiar lay people came from farther away, accepting the roles of pilgrim and patient to the monks' priest and doctor; they, too, offered donations to the monks in return for being allowed to approach the saint. And just as the saint's relics became the focus of the physical and sacral landscapes, the saint also presided at the center of the monks' social networks. The saint was the father or mother of the monastic family, the landlord of the monks' clients, the ultimate political ally, the true healer of pilgrims.

Of all these friendships, alliances, and exchanges, most important to the monks were the relationships they formed with each other. Inside their holy walls, the monks joined together, in their words, as a *familia*. While historians have noted the monks' use of kinship vocabulary to describe

[85]

their communities, none has understood just how thoroughly the monks adopted the kinship model.[1]

Monastic leaders urged monks to abandon blood kin and patrimony and to give their inheritances and their unfettered allegiance to their monastic *familiae*. At the same time, blood relatives demanded aid from influential monks and tried to dominate their settlements. The monks constantly had to choose between obligations to blood kin and to their abbatial fathers and monastic brothers. More was at stake than a monk's affections, for the family that won a monk's heart also gained his lands, goods, and political support. Canonists and jurists did their best to reconcile the monk's obligations to both carnal and spiritual kinfolk. Still, according to the *vitae*, issues of affection, loyalty, and property repeatedly assaulted each monk, challenging the stability of his social network and the solidarity of the entire religious elite.

The Kinship Model of the Religious Elite

Kinship was one of the most important organizing principles of early Irish society, as it was in most medieval European societies. In the Irish laws, probably first recorded in the seventh century, the basic landholding and legal unit was the extended family (*fine*). The *fine* owned the *fintiu*, the kin-group's land, although smaller family units actually occupied and farmed their own parcels. Theoretically, the *fine* controlled the alienation of its members' lands, except those acquired by purchase or gift, and it worked to make sure that each of its members had an adequate share of the kin-group's land. The *fine* was also legally liable for the penalties and wergilds of its individual members. The group could prevent any member from becoming the client or tenant of a wealthier man, since it was also liable for defaulted rents or dues. The *fine* also probably filled less formal functions, acting as a farming cooperative and offering protection and support to its members. Finally, if someone killed a member of the group, the *fine* claimed the victim's wergild (*éraic*) or prosecuted a blood feud against the offender. Those who evaded their duties as part of the *fine* were deprived of all the kin-group had to offer.[2]

---

1. John Ryan, *Irish Monasticism: Origins and Early Development* (Dublin, 1931), 263–85; Kathleen Hughes, *The Church in Early Irish Society* (London, 1966) 157–72.
2. On cooperative farming: Fergus Kelly, *A Guide to Early Irish Law* (Dublin, 1988), 99–109; D. A. Binchy, ed., *Críth Gablach* (Dublin, 1941). On alienation of the kin's land: CIH 1:247; ALI 5:510. On the individual's land: CIH 2:532; ALI 3:44. On contracts: CIH 2:489–

The extended family also provided the conceptual framework for Irish political structures. Although ruling groups had long been anchored to distinct territories, people called them first by tribal names, such as the Uí Néill (descendants of Níall) or the Eóganachta, from the Munster eponym Eógan Mór. Distinct political factions often formalized alliances with fake genealogies, hypothesizing blood ties between the ancestors of each group as kinsmen.[3]

However, the hagiographers promoted the nuclear family as the basic, coresident, affective family unit. They believed that households should include parents, children, occasionally foster children, and servants; secondary wives or mistresses may also have resided in elite households. Extended kin and adult foster relations lived in separate households. Such nuclear units existed within the framework of the *fine;* individuals of this smaller family retained legal rights and property, despite the laws' emphasis on the *fine.*[4] Churchmen actually campaigned to reduce the property-owning unit to the nuclear family and encouraged the rights of individuals over those of the kin-group, in Ireland as elsewhere.[5] The monks and priests of early Ireland also used ecclesiastical canons and secular laws to battle polygamy, concubinage, and easy divorce, practices that not only were morally offensive but also reduced donors by producing multiple heirs.[6] In sum, the hagiographers suggested that the *fine,* the nuclear family, and the individual each had social and economic functions and legal rights, although these sometimes clashed, particularly when the church became involved.

Yet kinship was the only influential model available to monks and nuns for the organization of their communities. No Roman-style urban corporations or representative assemblies of native nobility existed in Ireland to provide alternative inspiration. Even the process of becoming a monk or a

---

90. On liability of the *fine* for members: CIH 2:411; ALI 1:260. On blood feud: CIH 2:733. On division of the kin's land: CIH 1:217; 3:1034. See also Gearóid Mac Niocaill, *Ireland before the Vikings* (Dublin, 1972), 50–51; Nerys T. Patterson, *Early Irish Kinship: The Legal Structure of the Agnatic Descent Group,* Working Papers in Irish Studies 88-2 (Boston, 1988).

3. John V. Kelleher, "Early Irish History and Pseudo-History," *Studia Hibernica* 3 (1963), 113–27.

4. David Herlihy, *Medieval Households* (Cambridge, Mass., 1985), 34–43.

5. Donnchadh Ó Corráin, *Ireland before the Normans* (Dublin, 1972), 44; Jack Goody, *The Development of the Family and Marriage in Europe* (Cambridge, 1983).

6. Nancy Power, "Classes of Women Described in the *Senchas Mar,*" in R. Thurneysen et al., *Studies in Early Irish Law* (Dublin, 1936), 81–108; Wasserschleben, *Collectio,* 111–18, 180–95.

[87]

nun was essentially one of assuming a new family, a new home, and a new inheritance. For adult recruits, which included all religious women, crossing the threshold into the saint's enclosure demanded a reordering of thought, behavior, and social relationships, just like marriage or adoption. Novice monks or nuns lost kin rights and duties for new obligations; they gave up property for a dwelling place behind the enclosure's walls, and pride of social status for humility. They lost the power derived from kingroup and instead sought total obedience to their abbot or abbess; they relinquished names for anonymity, speech for silence.[7]

A new monk faced a multitude of choices: whom to take as a friend, as an enemy, as a tutor, confessor, or abbot. Within extended families, individuals could not make full use of all of their blood ties and had to choose allies from among their many relatives. Similarly, monks selected friends and allies from the community within the enclosure.[8] They chose their abbots much as members of a noble ruling group determined which patriarch was to be their king. For example, Munnu was filling in for the absent Áed Gobbán as temporary abbot of Ard Crama, a subsidiary house of Bennchor, when Bennchor's abbot, Comgall, died. The community at Ard Crama gave Munnu a choice: He could continue, as a son of Saint Comgall, to live at Ard Crama; he could become head of the family of Bennchor as Comgall's successor; or he could sever his affiliation and leave both communities. Munnu chose to abandon Comgall's family and begin one of his own.[9] The process of negotiation and Munnu's choice were set entirely in kinship terms. If Munnu wished to stay, he had to become a permanent member of the family, and choose his place within it.

Women used a different model for their entry into religious communities. When they became nuns, women married Christ, with all the social and economic connotations such an alliance implied. Samthann was one of many women who rejected a mortal spouse to be the bride of Jesus. She requested of her guardian "that you should now offer me to God, and not to a man, in marriage."[10] Other, less independent women may have been

---

7. Victor Turner, *The Ritual Process* (Ithaca, N.Y., 1969), chap. 3, "Liminality and Communitas"; Turner, *Dramas, Fields and Metaphors* (Ithaca, N.Y., 1974), chap. 6, "Passages, Margins and Poverty: Religious Symbols of Communitas." On kinship models, see Nerys T. Patterson, "Kinship Law or Number Symbolism? Models of Distributive Justice in Old Irish Law," *Proceedings of the Harvard Celtic Colloquium* 5 (1985).

8. Marc Bloch, *Feudal Society,* trans. L. A. Manyon (London, 1961), 123–42; J. A. Barnes, "Social Networks," *Addison-Wesley Modules in Anthropology* 26 (1972), 1–29; J. Mitchell, "Social networks," *Annual Review of Anthropology* (1974), 279–99.

9. HVSH, 202–3.

10. PVSH 2:253–54; see also 65–66.

guided by male relatives into the religious life, much as fathers arranged marriages for their daughters. The process of entering a religious community was thus gender specific, copied from the various ways of changing kin affiliation available to men or women. Men selected and cultivated useful alliances with members of their extended families, while women married men, preferably from the same kin-group, who could bring support and resources to their families.[11]

The men and women who lived with abbots and abbesses comprised a *familia* or *muinter*. In fact, *muinter* may have derived from Latin *monasterium*, making the equation of family and monastic community easier, although the terms also referred to the larger religious community, and not just to the monastic elite.[12] God was the ultimate *paternoster* of the monastic *familia* as to all Christians. He was also *ap archaingel* (abbot of the archangels) and *ar nabb* (our abbot).[13] Just as God was father and abbot, saints and abbots were also fathers and representatives of God's paternal authority. God's premier delegate on earth was *ab Romha*, the holy father of the family of Saint Peter.

The abbot of even the humblest community was first and foremost a father to his monastic sons.[14] When Comgall's monks finished their clerical training, he ordered each of them to become *pater aliorum* (father of others). Comgall had trained his monks specifically to lead ecclesiastical families.[15] Even before his birth Cóemgen was destined to be "father of many monks," according to an angel who visited his mother.[16] Similarly, abbesses were mothers, aunts, and nurturers. Íte was *multorum matrona* and *matertera*, mother and maternal aunt, to her community and lay devotees; Brigit was also a *mater spiritualis*.[17]

Abbots performed many of the duties appropriate to heads of large kin-groups. They were responsible for protecting the rights of the community's inhabitants, "from the small to the great."[18] They ordered the group's estates and, sometimes with the help of a steward or *oeconimus*, kept track

---

11. HVSH, 15; Herlihy, *Medieval Households*, 32–36. See also Suzanne Wemple, *Women in Frankish Society: Marriage and the Cloister, 500 to 900* (Philadelphia, 1981).

12. DIL, 191–92. See Heinrich Fichtenau's discussion of familial models in *Lebensordnungen des 10. Jahrhunderts* (Stuttgart, 1984), 1:165–84.

13. *Saltair na Rann*, 1.831, cited in PBNE 2:338n; Joseph O'Neill, ed., "The Rule of Ailbe of Emly," *Ériu* 3 (1907), 106.

14. PBNE 1:103.

15. PVSH 2:168.

16. HVSH, 361.

17. PVSH 2:119, 167, 268.

18. Mac Eclaise, ed., "The Rule of St. Carthage," IER 27 (1910), 498.

of production, making sure that everyone had clothes, supplies, and, most important, food. Columcille, for instance, checked the barn at Í before he died and was pleased to see it filled with enough grain to feed his monks for a year.[19] An abbot also controlled his community's finances and dealt with visitors and traders, who were always taken to see the head of the community at a suitable interval after their arrival.[20]

Abbots and abbesses ordered the rituals of their families, signaling when to begin praying and when to finish.[21] They also directed more mundane affairs within the community. They regulated meals and bedtime. They conducted lessons and ordered punishments, oversaw the labor of tenant farmers, and solved problems with farm equipment and cart animals.[22] At home and abroad, in the annals and in the *vitae,* the name of the abbot or abbess—often called the *comarbae* or "heir" of the saint—symbolized the entire monastic family and its orderly existence.

Ideally, abbot and monks loved each other.[23] Parents in early Ireland cherished their children, as many episodes from the lives showed: mothers wept at the disappearance of their babies, and parents rushed to save their children from disaster.[24] So, too, saintly abbots felt fatherly love for their children and tended to their welfare. Columcille worried about his sons at Í when they worked too hard. Once, when their enthusiasm flagged on the long trek back to the enclosure after a day's work in the fields, Columcille sent his spirit to refresh and cheer them.[25] Mac Nise could not bear to see his monks become depressed at the dreariness of daily labor, so he arranged some feasting and celebration for his sons.[26]

The monks responded affectionately. When Máedóc's disciple, Dallán, discovered that his abbot would die within a year, the monk felt the grief of separation "like a woman from her son, or of a cow from her calf, or a bitch from her whelps, or a duck from her pool."[27] Columcille's monks wept at his parting; even his horse shed tears.[28] But imminent death did not bring the only proof of devotion; the saints and their spiritual sons

---

19. Adomnán, 520–21; see also USMLS, Conchubranus III, 430–33.
20. Adomnán, 209, 215, 220; HVSH, 129–30; PVSH 1:27, 168; 2:257.
21. PVSH 1:160; USMLS, Conchubranus III, 434–37.
22. PVSH 1:186–87, 206; USMLS, Conchubranus II, 434–47; Mac Eclaise, "Rule of St. Carthage," 498–503.
23. Ryan, *Irish Monasticism,* 276–78.
24. HVSH, 133–34, 191.
25. Adomnán, 282–86.
26. HVSH, 406.
27. PBNE 1:267; 2:259.
28. Adomnán, 522–25; 528–29.

also displayed affection for each other while alive. Columcille's monks at Dermag ran joyfully to meet him when he visited, jealously protecting him with branches from an eager crowd of their lay neighbors.[29]

Some hagiographers represented the abbot as more like a foster father than a father. Traditionally, elite families sent their children to the households of clients or relatives, where the fosterer supplied love, protection, and practical education.[30] A boy in secular life lived with his mother or foster mother until he was old enough to be sent among men and committed to a foster father's care, there to learn the manly arts. A boy destined for religion went to men or women who could teach him the skills appropriate for his future career. Brénainn, for example, spent his early years under the care of his foster mother, Saint Íte, but at the age of six or seven he went to a foster father, Bishop Ercc.[31]

Colmán Ela's hagiographer let his imagination take flight when he described the relationship between the saint and two fosterlings who became his pupils.[32] Saint Columcille brought the babies to Lann Ela. The boys were the product of incest between Columcille's sister and their cousin, and the great saint was ashamed to let them live, but afraid to expose or abandon them. Evidently, Colmán's hagiographer believed Columcille to be more attached to his aristocratic lineage than to his sister's sons; Colmán, on the other hand, represented the ideal abbatial fosterer. Colmán offered to raise the babies, explaining "I have two paps such as no saint ever had before, a pap with milk, and a pap with honey, and these I will give to them (to suck)."[33] The metaphor is beautiful; Colmán was father, mother, and fosterer to the abandoned children. Colmán's role also extended to teacher, a job for which he was well qualified, since he was "full of generosity and righteous knowledge."[34]

In small communities, the abbot himself may have been the affective substitute for a monk's father, as Colmán was for the nephews of Columcille, Ultán and Baíthín. In later centuries and larger communities the

---

29. Ibid., 214–17.
30. Secular jurists recognized affective fosterage ties; see the legal tract on fosterage, CIH 5:1759–70, esp. 1762, 1764, ALI 2:146–93.
31. PBNE 1:45–46.
32. Ibid., 173–80; 2:167–73. For a motif similar to Colmán's nursing see Eoin Mac Néill, *Celtic Ireland* (Dublin, 1921; rpt. 1981), 55.
33. PBNE 1:174. This image may derive from Continental influence; see Caroline Bynum, "Jesus as Mother and Abbot as Mother: Some Themes in Twelfth-Century Cistercian Writing," in Bynum, *Jesus as Mother: Studies in the Spirituality of the High Middle Ages* (Berkeley and Los Angeles, 1982), 110–25.
34. PBNE 1:180.

abbot probably became psychologically more distant from his monks. Other officers then shared his many responsibilities.[35]

An Irish monastic community usually included both *seniores* (or *sruithi,* elder monks) and *juniores* (young monks), as did Benedictine communities on the Continent. According to the many early Irish monastic rules, the relationship between young and old monks was hierarchical. One such rule advised a young monk to seek out an *ecnaid craíbthech* (devout sage), not necessarily the abbot, to guide him, rather than trusting his own immature self-discipline.[36] The novice was to revere older men and obey them, while his seniors were to instruct the youth diligently, according to Mochuda's rule.[37]

One of the most important relationships between older and younger monks was that of *anmchairde,* soul friendship.[38] Sometimes, a monk's *anmcharae* or confessor performed a fosterer's function, while the abbot filled a strictly paternal role. Saint Bairre, for example, was baptized by Colingus, later his *anmcharae* (soul friend or confessor). Colingus loved his charge so much that he offered his service and his *locus* to Bairre, and asked for nothing in return but that he be resurrected with Bairre on Judgment Day.[39] According to Ailbe's *Rule,* an older confessor was to reprove an errant monk kindly and carefully, and if the monk would not confess his guilt, the confessor was to send him somewhere to sulk in private and consider his sins. The abbot was not involved in this private interaction between monk and soul friend, for the confessor replaced him as father to the monk.[40]

The *céili dé* (clients of God), reforming ascetics of the eighth and ninth centuries, placed great importance on confession and on the relationship between monk and *anmcharae.* Commentary on the *Félire Óenguso,* a ninth-century text supposedly written by the *céile dé* Óengus mac Óengobán, told this story of Brigit and one of her foster-sons:

"Well, young cleric, there," says Brigit, "hast thou a soulfriend?" "I have," replied the young cleric. "Let us sing his requiem," says Brigit, "for he has

---

35. PVSH 1:cxvii–iii.
36. John Strachan, "An Old-Irish Metrical Rule," *Ériu* 1 (1904), 197.
37. Mac Eclaise, "Rule of St. Carthage," 508–9.
38. Ibid., 502–4. Columbán's rule, which lays heavy emphasis on the hierarchical relationship between junior and senior monks, ordered monks to confess daily; see G. S. M. Walker, ed., *Sancti Columbani Opera* (Dublin, 1957), 144.
39. PVSH 1:72–73; HVSH, 358.
40. O'Neill, "Rule of Ailbe," 104–5.

died. I saw when half thy portion had gone, that thy quota was put into thy trunk, and thou without any head on thee, for thy soulfriend died, and anyone without a soulfriend is a body without a head; and eat no more till thou gettest a soulfriend."[41]

Although a monk's *anmcharae* was not always close at hand, as documents from the *céili dé* monastery of Tamlachta show, the bond between a monk and his tutor or confessor was strong enough to be maintained over great distances. Ordinary monks also refused to let physical separation hinder the relationship. For example, when Finnian sensed that his tutor, Ciarán of Saigir, was approaching death, he journeyed all the way from Cluain Iraird to see his old teacher; for, as the hagiographer explained, "it was with him he studied his psalms and every kind of learning that he had."[42] The spiritual dimension of the confessor- or tutor-student relationship elevated it above ordinary family ties.

According to the hagiographers, the saints were able to switch tutors and confessors as they grew older and their needs changed.[43] Some houses seem to have had special reputations as schools, such as Cluain Iraird. Other communities produced so many scribes and manuscripts that they clearly supported important scriptoria and schools.[44] Young would-be scholars flocked to these monasteries, hoping to study with masters of theology and other arts and sciences.

Still, although the saints supposedly wandered from tutor to tutor, most monks of the ninth century and later may have been less mobile, and had more limited options. Many were brought up in the communities where they spent their entire lives; they changed tutors or confessors not by seeking different communities but by forming new relationships with older monks already familiar to them. In fact, saintly vagrancy may simply be a motif of the standard Indo-European hero tale, in which kings and warriors meet as many famous figures as can be crammed in the story; certainly, the hagiographers may have shown their protagonists moving from monastery to monastery more often than was common for most

41. FO, 64–65; see also 180–83.
42. Gwynn and Purton, "Monastery of Tallaght," 143–44; see also PBNE 1:111, 2:107–8.
43. PVSH 1:99–100, 2:167.
44. For the school at Cluain Iraird: HVSH, 80, 101, 137, 161, et passim. For other houses of learning: Kathleen Hughes, "The Distribution of Irish Scriptoria and Centres of Learning from 730 to 1111," in Nora K. Chadwick et al., eds., *Studies in the Early British Church* (Cambridge, 1958), 243–72.

monks, just to promote a saint's importance by bringing him into contact with as many of his holy colleagues as possible.[45]

But the patterns are too persistent to be completely formulaic. For one thing, monks other than saints were educated and nurtured at home or at local churches before formally entering a monastery; some of the fosterers and tutors of saints were not famous holy men themselves and so could add nothing to a saint's status.[46] Whether or not the saints moved from monastery to monastery and tutor to tutor, the stories of wandering scholar-saints emphasized the voluntary nature of tutor-student relationships. Monks chose men who could provide them with education and something more; free of the tensions over inheritance, authority, and duty that troubled a father and son, the relationship between a monk and his chosen confessor or teacher provided a fosterer's support to the younger man and companionship and affection to both.[47]

Disaffection and Fraternal Competition

Relationships between monks of the same age or status were fraternal. In general, the brothers lived and worked together peaceably enough. Scenes from the lives showed them sharing meals, laboring in the fields in small groups, and sitting companionably around the *proindtech*, warming their feet in hot-water baths.[48] However, cooperation among members of a community did not always indicate love, for the fraternal bond was not necessarily affective. While the hagiographers may have assumed positive relationships among groups of monks, they rarely described affection or friendship between individual monks of the same generation.

The writers of monastic rules enjoined the monks to pray diligently and constantly, to obey their abbots and elders, and to practice many virtues. These individualistic rules, ordering monks to be "ever at prayer of oblation," directed their eyes away from each other and toward God only.[49] Those who wrote monastic rules worked harder to curb hostile relationships than to promote brotherly love. They sternly ordered monks to be "without murmuring, without insulting anybody, without jealousy,

45. Dorothy Ann Bray, "The Lives of Early Irish Saints: A Study in Formulaic Composition and the Creation of an Image" (doctoral thesis, Edinburgh, 1982), 111ff.
46. PVSH 2:36–37.
47. Herlihy, *Medieval Households*, 41–42.
48. Adomnán, 328, 364, 388–90, 494, 516; HVSH, 379–80; PBNE 1:30.
49. O'Neill, "Rule of Ailbe," 98–99.

without pride. Without contention, without willfulness, without disputes, without anger, without persecution, without special dislike, without ferocity, without force" and without a dozen other disruptive vices.[50] But hate, insult, and murmur against each other the monks did.

The hagiographers' use of *fratres* for the monks is instructive. In secular society, kinship ties between men of the same generation were less important and less affective than the ties between foster brothers, comrades, and even patrons and clients. Such allies were never liable to inherit from the same source, so they were free to develop supportive and loving relationships. But relations between monastic brethren often followed the pattern between blood relations of the same generation, and were frequently poisoned by competition.

The saints' lives contain many hints of dissension and dislike among the brothers, as well as general dissatisfaction with the monastic life. While he was staying in Saint David's community in Wales, Máedóc's miracles and piety made him so unpopular that one of the monks hired an axman to trail the Irishman into the woods and hack him to death; fortunately, David arrived in time to save his Irish novice. The hagiographer neglected to mention whether the jealous instigator was punished.[51] Conflict in this and other cases often derived from jealousy over a brother's higher status or anger over shirked responsibilities. The hard life of labor and asceticism often inspired anxiety and anger among the monks when one brother did not work hard enough to support the community.[52] The twelve brothers in Fínán's community, including the saint-to-be, Colum, each took a daily turn at scrounging food for the rest. But when Colum, preoccupied with spiritual matters, forgot his turn, the others began to grumble until God provided dinner.[53] Colum had let his brothers down. The community's survival depended upon the collective efforts of the entire monastic family, including future saints.

Monastic brothers even fought over who was to succeed to positions of authority within the community. British monks in Mochuda's community tried to kidnap him and dispose of him in order to take over Rathan. Mochuda punished the dissenters by decreeing that British monks would never rule his community.[54] Such solutions were effective only when the

---

50. Mac Eclaise, "Rule of St. Carthage," 506–9, modified text and translation (see DIL, 396); Walker, *Sancti Columbani Opera*, 150–56, 158, 160, 164.
51. PBNE 1:184–85; cf. PVSH 2:298.
52. PVSH 1:186–87.
53. HVSH, 225–26; see also PBNE 1:162–63.
54. PVSH 1:187–88.

abbot's power within the community was already secure. But the annals showed that disputes over the abbacy and other offices could become serious indeed, leading to armed encounters within the saint's enclosure. In 836, rival factions of Ard Macha monks had already been fighting for control of their community for years; when visiting Cell Dara, they actually came to blows within Brigit's sanctuary.[55]

Abbots seem to have been unable to prevent or control tensions in some communities. Those who struggled to maintain their own positions found it difficult to keep all of their rebellious brothers within the monastery. Ailbe's *Rule* suggested that the monk be steady and never restless, but reminded the abbot not to provoke monks into leaving the enclosure by trying to enforce a harsh rule.[56] The monks must have sought better circumstances in other communities, for both canonists and penitentialists pleaded that monks stay home; the penitentials decreed that "there should be no vagrant cleric in the community" and that "a monk who goes wandering without consulting his abbot is to be punished."[57] The law tract *Córus Béscnai* stated that only dire circumstances, such as financial failure or famine, or such noble objectives as pilgrimage justified a monk's departure from his community.[58] Yet monks and nuns did escape the enclosure, sometimes to satisfy lust, sometimes for purportedly pious but all-too-independent motives.[59]

The *vitae* admitted that men and women left their communities, but tried to prevent this with warnings of the consequences. In the saints' lives, dissatisfied monks who abandoned their brothers met sudden, violent death.[60] The lessons of the lives merely reinforced secular laws and penitentials, and the desperate desire expressed most clearly in Ailbe's rule for stable and peaceable monastic communities. The very survival of communities shows that some spirit of cooperation must have prevailed inside the holy walls. But hagiographers and monastic leaders clearly feared competition and dissension within their communities, even if actual instances of open hostility, which compelled monks to feud and to flee, were rare.

55. AU, 292, 296, 306, 430. Cf. entries regarding the change of abbots at Ard Macha in 835, 839, 848, and 1001.
56. O'Neill, "Rule of Ailbe," 96, 104.
57. Ludwig Bieler, ed., *The Irish Penitentials* (Dublin, 1975), 54, 58.
58. CIH 5:1818; ALI 3:64–65.
59. PVSH I, 227; II, 121; cf. PBNE I, 42; Wasserschleben, *Collectio*, 165–66.
60. HVSH, 242.

Monastic Family and Monastic Property

The origins of fraternal rivalry lay quite literally outside the sacred walls, in the property of the monastic community and the clients whom it commanded. Among the secular elite, battling over inheritances and political power, it was common enough for one brother to kill another, or at least to take his kingship or territory. Nephews fought uncles, cousins quarreled, sons even deposed fathers.[61] Issues of property and power also invaded the monastic enclosure, since members of one or two secular kin-groups often dominated a monastic community or even an entire network of monasteries. Communal and personal property, already subject to the ambiguity of the secular laws regarding the family, easily became confused in the monks' struggle for control. The religious elite also feuded with secular dynasties in order to resist infiltration and domination by outside interests, and to retain control of their own holdings and offices within their communities.

Legal problems began as soon as Christian converts acquired property for monastic settlements. A community of monks inhabited property as a corporate unit. Lawyers formally distinguished between these men, who lived in the settlement, and the people who owned the land beneath the enclosure. But normally the landowners were related to some of the monks; even more commonly, one family or a few related families from the monastic community itself owned the land on which the community lived. Monastic estates, and with them the leadership of the community, passed from one member of the landowning family to another according to the laws of inheritance:

> The tribe of the patron saint shall inherit the church as long as there is a person of the patron saint's tribe fit to be an abbot; even if there is only a psalm-singer of [that tribe], he will take the abbacy. Whenever there is no one of that tribe fit to be an abbot, [the abbacy] is to be given to the tribe to whom the [settlement's] land belongs, until a man from the patron saint's tribe shall be qualified to be an abbot; and when he is, [the abbacy] is to be given back to him, if he is [a better candidate] than the [other] abbot, of the tribe to whom the land belongs, and who has [already become abbot]. If

---

61. AU, 254, 257, 308, 332, 374, et passim. See the index in W. Hennessey and B. MacCarthy, eds., *Annals of Ulster* (Dublin, 1887–1901), 4:43: "Brother, respective, slew" and "Brothers, respective, slew."

[the candidate from the patron saint's tribe] is no better, he shall succeed [to the abbacy] only in his turn.[62]

As this legal author acknowledged, the saint's family, that is the abbot's family, and the family that owned the monastery's lands were often one and the same.[63] The same kin-group supplied other officers to the community, such as the man designated to succeed to the abbacy, often called a *tánaise ap,* literally "secondary abbot" or "next abbot." This made keeping property and power in the family even easier, at least from a legal standpoint.

The religious elite gladly adhered to secular laws of inheritance, with a few minor modifications. They particularly approved of laws that encouraged the acquisition of ecclesiastical properties. According to legal compilers, the Christian elite retained all pagan laws that were acceptable to Pátraic; the saint must have accepted property law, so long as devout lay people were allowed to alienate land to churches.[64] Both eighth-century canonists and recorders of secular law promoted the transfer of property to churches; indeed, lawyers may even have adapted some of the Irish laws from Latin canons.[65] Churchmen were particularly concerned with women's donations, since women traditionally had severely limited rights to dispose of property. The canonists repeated strict limits on women's ownership and inheritance of property, often in legal terms almost identical to secular law; but they made an exception for a lady who donated to ecclesiastical establishments, especially those run by her family members.[66]

On the other hand, the monks supported laws that prevented the alienation of ecclesiastical properties and the property of monastic clients. For example, a monk, like minors and women, could not buy, sell, or give away property without the approval of his male guardian, the abbot.[67] Thus,

62. CIH 5:1820; ALI 3:73. See also VT, 338–41, where the situation is more complicated because it involves not only the family that originally owned the land and the abbot's family, but also the families of Ard Macha, the mother settlement of the community in question.

63. CIH 5:1829.

64. Ibid. 2:341; ALI 1:15–17. See also Kim McCone, "Dubthach Maccu Lugair and a Matter of Life and Death in the Pseudo-Historical Prologue to the *Senchas Már,*" *Peritia* 5 (1986), 1–35.

65. L. Breatnach, "Canon Law and Secular Law in Early Christian Ireland," *Peritia* 3 (1984), 439–59.

66. L. Bitel, "Women's Donations to the Churches in Early Ireland," *JRSAI* 114 (1984), 9–10. See also the articles on women's property and rights in Thurneysen et al., eds., *Studies in Early Irish Law.*

67. CIH 2:528–84; ALI 2:344–45.

the canonists maintained the bias of the laws in favor of the rights of families over those of individuals, but insisted on more rights for the individual lay person when he or she tried to give property to monasteries.

The issue of private property within the monastic community was more difficult for clerical lawyers. Canonists echoed secular jurists in their decisions regarding the private property of monastic officers, and the vexing problem of keeping it distinct from the community's holdings.[68] Such a problem arose on the rare occasion when a property-owning monk left the enclosure. A departing abbot who was not ordained could take away his personal property, but an abbot-priest had to leave what had been his property with the community. The rules were the same in the monastery as on any estate: any member of a family, even the father, could take away or alienate what he had acquired by gift or purchase, but he could not diminish the corporation's property. Of course, the landowning abbot and his heirs could not alienate the settlement's estates to a secular owner if he thus displaced the saint's *familia*. For women, however, the laws were different. Women's communities often dispersed at the death of their landlady and abbess, since the abbess could only hold family lands for her lifetime; after that, the property reverted to her male kin and the nuns had to go elsewhere.[69]

The monastery's methods of obtaining, using, and alienating land were thus similar legally to those of any other kin-group. Even income derived from donations was regarded as part of a larger economic exchange that included other dues and services, similar to the exchanges of labor and rents on secular estates. The duties of the abbot and monks to protect and expand their holdings whenever possible were also those expected of any landowner and his heirs. Hagiographers repeated this legal principle in their tedious lists of dues and donations owed the saints, and in vivid descriptions of the drastic revenge taken by holy men on thieves and intruders. By the eighth century, then, saints, jurists, and canonists agreed: The monks had both an obligation and a right, as a legal corporation, to hold their property and use it according to the laws of kinship.

Still, such extensive laws and canons, intended to prevent any disputes over monastic property, suggest exactly what kinds of trouble arose between the monastic *familia* and the smaller kin-group and individuals

68. Breatnach, "Canon Law"; Liam Breatnach, Donnchadh Ó Corráin, and Aidan Breen, "The Laws of the Irish," *Peritia* 3 (1984), 382–438.

69. Wasserschleben, *Collectio*, 173, cited in Hughes, *Church in Early Irish Society*, 159; CIH 2:534; cf. 532–33. See also Kathleen Hughes, *Early Christian Ireland: An Introduction to the Sources* (London, 1973), 234–35; CIH 5:1818, ALI 3:66–67.

within it. Ecclesiastical propaganda against the extended kin-group succeeded too well. Given the economic organization and the dominance of
family in early Ireland, the introduction of private-property interests into
the monastic community were inevitable. But this intrusion led to dynastic disputes, such as those at Ard Macha, and many of the petty squabbles
among monks in the *vitae*.

The hagiographers made clear their disapproving opinion that property
not only caused conflict among the brothers and distracted a monk from
his prayers; it also opened the gates of the saint's settlement to the monks'
relatives, further exacerbating any existing tensions. Saint Molua got this
advice about family trouble from a kinsman, King Fáelán of the Uí
Fidgeinte, whom he visited in order to ask about the possibility of an
endowment. According to the hagiographer, Molua found Fáelán playing
dice, "as was the custom of kings," but the king ignored him. Fáelán
eventually explained rather coolly to the naive churchman:

> If you would live among your kinsmen, your settlement will not be extensive,
> nor will it grow. Indeed, a cleric in his own homeland does not get any respect
> and your own kinsmen, by keeping out pilgrims, will control your settlement
> forever. If, however, you would set up your settlement in exile, it will be great
> and will be honored by all and will grow greater daily.[70]

Go to Leinster or Munster, the king told the saint. Not only would he be
free of quibbling kinsmen there, he would also gain the authority and
power that a holy man could acquire only in a strange land.[71]

Although Molua accepted the king's advice without questioning his
motives, at first he ignored Fáelán's sage words. He left his *patria* but only
went as far as his mother's homeland, where two maternal uncles involved
him in a feud over property. One offered him a portion of the family's
land, but the other destroyed the church that Molua built on it.[72] After
that, the saint finally followed the counsel of Fáelán, reinforced by an
angel's suggestion that he head for Slíab Bladma. Molua realized that
family and its property were nothing but trouble for a devout monk, and
could complicate his organization and administration of a monastic
community.

70. HVSH, 137.
71. Peter Brown, "The Rise and Function of the Holy Man in Late Antiquity," *Journal of Roman Studies* 61 (1971), 80–101.
72. HVSH, 137.

Other hagiographers made the lesson more obvious. When Mochua's maternal uncle donated a *villa* to his community, the saint burned it as an example to his monks, "lest a servant of Christ should acquire some property from the alms or goods of a sinner."[73] The monks unquestionably considered conflict over family property a very serious problem. Many saints other than Molua were clever enough to realize this and to avoid the entanglements of kin and its lands.[74]

The Rhetoric of Rejection

The ideal of monastic withdrawal and the renunciation of worldly goods permeates the *vitae*. Hagiographers insisted that Irish saints of the fifth, sixth, and seventh centuries had renounced their families and inheritances to found monastic communities where they secluded themselves and lived in radical asceticism with religious celibates of the same sex. At the same time, it must have been obvious to the hagiographers that monks and nuns retained close kinship ties and often even lived among their blood kin. The rejection of kin was hagiographic rhetoric, but it held great symbolic importance. In their stories of saints who abandoned their parents and patrimonies, hagiographers described two trends: the ideal, wherein ecclesiastics of the early centuries actually left their patrimonies and home territories to found churches elsewhere; and the post-800 reality, when ordinary monks like the hagiographers themselves made vows to shift allegiance to their monastic families and to reorient their corporate identity accordingly.

The hagiographers tried to convince their fellow monks that the saints had coldly detached themselves from their kinfolk when they left home for the enclosure. Brénainn's monks, eager to abandon their families and join him on his perilous quest for the Land of Promise, provided the ultimate example: "Father Abbot," they declared, "your will is ours. For did we not reject our parents for you and God, and did we not revile our inheritances, and did we not give our wills and bodies into your hands? So we are prepared to follow you, whether to life or to death."[75]

In the hagiographer's view, the severance of affective ties was the first step toward becoming a religious professional.[76] Not only Brénainn's

73. PVSH 2:185.
74. Ibid., 107–8.
75. Bieler, *Irish Penitentials*, 58, 59.
76. PVSH 1:107.

monks left home for the enclosure; Brénainn himself departed as soon as he heard the gospel words: "He who relinquishes father and mother and sister will receive one hundredfold in the present and will possess eternal life."[77] A monk's decision to leave the security of his home and transfer loyalty to a new community was permanent. An old Irish rule counseled mature recruits: "If you have a son or household that you determined to part from, you shall not seek them out, shall not think of them, just as if you were [dead] in the ground."[78] Monks who left home were to follow Munnu's example when he returned to his birthplace of Donegal: the saint, according to his hagiographer, "did not see that land, nor so much as the road upon which his feet walked, nor did he greet anyone, neither father nor brothers nor sisters, all of whom were living there then."[79]

Hagiographers knew that when a person rejected his kin, he also left behind, as Brénainn's hagiographer put it, "his land and his country, his parents and his patrimony."[80] The saints, who were generally of noble birth, dismissed their heritages with exemplary gestures. Áed, for example, readily agreed when Bishop Illundus asked him to leave his family, a branch of the powerful Uí Néill. "My son," asked the bishop, "now can you become a plowman and put your hand on the plow?" Áed, appreciating the peasant metaphor applied to the offspring of an aristocratic warrior family, was indeed ready to suffer a loss of social status and take up the hard labor of monasticism.[81] The saints' decision to discard status and ancestry was quite conscious, and as Mochuda's hagiographer showed, brought its own rewards. When only twelve years old, Mochuda formally renounced his father and the genealogy that he represented; the child was then adopted by his Father in heaven and honored as God's son before kings and princes.[82]

Some saints fled their families to distant lands, where no kin lived to remind them of their secular origins. Their migration proved their commitment to the religious life, since leaving the ancestral homeland took the saints from familiar and secure environs into a hostile world. According to tradition, many of the most famous holy men established their major churches outside their families' territories. Cainnech, for instance, was born among the Ciannachta Glinne Gaimin, near Cúil Rathain; he set

77. HVSH, 56; Matt. 19:29.
78. Strachan, ed., "Old-Irish Metrical Rule," 200–201.
79. HVSH, 200; see also 160–61.
80. PBNE 1:48, 2:48.
81. HVSH, 169.
82. Ibid., 335; see also HVSH, 383, 404; PVSH 1:202–3; USMLS, Conchubranus I, 258.

up the community of Druim Coos there, but his most important church was Achad Bó, in Osraige. Énda came of the Airgialla, but dwelt most of his life on the remote island of Ára. Máedóc went from Connacht to create Ferna Mór, in Leinster. Columbán left his adoring mother and went all the way to Italy, but other saints only got so far as the next province. Hagiographers emphasized that crossing the nearest political border was enough of a flight from family for some saints.[83] Others could not disguise the fact that their holy patrons had left paternal territory for that of maternal kin; these saints avoided troublesome questions of inheritance, but gained endowments from sympathetic kinfolk.[84]

Still, strong local traditions held that many saints had established churches in their homelands. Hagiographers had to admit that saints continued to live near their families, but explained that they had found ways to create a spiritual distance between themselves and their kin. Monenna, for example, began her career as a nun by living at home with her parents, and yet remained *seorsum,* "apart."[85] She and other saints cast aside all the lands, clients, goods, and obligations that came with their names and became aliens in their own homelands. Abbán enraged his royal parents by arrogantly dismissing a future as his father's heir and successor, according to one of his hagiographers. "Son," they cried, "you ought to ride more, go hunting, practice military exercises, so that when your father grows old you can lead out the Leinstermen against enemies, to fight for your birthright." But Abbán lectured them on the Trinity and announced that he was a servant of God, not a soldier of the *saeculum.* His annoyed father had him put into chains, but Abbán miraculously burst his bonds. Eventually, his parents let him wander away into religious life

83. For example:

Saint	Born	Major foundation
Áed m. Bricc	Múscraige Tíre	Cell Áir (Westmeath)
Ciarán	Corcu Loegde	Cluain Moccu Nóis (Offally)
Colmán Ela	Dál nAraide	Lann Ela (Offally)
Crónán	Éile	Ros Cré (Tipperary)

See also D. Ó Laoghaire, "Irish Spirituality," in Proinséas Ní Chatháin and Michael Richter, eds., *Ireland and Europe* (Stuttgart, 1984), 73–82. For Columbán on the subject: Walker, *Sancti Columbani Opera,* 94–95, xliii. Cf. 166, "Si parentum . . . superpositione."

84. See, e.g., PVSH 2:185; see also Dorothy Africa, "Women and Female Kin in Irish Hagiographical Tradition" (Ph.D. diss., Center for Medieval Studies, University of Toronto, 1990).

85. USMLS, Conchubranus, I, 256.

under the care of his mother's brother, Saint Ibar, at a nearby monastery.[86]

To men and women of high social status, accustomed to controlling people and resources and never questioning their duty to do so, the rejection of birthright was a shocking violation. Family rows erupted over many of the saints' attempts to leave the world behind. Their parents and brothers were often furious when noblewomen refused the bridegrooms chosen for them. Monenna, Samthann, Íte, and Brigit all waged emotional battles with kinsmen in order to escape destinies as wives and political links in alliances between different kin-groups.[87]

Since family, status, and property proved inseparable legally, socially, and economically, the hagiographers could not help but teach a muddled lesson about the rejection of family. The issues of personal and collective loyalties were too confused, and the legal and extralegal problems of property too complicated, for them to do otherwise.

Monastic Family and Blood Kin

The monks fought with their consciences and with each other over property and power; they wrangled with their kin over inheritance and allegiance. But, paradoxically, the monks' relationships with blood kin also provided a compromise solution to these problems within the monastic community. Monastic leaders consolidated their positions within the enclosure with the aid of fathers, brothers, and other kin. Their aim was only partly selfish. Abbots and officers needed to organize their communities and properties in the most efficient way possible. They had to institute formal precedents for the division of authority, and for the assignment of managerial roles to trustworthy aides. They also needed to pass on property and skills in order to maintain the settlement over many generations. To solve their problems, the religious elite resorted to well-tested models, relying on ties to their blood relatives to help check the potential instability of the monastic community.[88] In return, however, their families

86. PVSH 1:5–6.
87. L. Bitel, "Women's Monastic Enclosures in Early Ireland: A Study of Female Spirituality and Male Monastic Mentalities," *Journal of Medieval History* 12 (1986), 21–22.
88. For an in-depth case study of relations between a saint, his monastic *familia*, and his blood kin, see Máire Herbert on the Uí Néill and the Columban *familia* over many generations: *Iona, Kells, and Derry: The History and Hagiography of the Monastic Familia of Columba* (Oxford, 1988), 27–46, 124–26.

expected and sought some share of control over the monastic community and its wealth. As King Fáelán warned Mochuda, this arrangement often caused still more contention among kin and spiritual brethren.

To monastic leaders, the most obvious method of ensuring the community's stability was to pass property and power to designated heirs. Although sex and the fathering or bearing of children were contrary to the ideal of celibacy, some monks let slip that ideal in order to perpetuate their communities. Of course, if the saints' lives are to be believed, most monks were chaste, living and working together as virtuously as Egyptian hermits. The annals also repeatedly mention *anchoritae,* ascetics, as members of major monastic communities.[89] Yet even when a core group of monks maintained themselves as a celibate elite within a community, their rulers and their associated lay brothers often provided the stock from which they drew recruits. Kathleen Hughes and John Kelleher have shown that major monasteries such as Sláine, Lusca, and Cluain Moccu Nóis contained monastic families that were bound by blood as well as by consciously created family-style ties. Abbots and officers openly supported wives, sons, and other kin. They sent their relatives to become officers in nearby monasteries, or they kept sons, brothers, and nephews within their own communities to succeed to offices there. Successive generations of the Maicc Cuinn na mBocht, for example, controlled major monastic offices at Cluain Moccu Nóis for about three centuries. Another family, the Uí Sinaich, battled for and won control of Ard Macha, remaining in power for generations.[90] There is no reason to assume that other monks ignored the example of their abbots and officers.[91]

Kinship within monastic communities allowed the religious elite to pass knowledge and responsibility, as well as property, to sons and other family members. One tenth-century poem suggests that abbots, like craftsmen and secular rulers, could most efficiently be succeeded by their sons.[92] The process also promoted a permanent population within mon-

---

89. AU, 202, 206, 210, 250, 266, 268, et passim. AU contains at least forty-two such references before 950. See also Aidan McDonald, "Notes on Monastic Archaeology and the Annals of Ulster, 650–1050," in Donnchadh Ó Corráin, ed., *Irish Antiquity* (Cork, 1980), 314–17.

90. John V. Kelleher, "The Táin and the Annals," *Ériu* 22 (1971), 107–29, esp. 125–27; Hughes, *Church in Early Irish Society,* 161–66; Tomas Ó Fiaich, "The Church of Armagh under Lay Control," *Seanchas Ard Mhacha* 5 (1969), 82–100. See also Donnchadh Ó Corráin, "Onomata," *Ériu* 30 (1979), 165–80.

91. See the genealogical chart in Kelleher, "Táin and the Annals."

92. T. O'Donoghue, "Advice to a Prince," *Ériu* 9 (1921), 43–54, cited in Hughes, *Church in Early Irish Society,* 163–64.

astic settlements. Monasteries needed their families of administrators, their abbots and scribes, stewards and tutors, more urgently than the ideal of celibacy allowed.[93]

The Irish were not unique in this attitude. The marriage of clergy was not finally and officially prohibited on the Continent until a series of reforming councils in the eleventh century, even though councils and popes had denounced the practice regularly since the fourth century.[94] Bishops of Rome and elsewhere constantly repeated the plea for monastic celibacy—which suggests that European monks and priests continued to reproduce. The majority of Irish monks could mark their religious identity in other ways that interfered less with their social functions, and allowed them to marry and successfully perpetuate their religious families. As Colmán Ela explained of two novices in his community, one was bound for heaven and one for hell, and asceticism would change neither of them.[95]

The monastic kin-group also perpetuated itself by bringing in new brothers from elite families outside the enclosure. Although the hagiographers suggested that adult recruits were common at first, once Christianity had established itself in Ireland children also entered the enclosure. For one hagiographer and the saint whom he praised, childish prayers were synonymous with the religious life; he related how Mochuda was drawn to the site for Rathan, his *locus,* by the ghostly sound of boys reading aloud.[96] The recruitment of young boys signaled secular society's acceptance of monasteries as property-holding, kin-based communities like any other. Parents knew that their sons would learn useful skills and begin promising careers under the tutelage and care of the monks.

The local nobility was happy to infiltrate monastic communities, gaining influence over property and prestigious religious offices, by allowing their children to become monks. Rejects from royal politics filled the upper strata of the monastic hierarchy in large communities. The Dál Cais clan, which produced Brain Boru and the O'Brien kings of Munster, attempted with mixed success to dominate the abbacies of old commu-

93. There are no explicit Irish references to the situation described by Wollasch in eleventh-century France, where entire families joined monastic communities, bringing their property with them. See J. Wollasch, "Parenté noble et monachisme réformateur," *Revue Historique* 535 (June–September 1980), 3–24.

94. Karl Joseph Hefele, *Histoire des conciles d'après les documents originaux,* trans. Henri Leclercq (Paris, 1907–1952), 5:215, 245, et passim; Ryan, *Irish Monasticism,* 86n.

95. PBNE 1:182.

96. PVSH 1:185; HVSH, 136, 204, 398.

nities such as Inis Chathaig, Inis Cheltra, Tuaim Greine, and Tír Dá Glas. At various times from the tenth to the twelfth century, peripheral members of the Dál Cais held important posts in all of these communities. They virtually controlled Cell Da Lua both before and after the twelfth-century reform movement. The men who assumed these monastic offices, and the children who grew into them, came from politically weak branches of the ruling dynasty, and were themselves often displaced by families more recently excluded from secular power.[97] Whether this pattern held in other regions and in other types of monastic establishments remains to be shown. However, as the annals repeatedly demonstrate, secular lords throughout Ireland interfered with monastic government whenever possible. Recruitment and replenishment of monastic populations was less of a problem to many communities than the political manipulation of their administrative offices by local nobility and their offspring.

Even when parents hoped to gain from their sons' monastic careers, they still may have recognized a genuinely spiritual or intellectual vocation in a child and honored it by allowing his or her recruitment by the monks. Mochóemóc's parents gave him to Íte, his foster mother, because they were *carnales,* but she a spiritual *matertera* who would teach him the religious life.[98] Monks did not always seek the healthy offspring of the politically powerful. They used recruitment for authentically charitable and religious purposes, taking in children with physical defects and abandoned children. When children were not likely to survive a crueler world outside the sacred space, parents left them with the monks. For example, when an aristocratic boy suffered damage to his eyes as a hostage of the king of the Uí Cheinselaig, his parents offered him to Cainnech's community, where he went on to become a successful monk, founding Cell Da Lua.[99]

Secular folk who recognized the monk's mark on a son, or wanted a link with the local saint, or simply wanted to provide support for a weak child instead of killing him, abandoned their baby sons to the enclosure.[100] In an age when infant health was generally poor and mere survival almost a

---

97. Donnchadh Ó Corráin, "Dál Cais—Church and Dynasty," *Ériu* 24 (1973), 52–63. See also the involvement of Énda's kin in his monastic career, PVSH 2:60–63.

98. PVSH 1:66–67, 99–100, 172; see also HVSH, 399.

99. HVSH, 193; see also 219–20.

100. John Boswell, "Expositio and Oblatio: The Abandonment of Children in the Ancient and Medieval Family," *American Historical Review* 89 (February 1984), 16–33; cf. Wasserschleben, *Collectio,* 168–69.

miracle, child abandonment represented little more than an excuse for sending a spare son off to the safety of the monastery.[101]

A tradition of adult recruitment also lingered from earlier, more zealously ascetic days. Some men were voluntary recruits, some forced by society to leave other careers. Many men and women appeared in the saints' lives simply as *penitentes,* whose presence in monastic communities needed no further explanation. One of Monenna's nuns, for example, came to live with the saint after a sinful career that included at least one generous illicit lover; only after she had discarded all traces of her past life, including a precious pair of shoes given her by her former lover, could the woman devote herself to her new lord.[102] Kings, such as Mochuda's protégé Cusantin of Alba, and Cormac mac Diarmata of Leinster who joined Comgall's community, were welcome to shed their royal cloaks for a monk's tunic.[103] Not all penitents came willingly; monasteries may have functioned as prisons for political and social dissenters. The hagiographers' picture of outlaws-turned-monks suggests that many criminals were men of free or high status, perhaps bereft of an inheritance, who could not find any other safe, acceptable place in society.[104]

Adult recruits were not as well integrated into the community as the men who had trained for it from an early age. They usually needed extra instructions in prayers and doctrine.[105] But their lack of vocation also allowed them a measure of security not available to others in the enclosure. Since they were not essential members of the monastic family, they were allowed to come and go more freely. A man bound to Colmán Ela's rule left the community to return to his kin when the monks lacked enough food to feed themselves.[106] *Athláig* (former laymen) remained laymen in some monastic eyes. Munnu's hagiographer even mentioned "a certain layman, a monk of saint Fintan" (*quidam laicus, monachus sancti Fintani,*) seeing no contradiction in this description of an *athláech.*[107] Adult recruits were also the butt of hagiographical snobbery on many occasions. Hagiographers portrayed them as shallow in vocation and

---

101. HVSH, 143, 337.

102. USMLS, Conchubranus III, 434–47.

103. PBNE 1:181–82, 166–68; see also Adomnán, 252–56, 266–68.

104. Kathleen Hughes and Ann Hamlin, *Celtic Monasticism: The Modern Traveller to the Early Irish Church* (New York, 1977), 15; see also Richard Sharpe, "Hiberno-Latin *Laicus,* Irish *Láech* and the Devil's Men," *Ériu* 30 (1979), 75–92. For outlaws turned penitent monks, see VT, 240; HVSH, 351, 393, 399; PBNE 1:47; Adomnán, 252–56, 420–34; PVSH 1:225–26.

105. Gwynn and Purton, "Monastery of Tallaght," 127.

106. HVSH, 211–12.

107. Ibid., 206; compare the *vita altera,* 253.

overenthusiastic in practice. For example, they mocked the new monks who refused to eat meat when there was nothing else to eat, even though their monastic betters consumed a little flesh.[108] In secular communities, kinless and propertyless men who married into a community and wanderers who came to stay were subject to discrimination in social status and property rights.[109] Similarly, *athláig* remained on the periphery of the religious elite, marked by specific connotations of penitence and punishment.

Whatever the monks' reasons for accepting these different sorts of recruits, the process of recruitment itself derived from kinship. The community gave birth to, fostered, or adopted novices. Neither the tarnished celibate ideal, nor lower recruitment standards, nor the maintenance of blood ties necessarily affected the monks' spiritual vocation, or limited their spiritual purpose, or diminished their allegiance to their monastic families. These solutions simply addressed the need of the religious elite to organize and perpetuate itself.

Clearly, the monks could not completely divorce themselves from their secular families and still survive as a community in a kin-based society. No community in early Ireland could survive in isolation without supportive links to other groups. Even when monks succeeded in enlarging their communities, and even when families of monks became stable, permanent, and prosperous, they sought additional support from beyond their walls.

In the *vitae*, the interaction of monks and nuns with their blood relations functioned on two levels. When monks consorted with parents, siblings, or other kin, they demonstrated the genuine value of blood ties. But their alliances and friendships also symbolized the relations between an entire monastic community and other communities, both religious and secular. Hagiographers consistently described these encounters between different communities in terms of kinship. They also made it plain that the ultimate purpose of any monk's ties with his blood kin was the support of the monastic community (Fig. 14).

Many saints, monks, and nuns kept up personal relationships with family, according to the lives, because of the affection they felt for their rela-

---

108. PVSH 2:73, 139.

109. CIH 2:426–27, and ALI 5:517, describe three kinds of men who have no families or lords of their own and must depend upon their wives for property, status, and the support of kin-groups. One of these men, the *cú-glas* (wolf) or outsider from overseas, is also described in CIH 1:31, and ALI 5:235. The social stigma attached to the *cú-glas* also affected his son; see CIH 1:22 and ALI 5:203.

1. Saints of the Cenél Conaill

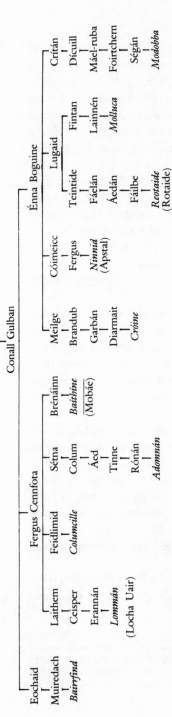

Níall Nóigiallach
Conall Gulban

Fergus Cennfota   Énna Boguine

Eochaid   Laithem   Sétna   Brénainn   Meilge   Cóimeicc   Lugaid   Crítán

Muiredach   Feidlimid   Colum   *Baíthíne*   Brandub   Fergus   Teintide   Fintan   Dícuill

Bairrfhind   Cetsper   Áed   (Mobáe)   Garbán   *Nínníd*   Fáelán   Lainnén   Máel-ruba

    Erannán   Tinne   Diarmait   (Apstal)   Áedán   *Molluca*   Foirtchern

    Lommán   Rónán   *Cróne*   Fáilbe   Ségán

  (Locha Uair)   *Adomnán*   *Reotaide*   *Modobba*

                                          (Rotaide)

Columcille

2. Cenél Conaill kings of Temair

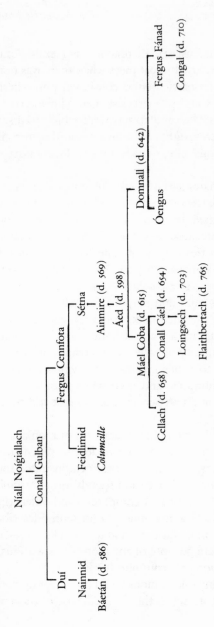

Níall Nóigiallach
Conall Gulban

Duí   Fergus Cennfota

Nainnid   Feidlimid   Sétna

Báetán (d. 586)   *Columcille*   Ainmire (d. 569)

                         Áed (d. 598)

                       Máel Coba (d. 615)

    Cellach (d. 658)   Conall Cáel (d. 654)   Domnall (d. 642)

             Loingsech (d. 703)   Óengus   Fergus Fánad

            Flaithbertach (d. 765)   Congal (d. 710)

14. Genealogies of Columcille. The importance of saintly kinship connections and pedigrees should be evident from the by-no-means-exhaustive genealogical charts of saints and kings related to Columcille. The charts are constructed from twelfth-century manuscripts based on ninth-century or earlier materials. See Pádraig Ó Riain, *Corpus Genealogiarum Sanctorum Hiberniae* (Dublin, 1986), 4–9, 12, 13–14, 53, 54; Máire Herbert, *Iona, Kells and Derry* (Oxford, 1988), 310–11; Gearóid Mac Niocaill, *Ireland before the Vikings* (Dublin, 1972), 153.

tives. An *athláech* in Mochuda's community was one of the few monks in the *vitae* allowed to visit his former home; the saint sympathized with the man, who was overcome by homesickness and loneliness for his people.[110] Other monks remained in contact with relatives and even rushed to their aid when they needed support.[111] Máedóc, for instance, rescued his brother, who had been taken hostage by the Uí Chonaill Gabra. He fasted for three days before the gates of the tribal king and even caused the death of the king's daughter in order to win the hostage's release.[112] Apparently monks who had renounced inheritance claims could be allies with their brothers rather than competitors.

Monks also maintained affective ties with female relatives. Columcille, who fled to Í to avoid kin entanglements, rushed to pray for a kinswoman who invoked his aid during childbirth.[113] Others at Í were anxious about relatives left outside the sacred space. Colcu mac Cellaig begged a lump of blessed rock salt from Columcille for his sister, who was also his foster mother, to hang above her bed, in the hope that it would cure her inflamed eyes.[114] Even God approved of contact between monks and their mothers. When Colmán's mother begged to see and speak with him, the saint tried to maintain an orthodox distance between them. He told his mother that she could either speak to him separated by trees or look at him, but not both. She chose to speak to her boy. But God cleared away the trees between mother and son even as they spoke.[115]

These examples appear to represent nothing more than the hagiographer's positive interpretation of personal ties between monks and their close kin. But the hagiographers also used kinship to symbolize the relations between entire communities. For example, in the famous story that culminated in the saints' cursing of Temair, kinship provided the symbolic vocabulary for ties between monastic communities and secular leaders. The story goes that many clerics were moved by family feeling to come to the rescue of Áed Guaire, king of Uí Maine in Connacht. His cousin, Bishop Senach, sheltered the king, who was on the run from the Uí Néill king, Diarmait mac Cerbaill, "because of the kinship between them, for their two mothers were sisters."[116] Senach's foster mothers begged Saint

110. PBNE 1:300.
111. HVSH, 157–58.
112. PBNE 1:187.
113. Adomnán, 434–36.
114. Ibid., 340; see also 240–42.
115. HVSH, 360.
116. PBNE 1:322; 2:313.

Ruadán, their brother, also to give refuge to the bishop's cousin. Áed depended on the ties of blood and affection to preserve him from his enemies. But to the hagiographer, Ruadán and Diarmait mac Cerbaill represented groups, not individuals, in their battle over Áed, who also symbolized more than his troublemaking self in the episode. Diarmait signified Uí Néill rulers of Temair; Ruadán symbolized churches, specifically his own at Poll Ruadáin and its mother settlement, Lothra; Áed was the Uí Maine, in whose territory Lothra lay. Ruadán's hagiographer demonstrated the utility of personal relationships based on kinship at the same time that he used a network of kinship ties to represent larger alliances between ruling groups and monastic communities. Although the story itself is fantastic propaganda, it also reveals some of the hagiographers' assumptions about kinship: Individual monks as well as whole monastic families could effectively use their ties to kinsmen and foster relations to benefit themselves and their allies.

Many monks drew on the material support of blood kin in order to establish religious communities.[117] One hagiographer described how a religious woman called Brigit took the dowry given her by her father, a fort built next to her parents' enclosure, and created a community of nuns within easy reach of parental support.[118] Déclán went home to Brega in order to seek donations from his family, who obliged him "because of the primary blood tie," giving him a field on which to build a monastery and name it after himself.[119]

Some family members worked together to build networks of religious communities.[120] According to Ciarán's hagiographer, two brothers named Midrán and Odrán, both monks, traveled together around Ireland on pilgrimage. When Midrán wanted to remain at Saigir with Saint Ciarán, Odrán objected; he only allowed his brother to stay after Midrán proved his sincere desire with a miracle. Odrán was mollified when Ciarán predicted that he would establish a famous house, Leitrecha Odráin. The hagiographer's purpose in this episode was to illustrate Ciarán's wisdom and justice, and to explain the origins of Leitrecha Odráin. Yet the entire interaction was based on the assumption of brotherly feeling between the

117. HVSH, 397–98. See Donnchadh Ó Corráin, "Early Irish Churches—Some Aspects of Organisation," in Ó Corráin, *Irish Antiquity*, 337–38. For similar situations in France, see E. Lesne, *Histoire de la propriété écclesiastique en France* (Paris, 1943), 1:132–33.

118. HVSH, 397–98.

119. PVSH 2:51.

120. Ludwig Bieler, ed., *Patrician Texts in the Book of Armagh* (Dublin, 1979), 132, 148, 150–52, 156–58.

two monks and of relations between Saigir and Leitrecha Odráin.[121] Ciarán's hagiographers seem to have been particularly sensitive to family relations. When Ciarán's fame spread throughout Ireland, many of his relations (*coibnesa*) gathered around him. His mother came to live near her son, bringing along some virgins, including his sisters, with whom she established a nunnery.[122] No doubt the saint's symbolic authority over his mother's foundation represents Saigir's special relations with a neighboring women's community.

To monastic scholars, kinship connections among saints signified political alliances between their communities, just as secular genealogies represented confederations of ruling groups and other tribes. Many of the most famous saints were related by blood, as their genealogies showed. Colmán Ela sent for Columcille to help him convert a recalcitrant pagan king because, as the hagiographer explained, Columcille's father was Colmán's grandfather. Columcille held the crozier, Colmán preached, and they called in another kinsman, Manchán, to sprinkle the holy water.[123] No doubt the communities of Lann Ela, Cenannas, and Liath Mancháin appreciated this symbol of their relations. Yet even when the hagiographers used saints and their kin to symbolize ties between communities, they still depicted personal and loving friendships between the characters in their episodes. For example, Brénainn's biographer showed how he sought out his sister just before his death, to bless her and bid her a fond farewell. The scene probably represented some positive connection between the siblings' communities, but that did not diminish the literary effect of their parting.[124] As long as Brénainn and his sister recalled that they were religious professionals first and siblings second, they were free to demand love and support from each other.

Although they never thoroughly solved the problems of tangled alliances and the difficult position of monks and nuns caught between spiritual kin and monastic family, hagiographers sent one clear message to the religious elite: Monks had to give their primary allegiance to their monastic families. They hid this message in their stories of fierce, kinless ascetics who roamed Ireland, laying down cemeteries and erecting protective walls in the days of the Christian frontier. Monastic scholars may even have believed these early exemplars to be genuinely self-sufficient. Monks

121. PVSH 1:227–28.
122. Ibid., 220–21; PBNE 1:104.
123. PBNE 1:168.
124. PVSH 1:149–50; PBNE 1:93.

and nuns throughout the Middle Ages mouthed this same rhetoric of rejection, pretending to abandon family and inheritance. They claimed to discard blood kin for another family, the monastic community, and its property, the saint's enclosure. They left father and mother for abbot and brother; they shed the obligations of inherited positions for their responsibilities as intercessors with the saint.

But, as the hagiographers admitted, there was no such thing as an isolated self-sufficient community that could weather the dangers of life in pre-Norman Ireland. The nuclear family was enmeshed in ties to the larger *fine;* and no individual relied for support on one social group only. The vow taken by Brénainn's monks and countless others to ignore their parents and forfeit their inheritances became merely the symbol of a monk's choice to affiliate himself with a particular monastic settlement and its community. Brénainn's monks gave their hearts and wills to him but, after their fantastic voyage to the Land of Promise, they returned to the waiting arms of monastic brethren and blood kin. Far from abandoning one family for another, most monks and nuns actually enjoyed the benefits and suffered the troubles of two.

Ultimately, neither monastic *familia* nor blood kin completely dominated any monk's social network. Each monk had to choose friends and allies from his brothers by blood and by spirit, his cousins, aunts, uncles, and dozens of other relatives. Usually the monks tried to balance ties to other monks and to kin. As a group, the monks worked to maintain the solidarity of their monastic *familia,* supplementing it, when necessary, with ties that reached beyond the blessed walls to blood kin.

CHAPTER FOUR

Clientship and the Division of Labor

M ONKS OF PROSPEROUS, POPULOUS MONASTERIES ENCOUNTERED a variety of lay people with whom they formed social ties, some brief, some permanent. Even the tiniest monastery attracted visitors of one kind or another, and monks of the poorest, shabbiest settlement had neighbors. The simple ideal of the monastic *familia* could not accommodate all these people and relationships. Monks maintained their kin-style ties among themselves, but they formed other kinds of contractual relationships with lay people who lived in or near the enclosure.

The larger community, composed of monastic *familia* and laics, caused the monks three chronic problems. First, they needed to support a large and varied settlement with extensive population and property. Second, they had to divide labor within the community. Third, the brothers sought to define more precisely the limits of the monastic community; in particular, they needed to identify the monastic elite among the lay people and secular business that intruded on the sacred space. To solve these complicated problems, the monks assigned to lay clients the job of material support, while themselves turning to more elite occupations, such as prayer and managerial work.

Legal *Manaig*

Most monastic settlements did not survive by either the monks' prayers or their labor, but by the labor of tenants and *manaig* (sg. *manach*, "monastic client"). The contractual relationships between the *familia* of monks

[115]

and its laborers, modeled on secular clientage, provided the monks with all they needed to live while they devoted themselves to more important business.

Monks placed their communities in the midst of lands that they owned, which had to be farmed or used as pasture or in other productive ways. Clients, tenants, and servants lived and worked on monastic lands. These men and women of varying social status owed different kinds of rents or labor to the monks and received returns appropriate to their stations. Some *manaig* and tenants were free farmers whose families had occupied the land long before any saint had thought to enclose its sacred space; others were chattel granted as part of an endowment to the monastery. However, all worked for only one purpose: to support the monks and to be supported by them. Neither slaves nor clients nor tenants shared the spiritual kinship of the monks, but all of them were members of the larger monastic community. In exchange for their sweat and their rents, monastic clients gained spiritual protection and special participation in Christian rituals, assets of immense value in this Christianizing world.

The legal writers, especially post-eighth-century glossators and commentators, had much to say about the class of farmer called a *manach* and about his contractual relations with the monastic elite.[1] *Manach* derived from Latin *monachus;* in the saints' lives, *manach* generally meant a man with a tonsure, a member of the saint's *familia*. But according to legal usage, a *manach* came from a different social group. Later medieval commentators on the *Córus Béscnai,* an eighth-century tract that supplies more evidence about *manaig* than any other single source, explained that monks were of the *fine erluma,* kin-group of the patron saint of a monastery, while *manaig* had a kin-group to themselves (*fine manach*).[2] The commentator did not necessarily mean this kin terminology literally, although Thomas Charles-Edwards has argued that the *manaig* of a church may originally have been a single kin-related *túath* (tribe).[3] But just as the monks chose to use kinship as an organizational principle, so legal writers employed the familiar vocabulary of kin relations to express all sorts of

1. Kathleen Hughes, *The Church in Early Irish Society* (London, 1966), 136–41; Charles Doherty, "Hagiography as a Source for Irish Economic History," *Peritia* 1 (1982), 301–28; T. M. Charles-Edwards, "The Church and Settlement," in Proinséas Ní Chatháin and Michael Richter, eds., *Ireland and Europe* (Stuttgart, 1984), 167–75; Fergus Kelly, *A Guide to Early Irish Law* (Dublin, 1988), 33, 39. But see CIH 3:1348, where *manach riagalta* refers to a monk in orders.

2. CIH 5:1820, 2:530.

3. Charles-Edwards, "Church and Settlement."

social and economic ties, including clientage. *Córus Béscnai* was a tract written by and for clerics, hence subject to their organizational concepts.[4]

Thus, a monk was not a *manach*. *Manaig* were farmers, clients and tenants of the monastic family. The relationship of a *manach* to the monastic elite was formally contractual, based on the relations among secular lords and clients. Just as the secular lord acted for his family's interests and lands, so the abbot acted for the saint and the monastic *familia* when forming contracts with clients. But ecclesiastical clientage differed both in the dues offered and the returns expected by clients.

Legal minds divided monastic clients into two neat categories of status, *doer* and *soer*, base and free, similar to the *doerchéile* and *soerchéile* of secular clientage.[5] Both were essentially agricultural tenants, although many received loans of stock, cattle, or equipment from their lord rather than land. In return, clients owed dues of a certain percentage of the stock, along with rents in the form of meat, grain, and dairy products, or the provision of formal hospitality. The laws described these rents and dues in Old Testament terms as *dechmada*, *prímiti*, and *almsana* (tithes, firstfruits, and alms).[6] Thus, for example, a *manach* who received stock of fifteen or twenty breeding cattle at the start of his clientship owed his lord an annual 10 percent, two calves, as tithes plus one of each kind of his animals born in the spring as firstfruits, along with food-rents as alms.[7] As his herds increased, his tithes grew. Both a free and a servile *manach* also paid the amount of his legal worth, his honor-price, to his lord when they formed their contract, and at his death his heirs paid the lord a sum equal in value to one third of his honor-price; in return, his lord protected him as guardian in legal disputes and other kinds of conflict.[8]

The *soermanach* was a free man who entered clientship with lands of his own, receiving only stock from his ecclesiastical lord. Free clients often included nobles of considerable power and status as well as prosperous peasant farmers; the more aristocratic and wealthy the patron, the more noble his clients. As in secular clientage relationships, the rents of a free client were lower than those of base clients, and his duties of a higher order. For instance, he was a valuable member of his ecclesiastical lord's

---

4. Liam Breatnach, Donnchadh Ó Corráin, and Aidan Breen, "The Laws of the Irish," *Peritia* 3 (1984), 382–438.

5. Kelly, *Guide to Early Irish Law*, 29–36; D. A. Binchy, *Críth Gablach* (Dublin 1941), 69–109.

6. CIH 2:503.

7. Ibid., 503, 529, 530; Charles-Edwards, "Church and Settlement."

8. CIH 2:503.

retinue in legal matters, as he could provide oaths of witness and help enforce guaranties.[9] He was also expected to bear arms for his lord.

The firstlings that the *soermanach* owed to his lord included a due with which no secular client was burdened, his first-born son.[10] This seems to have been a devious legal device that made so-called free clientage heritable from father to eldest son; the laws neglected to mention the status of the *soermanach*'s other sons. The author of the *Córus Béscnai* decreed that the firstling was to bring his share of his father's land with him and to live on it himself, and to act generally like a *soermanach*. Whether he was allowed to maintain ownership of his lands remains unclear. As the purpose of free clientship was for the lord to reap returns without lending out any of his own lands, most likely the client kept his lands.

Doermanaig were men of lower social status who paid higher rents and owed a set number of hours of manual labor dues. Some had to work on the lord's estates, as well as keeping their own farms, for which they paid rents. The semilegal text *Ríagal Pátraic* suggested that a *manach* paid an annual rent of a day's plowing to each ordained cleric who inhabited a small ecclesiastical community, along with the amount of seed sown and land plowed in one day; he also provided the cleric with clothing and refection for three major feast days.[11]

Doermanaig had more restricted legal rights than freemen. Like minors and women, they could not make legal agreements or contracts of any kind without the consent or possibly even the presence of their lords.[12] They also found it more difficult to break their clientage contracts with their lords than a freeman might. A commentator on the *Córus Béscnai* allowed seven "necessary desertions" of a church by a *manach*, a parallel to the seven reasons for breaking clientage relations listed in other legal texts.[13] These included the failure of the church and its representatives to provide material or spiritual support, a natural disruption of rents such as famine, the client's loss of his land, or lengthy journeys for religious purposes, such as the pursuit of learning or pilgrimage. The commentator apparently found the last two less necessary, because he assigned the client fines for them.[14]

But the *Córus Béscnai* did not allow for the mutual dissolution of a

9. Binchy, *Críth Gablach*, 90–91; see ll. 19, 26, 43, 137, et passim.
10. CIH 2:531; see also Hughes, *Church in Early Irish Society*, 136–37.
11. J. G. O'Keeffe, "The Rule of Patrick," *Ériu* 1 (1904), 220.
12. CIH 2:522; see also 593.
13. CIH 5:1818; ALI 3:64–67.
14. CIH 5:1818.

manach-monastery contract, nor did it give the community the right to send away its clients because of dissatisfaction with the contract. In fact, the legal writers tried to prevent *manaig* from switching ecclesiastical lords, by ruling that their inheritance be divided between one-third for their new lord and two-thirds for their abandoned lord for three generations; that is, the client, his heir, and that man's heir each loss 66 percent of his property, so that the third heir's land equaled only one-twenty-seventh of the original estate.[15] Such a law, if enforced, efficiently restricted the mobility of tenant farmers.

Ecclesiastical laws show how the status of *doermanaig* differed slightly from that of unfree clients of secular lords. The ninth-century canonical text *Cáin Domnaig* restricted the labors of clients on the Sabbath, prohibiting farmers and their families from chopping wood, washing laundry, chasing lost animals, and other common chores. Although the text theoretically applied to everyone, clients of religious settlements would more likely have been among those who suffered, or enjoyed, an enforced day of rest.[16]

Charles-Edwards has suggested that *doermanaig* may have been enfranchised slaves, whereas *soermanaig* were legally free men from birth. A passage from *Córus Béscnai* described the liberation of slaves who became churchmen: "He will free slaves [*mugo*], he will exalt base kindreds through the grades of the church [*gráda*] and through the service of penitence to God. For the kingdom of heaven is open to every kindred of men after the coming of the Faith, both free kindreds and base kindreds. So, likewise, is the Church open to every man whoever should submit to the Law."[17] But *Córus Béscnai*'s author wrote here not of turning an eighth-century *mug* (slave) into a *manach*. He specifically set the episode in the distant Patrician past to give it the authority of antiquity; he also used the term *gráda*, formal ecclesiastical orders, as the vehicle for achieving greater status. But *manaig* were not men in orders. The passage was meant to illustrate the powers of patronage and protection held by ecclesiastical lords, spiritual successors of the *mugo* of Pátraic's fifth century who had shed the shackles of paganism to become Christian monks and priests. *Doermanaig* were base clients unable to change their status or jobs, subject to the laws of the monks whom they supported by their labor.

The hagiographers also suggested that *manaig* were not the laborers of

15. Ibid.; ALI 3:66–67.
16. H. G. O'Keeffe, "Cáin Domnaig," *Ériu* 2 (1905), 200–202.
17. CIH 2:528; Charles-Edwards, "Church and Settlement."

lowest status on ecclesiastical lands. In the ninth-century *Vita tripartita* of Pátraic, the *senchléithi* attached to Énda mac Néill's endowment to Pátraic were men of even more servile status, not even free to enter into the contract of clientage.[18] The social line between such men and *doermanaig*, like the line between base and free clients, existed in theory, but their status and wealth cannot have been divided so neatly into categories. All worked the land for the benefit of professional holy men or women, in return for either land or stock or both, and for the religious privileges accorded members of the larger monastic community.

The hagiographers occasionally referred to an institution of clientage that was just as complex as that found in the laws. But the hagiographic vocabulary of clientage differed from legal usage. The Latin lives from all periods used *monachus* and *frater* to refer to monks under vows; *minister* (servant) and *discipulus* described the monk in relation to his master or mistress, the saint and abbot or abbess. Latin-speaking monks called the men who worked their lands and herded their animals *aratores* and *armentarii;* if their labor was not in the fields, they were *artifices, operarii, laborarii.* The *bethada* (saints' lives written in Irish) called only monks *manaig.* Ruadán's hagiographer distinguished between *manaig* and *aes timthirechta* (serving people), their laborers and tenants.[19] Others wrote of *lucht oibre* (laboring people).[20] A tenant farmer on one of Máedóc's estates was *toireamh*, a plowman.[21]

In some instances, the term *manaig* in the *vitae* could certainly be interpreted as referring to laboring clients rather than tonsured monks, simply because no detail identifies them as one or the other. But when the word has a specific meaning, it consistently denotes a man whose primary function was prayer rather than manual labor.[22] *Manaig* sat down to eat in Rathan's refectory while Cusantin of Alba, a mere ex-layman, labored outside. Ciarán's cook worried about feeding his *manaig*, hardly a concern if the men of whom he spoke were tenant farmers with families or clients

18. VT, 72; Doherty, "Hagiography as a Source," 313–14.
19. PBNE 1:320.
20. Ibid., 172.
21. Ibid., 222. See also Hughes's discussion of clientage vocabulary in *Church in Early Irish Society,* 137–38.
22. But see Doherty, "Hagiography as a Source," 320, where he takes the *manaig* mentioned for monastic tenants. See also CIH 1:318, 2:529. The *Additamenta* in the Book of Armach clearly used *muinter* to refer to tonsured monks, although elsewhere in the lives it referred to *manaig*. See Ludwig Bieler, *Patrician Texts in the Book of Armagh* (Dublin, 1979), 172.

with their own holdings.[23] *Manaig* said the prayers, and when angels came to earth they appeared as golden-haired *manaig*.[24]

Hagiographers were too busy seeking financial support from local nobility to offer much information about the men and women who were bound to contribute to monastic prosperity. But they confirmed the differences between secular and monastic clientage, and gave clues about the development of the latter. The hagiographers clearly believed that lay people had become the clients and tenants of the monks as early as the age of the saints, the sixth and seventh centuries. The *vitae* charted the shift from times when the brothers labored to support themselves to the point when they became a monastic elite clamoring to be supported.

An episode from Mochuda's life, in which he refused to allow his monks to make use of the available technology to aid their subsistence labors, encapsulated a development that actually took many years. In the hagiographer's version, local secular leaders persuaded the saint to release his monks from labor by showering him with so much income that no one at Rathan had to sweat in order to eat.[25] In reality it probably took Mochuda's community a long time to acquire property and the men to work it so that the literate, praying elite could afford to lay down their hoes. But this episode and many others like it revealed a common concern of the hagiographers: the perpetual problems of how to organize and support a populous community that consisted of many more than just a few noble and fraternally minded monks, as well as how to make certain that valuable endowments remained productive estates. Rules worked well on vellum, but the organization of production required more practical effort.

Some stories about the origins of monastic communities give clues as to how secular laborers came to work for the monks during the early centuries of Christianization. Ruadán's donor, for example, offered an estate (*civitas*) called Snám Luthair "and the people attached to it" (*et gentem sibi adherentem*).[26] In another episode, Ruadán ferreted out the lost gold of a different *civitas*, in return for which the settlement gave itself and the farmers in the neighborhood to the holy man (*civitatem et gentem que est in circuitu illius*).[27] Columcille forfeited one of his foundations to Fintan in

23. PBNE 1:301; see also 105.
24. Ibid., 237–38.
25. PVSH 1:177–78.
26. HVSH, 161.
27. Ibid.

thanks for hospitality; Columcille's gift included "an estate called Cell Mactogi with all its service and the obedience of its tenants" (*cum omni servitute et obedientia hominum suorum*).[28] Gerald accepted a *locus* that included three farms and ten men to work them.[29] Hagiographers considered clients part of the land, like stock or natural resources, and they thought clientage a system legitimately inherited by the monks from generous donors over many centuries.

Hagiographers tended to confuse clients with donors, and free clients with unfree tenants. Most likely, in Ireland as elsewhere in Europe, the distinctions between servile and free tenants, and between lord's lands worked by tenants and free allods worked by clients, slowly disappeared, leaving all nonnoble tenants and clients in the same vast social class. Yet the mercenary services of a craftsman differed from the sweaty plowing and reaping of Máedóc's *aratores*. The relationship between Mochuda and the deaf-mute whom he cured, and who gave the service of himself and his descendants, was not the same as the political protection and donations (*manchaine*) offered to the saint by the king of Munster and his noble retinue.[30] In the laws, *manchaine* meant the dues of manual labor. But King Cairpre was not offering to push a plow for Mochuda. Hagiographers and their contemporaries understood the range of obligations and services and the subtle variations in dues and status, all difficult to define precisely and legally, that characterized their clientage relationships.

Of course, such high-class supporters as kings and their henchmen were neither tenants of the monastic family nor the *populus* or *muinter* described by the hagiographers as part of the larger monastic community. Noble lay folk were part of a more geographically dispersed social and political network that brought monks and lay people together. Despite hagiographic claims that everyone owed support to monastic communities, all lay people were not members of the larger monastic community. Nor were outsiders the major source of material support for the monks, as the laws consistently showed.

If neither social status nor obligatory service necessarily defined a *manach*, perhaps settlement patterns help to clarify the identity of *manaig* and the limits of the larger monastic community. The laws never specified

28. Ibid., 117; see also 228.
29. PVSH 2:110. The *vita* of Gerald is post-twelfth century. The measurement of land in *villae* was almost certainly not pre-Norman.
30. PVSH 1:245–48. The hagiographers' depiction of Gobbán was unique because he was probably a euhemerized craftsman god. See ibid., clxiii–clxiv.

where *manaig* lived, but the *vitae* indicated that lay folk who were in some sense subordinate to monastic officials lived and farmed nearby. For instance, Saint Áed gave his iron coulter to a plowman in his neighborhood (*in locis proximis*), a gift that probably represented to the hagiographer the loan of stock from monastic lord to peasant client.[31] At Cluain Brónaig, Samthann oversaw the rebuilding of her church. When she needed men to move her oratory she sent for her dependents, and at least eight lived close enough to her settlement to appear, ready to help, the next morning.[32] Munnu's hagiographer also referred to farmers living in the neighborhood (*in circuitu*) of Munnu's community; they were near enough so that their women and children could take refuge within the sacred enclosure when raiders arrived in the area.[33]

The eighth-century canonists also assumed, with the hagiographers, that dependent secular settlements were attached to monastic communities. The compilers of the *Collectio* referred to the enclosure surrounded by what they called *suburbanes*. Basing their decisions on Mosaic law, the canonists declared that a wall must stand between the temple and laics; within the wall the priests and their *familiae* resided, while outside lived secular laborers. In a chapter on endowments and donations, they described the organization of monastic estates:

> A consecrated place containing the relics of saints, given to a church, ought to be occupied by holy men and ought not to be without a priest. But on land without relics, which is next to the enclosure and which has been given to a church, men (that is, the family of the church) can be allowed to live. However, on land not directly adjacent to a church, both sexes can live and even common folk. Fourthly, moveable wealth, cows and sheep and the rest, can be lent out to layfolk, namely to Christians or monastic tenants.[34]

Thus, according to the canonists, the most sacred of spaces belonged to the saint and to his most ascetic devotees, including a priest. The abbot and his regular monks dwelt beyond the inner sanctuary. Next to them lived the secular folk of both sexes, more distant but still integral members of the larger monastic community. The monks lent their stock to these laics as part of the clientage exchange. Already in the eighth century, then,

---

31. Ibid., 95–96.
32. HVSH, 169.
33. Ibid., 213.
34. Wasserschleben, *Collectio*, 174, 176; Donnchadh Ó Corráin, "Early Irish Churches: Some Aspects of Organization," in Ó Corráin, ed., *Irish Antiquity* (Cork, 1980).

the monastic community existed as a well-defined territorial and social unit, including secular dependents as well as the saint and the monks.[35]

Manaig and Community Identity

Yet something else marked a man as a *manach*. In return for their labor, *manaig* enjoyed a semireligious status that raised them from mere laborers and tenants of ecclesiastical lands to personal clients of the monastic *familia* and its saintly patron. While *manaig* owed dues and obligations not normally imposed upon secular clients, as the *Córus Béscnai* shows, they also enjoyed certain spiritual benefits not available to others. For although the *manaig* labored to support the monks and formed contracts with the abbatial representatives of the *familia*, they were actually clients of the saint. The saints, through the monks, offered their clients sponsorship in this world and the next; they watched over clients' lands, gave clients refuge when needed, and bestowed all the protection that proximity to the saint's relics and the sacred space could offer. In effect, *manaig* gained a diminished version of monastic privileges and shared a muted form of monastic identity.

The land worked by monastic clients, whether their own or the monks', remained under the special protection of its supernatural guardian. Saint Máedóc was particularly severe about trespass or destruction of land under his monks' management. He warned some of the local nobility against trespassing on his estates and advised, as the hagiographer put it, "Any living creature not to kill so much as a hare or an angled trout within the territory of his church or sanctuary, and if they should do so, they should have short life and hell, and disease and famine in return."[36] As part of his legacy to his monks and clients, Máedóc called on 210 saints to pray for the death of anyone who harmed properties under his guardianship.

According to the hagiographers, other saints arranged similar protection for their estates and those of their clients, to be enforced by the monks of their enclosures with rituals and, if necessary, by legal means or

---

35. The possibility that *manaig* independently operated and inhabited the smaller monastic settlements, sending dues to their mother churches, has no basis in the hagiography; the hagiographers consistently referred to men who inhabited the sacred spaces and consecrated buildings as monks, *oratores*. See PBNE I, 257; Charles-Edwards, "Church and Settlement"; Richard Sharpe, "Some Problems Concerning the Organization of the Church in Early Medieval Ireland," *Peritia* 3 (1984), 230–70.

36. PBNE 1:244, 2:237.

even force. Cóemgen left a protective blessing (*coimhétt*) to his *áonach* and his *muinter*, literally his "assembly" and "retinue"; the latter included both free and unfree clients and tenants of Glenn Dá Locha.[37] The hagiographer surely knew his legal terminology. According to the *vita*, the saint arranged for clients to be immune from the ordinary legal processes of suit, judgment, or debt, and provided proof of his patronage in "guarantees and ownership and protection to them all in coming and going."[38]

The hagiographers did not intend their tales for clients of the saints. The monks needed no favorable advertising to keep their clients; even free clients probably had little choice about maintaining amicable relations with their monastic lords if they wanted to keep their farms productive and their families well fed. The hagiographers hoped that their stories would reach those who might disrupt production by harming monastic clients or lands. For example, the marauders who pursued monastic tenants into the sacred enclosures might have realized their peril had they learned the lesson of the *vitae*. Máedóc killed a warrior who threatened the farmers from his neighborhood (*tír ancuimirce*) who took refuge at Ferna Mór.[39] The saints did not tolerate disruption of rents and dues or the loss of laborers. Hagiographers recorded the displeasure of the saints as a formal challenge to potential criminals of later ages: Harass monastic clients at your peril.

Besides a general protective blessing for properties and clients, saints and their representatives offered more specific safeguards to clients. During his lifetime, Saint Máedóc saved his plowman from death beneath an iron plowshare; presumably, he could do it again for loyal clients of his monks. Máedóc also provided a water source for the thirsty inhabitants of Ferna Mór.[40] Like Máedóc, Saint Daig protected his people from the everyday hazards of labor. Daig's community owned a mill used by his tenants for grinding their own grain. When a woman was assaulted and wounded en route to the mill and her son drowned in the millpond, Daig's disciple, Saint Berach, healed her and restored her son to life.[41]

Legal commentators declared that a free monastic client gained another benefit that was foreign to the secular farmer: "Let the church give him reading, because a divine legacy is more important than a human one"

37. Ibid. 1:130.
38. Ibid., 130, 2:126; see also 185.
39. HVSH, 251.
40. PBNE 1:186, 221–23.
41. HVSH, 391–92.

(dénadh in eacluis léginn dó, úair mó do díbaidh deoda beirius ná do díbaidh indeoda).[42] For his labors, the *soermanach* was to receive as his reward some small bit of that monastic treasure, literacy. Some historians have used this decree as evidence of a literate laity in early Ireland. Yet the language of the laws (*dénadh . . . léginn dó*) suggests that the clients were read to rather than actually reading for themselves.[43] The legal writer may merely have been suggesting that *manaig* be allowed to listen to the gospels at mass; most lay Christians probably did not enjoy even this privilege. The hagiographers occasionally stated the importance of reading aloud hagiography and other ecclesiastical texts to lay folk.[44] Most likely, farmers stuck to farming and monks to reading. Certainly no other texts indicated that the farmers of early Ireland could read, although a few kings, and also lawyers and poets, who may have been clerics or clerically trained, were literate.[45]

However, although most of them probably did not share the Scriptures with their masters, *manaig* living near the sacred space took part in certain of the monks' rituals. The *Ríagal Pátraic*, which hovers between secular law and ecclesiastical canon, rules that churches neglecting to offer proper rituals to their *manaig* do not deserve their rents and dues, listed here as tithes, inheritance taxes, and bequest. In fact, the *airchinnech* or manager of a monastic community was not entitled to impose his will on his *manaig* unless he provided them with appropriate rituals. The same tract lists the four main rituals of a church as baptism, communion, prayers of intercession, and mass.[46] The *Córus Béscnai* lists five clerical obligations to clients, including baptism, mass, and communion and also burial and preaching.[47] The *céili dé* offered even more extensive services to lay clients, including confession, but demanded semiclerical behavior in return; married couples, for example, were to abstain from sex on all feast days, Sabbaths, and Fridays.[48] Since the monks kept their rituals exclusive, it seems that the more rituals a person attended, the closer he or she advanced to ecclesiastical status.

The hagiographers also wrote of clients who took part in religious

42. ALI 3:38–40, 2:344.
43. Hughes, *Church in Early Irish Society,* 140; Doherty, "Hagiography as a Source," 313.
44. PBNE 1:203.
45. Breatnach, Ó Corráin, and Breen, "Laws of the Irish."
46. J. G. O'Keeffe, "The Rule of Patrick," *Ériu* 1 (1904), 219.
47. CIH 2:529.
48. Edward J. Gwynn, ed., "The Rule of Tallaght," *Hermathena* 44, sec. suppl. vol. (Dublin and London, 1927), 78–87.

rituals. The twelfth-century *vita* of Colmán Ela provides information about several kinds of spiritual returns owed by his monks to their *manaig*. After the saint's death, both monks of Lann Ela and lay people of his larger community participated in funeral ceremonies, including a grand procession or circuit with relics (fratres et populi per circuitam elevaverunt reliquias).[49] Such integrated rituals were unknown in the sixth century, when, according to Adomnán, the monks of Í sought a miracle to prevent mobs of lay folk from crashing Columcille's funeral.[50] But by the Viking period, the monks even made it easier for their clients to take part in certain rites. For instance, Colmán's hagiographer instructed that monks were to recite the hourly offices slowly so that those in attendance could better understand them. Further, the Paternoster was to be in Irish so that others besides learned monks could chant it.[51]

Clients enjoyed more than the uplifting nature of ritual in return for their labors. Heaven was assured those who celebrated the saints' feasts on a regular basis; no doubt monastic clients, with regular access to rituals, kept the feasts.[52] Their rights to formal burial services also brought clients preferential treatment on their own journeys to heaven. In return for their rents of two hundred cows, which marked them as free clients, the Uí Duibhginn and Uí Braccáin gained burial places in the choir of Colmán's church. The monks reserved the best spots in the cemetery for wealthy patrons outside the community, but they buried Colmán's free clients very near royal resting places.[53]

Other lay folk benefited from monastic services and saintly protection, but outsiders were not so securely tied to the religious elite by obligatory dues and services on both sides. Clientage was securely based on contract. Relations between outsiders and monks lacked the exclusive and formal nature of clientage ties. Even the lowliest clients of the saints enjoyed more intimacy with them than did other lay people. Their very name distinguished them from the clients of lay nobility and identified them as dependents of a powerful saint and his or her successors.

As Mochuda's biographer noted, three things made a successful monastic community: its foundation by a saint; the saint's miracles, which established it as a sacred center; and the rents and dues it brought in to

49. HVSH, 224.
50. Adomnán, 536–39.
51. PBNE 1:170.
52. Ibid., 174–75.
53. Ibid.; 2:168.

keep it prosperous in an unfriendly world.[54] Monks could not perform their precious functions of prayer and ritual if the *manaig* did not labor to support them. Yet monastic clients believed that they would not last long in the wilderness beyond the enclosure without both the loan of stock and the prayers and protection offered by their patrons. The exchange between monks and *manaig* was vital to both.

The Monastic Labor Ethic

Although the hagiographers knew that the labor of clients brought the brothers their bread and meat, they chose to fill the *vitae* with pictures of monks scratching at the earth with their hoes. At the same time that they wrote about monastic communities of thousands and about tenants and dues and services that supported the monastic elite, the hagiographers described whole families of tonsured monks laboring with an almost Benedictine zeal for the work of the hands. Yet hagiographers also described saints who neglected manual labor for the unique responsibilities that defined them as the religious elite. The hagiographers saw no contradiction in these images of monastic labor, because they believed in a labor ethic that had been developed and elaborated by generations of monks. Monks regarded manual labor not as essential to survival, but as a spiritual option. In fact, manual labor was not even a genuine option for most of the religious elite, because they lacked the skills with which to support themselves and their communities.

The hagiographers nowhere demonstrated more determination to confuse spiritual ideal and economic reality than in their depiction of monastic labor. Several saints toil their way through the pages of the *vitae*. Many of them began their careers in childhood as shepherds or swineherds, a common occupation for children in pastoral economies, but also a motif dear to Christian writers. Saintly abbots and their recruits brought these skills with them to their religious settlements, as well as other useful talents, for as Brénainn's hagiographer pointed out, "the monk is fed and clothed by the labor of his hands."[55] According to the hagiographers, the monks emulated their saintly leaders, engaging in all kinds of manual labor, from sheer drudgery to skilled craftsmanship. In the early days at Í,

54. PBNE I:III, 122.

55. PVSH I:131, cited in John Ryan, *Irish Monasticism: Origins and Early Development* (Dublin, 1931), 362. See also 360–65.

monks were forced by their isolation to perform all the labors of subsistence. Columcille himself carried sacks of wheat to his cook.[56] Others were fishers and sailors; still others tended and milked cattle. Some plowed and sowed and harvested. They were not always successful, as demonstrated by Columcille's relief just before his death at finding a barn full of grain.[57] Monks at other monasteries hauled water, cooked, baked, and brewed beer, skills practiced by men and women alike.[58] They also cultivated orchards and foraged in the forest to support themselves. Cainnech's *tota familia* went with their carts and oxen out of the enclosure, across the marsh, and into the woods to seek building materials or fuel.[59] Colmán Ela and his monks began by building their own enclosure and a causeway across the bogs to it. God blessed their labors, clearly, for swans sang to them as they toiled; hence the settlement's name, Lann Ela, church of swans.[60]

In the *vitae,* many monastic communities often lack basic supplies and equipment, yet still manage to perform common domestic and agricultural tasks. Féichíne's brothers lacked even the water to aid their "sweaty labors," and had to haul it in buckets to irrigate the fields they hoed.[61] At Cluain Eidnech, Fintan's brothers worked so hard without even cattle to support themselves that whenever their abbot visited them in the field they ran wildly to him seeking food, like ravenous serfs at the approach of their lord.[62] A saint might have no plow, no water, no knowledge of agriculture, but he labored on nonetheless. According to his later *vita,* Máedóc planted trees in his orchard and, although he was no agronomist and could not tell one tree from another, all of the trees bore fruit.[63]

Some of the brothers were supposedly expert craftsmen in various media. Comgall had a monk who could weave baskets.[64] Brénainn and his brothers knew all about boat building, as did his hagiographer, whose description of Brénainn's labor was elaborate in detail. The monks covered a frame with ox hides, secured it with iron nails, then smeared the joinings inside and out with myrrh, bitumen, pitch, and rosin to make the boat

---

56. HVSH, 370.
57. Adomnán, 242–45, 262–63, 364–65, 416–19, 520–21.
58. USMLS, Conchubranus III, 448–49; Adomnán, 486–87; HVSH, 117, 141, 215, 221; PVSH 1:189, 2:81–82, 193.
59. HVSH, 183; PBNE 1:184–85; cf. PBNE 1:209–10.
60. PBNE 1:172.
61. PVSH 1:189, 2:81–82.
62. HVSH, 147–48.
63. PBNE 1:239.
64. PVSH 2:15.

watertight.[65] Brénainn also employed a smith to make anchors for him.[66] In Adomnán's time, monks at Í knew how to make iron tools, as hagiography and archaeology both prove.[67] Members of other, later monastic communities were also smiths or metalworkers. Several excavated sites revealed evidence of iron smelting and other crafts.[68] The National Museum in Dublin, among others, contains many of the well-wrought products of monastic workshops of the ninth to twelfth centuries, such as the Ardagh chalice and the Derrynavlan hoard, as well as a host of elaborately decorated reliquaries, brooches, bells, and staffs.[69]

The hagiographers were proud of at least one of their saints who created things of beauty from precious metals. Daig mac Cairill prophesied of himself that he would be a scribe, a priest, and the maker of a *capsa*, a box for his own relics. He also made objects of gold and brass for other people, such as bells, cymbals, crosses, reliquaries, and portable altars, all adorned with gems.[70] But Daig and his hagiographer harbored doubts about the value of his work in metals. The saint much preferred to read and write, which he did at night after finishing his more menial duties.[71] Twice when commissioned to make a portable altar Daig claimed to lack the proper materials, and both times God provided him with what he needed; once the gold fell from heaven, and once the saint was instructed by an angel to look in the graveyard for brass.[72] An episode from another *vita* suggests that Daig's reluctance did not stem merely from bashfulness or bad temper. When Brénainn needed gold for his craftsmen to make a fine chalice, he sent to Cainnech to see if his brother saint had any to spare. Cainnech had none on hand but vomited up a pound or two and sent it off to Brénainn.[73] The hagiographers' association of graveyards and vomiting with precious metals hints at disapproval of such expensive objects and their working.

The aversion of Daig and Cainnech was not just a Christian rejection of

65. PBNE 1:52.
66. Ibid., 64.
67. Adomnán, 390–93; Royal Commission on the Ancient and Historical Monuments of Scotland, *Argyll*, vol. 4: *Iona* (Edinburgh, 1982), 14–15.
68. See, e.g., M. J. O'Kelly, "Monastic Sites in the West of Ireland," *Scottish Archaeological Forum* 5 (1973), 1–16; Thomas Fanning, "Excavation of an Early Christian Cemetery and Settlement at Reask, Co. Kerry," PRIA 81 C (1981), 67–172.
69. National Museum of Ireland, *Treasures of Early Irish Art, 1500 B.C. to 1500 A.D.* (New York, 1977).
70. HVSH, 389.
71. Ibid., 390.
72. Ibid., 392, 394.
73. Ibid., 196.

lucre; the work of hands was not as important or uplifting as other work, and was often neglected for labors of the mind and spirit. Hagiographers took an ambiguous position on all monastic crafts and, indeed, on all manual labor, a view that they shared with their monastic brothers. Although some saints were expert laborers, others manifested their virtue by ignoring their chores. Mochuda, for example, was supposed to mind pigs for his family. When an orderly train of clerics passed by, chanting their heavenly psalms, the boy forgot his charges and followed the monks all the way to Tuaim. As he explained later, he had heard singing like no other, and simply had to learn the songs for himself, pigs or no pigs.[74] Later in life, Mochuda slept on duty as a miller, while the mill miraculously powered itself.[75] Ciarán also neglected his miller's work, allowing angels to do the manual labor while he improved his mind with reading.[76]

When the saints remembered their assignments, they sometimes performed miracles in order to get the manual labor out of the way quickly, so that their monks might attend to other matters. Sometimes they recruited angels for the job. Máedóc's *familia* was building a wooden church but lacked some necessary materials, such as a cart in which to haul its wood. Rather than make one or borrow one, the saint dismissed his monks to their cells, telling them to forget carpentry and ordering them not to peek outside for a while. When one disobeyed, he saw golden-haired monks, whom any sensible cleric could recognize as angels, doing the construction work.[77] Other saints provided miraculously for their *familiae* without the help of outside talent. Ruadán fed his monks with the fruits of a magic tree, rather than bothering to sow and reap. His saintly colleagues complained that all their monks deserted them for Ruadán's community at Lothra, and urged him to run his settlement with more monastic conformity. He agreed to their terms in exchange for some estates from Saint Finnian, land that miraculously needed no plowing.[78] Similarly, if less dramatically, Samthann gave her sisters a jar that perpetually provided enough butter for them and their guests, saving them the trouble of churning.[79]

Some abbot-saints absolutely refused to let their monks labor when it interfered with other duties. As early as the sixth century, according to

74. PVSH 1:172–73.
75. Ibid., 179–80.
76. Ibid., 203–204.
77. PBNE 1:237–38.
78. Ibid., 320–21.
79. PBNE 2:254.

Adomnán, Columcille halted his monks putting on their workaday shoes and ordered them off to a feast in celebration of the bishop of Laigen's arrival in heaven.[80] According to a much later hagiographer, Moling would not allow his brothers to begin work when an officer of the community started the day with an invocation of the Father and Son, but forgot the Holy Spirit. Only when the monk got his blessings right could the others begin their labors.[81]

When the saints themselves slaved in the fields, rather than indulging in prayer and scholarship, other monks were actually astonished. Visitors to Liath Mochóemóc found Mochóemóc on his knees, digging at the ground like a peasant farmer. They marveled at the sight, wondering what religious significance it held.[82] Colmán Ela was just as surprised to find Mochua laboring with 150 of his brothers in some back pasture of Tech Mochua. Colmán had come at an angel's bidding to be healed of memory loss; for his trouble he got a stern lecture from Mochua on the difference between the wisdom of a simple life of labor and prayer and the spurious knowledge derived from book learning.[83]

But Molua, the scholar saint, understood differently the relative value of manual labor compared with other kinds of work. His abbot, Comgall of Bennchor, challenged his hours at his books rather than in church or with his hoe. "Many have been deceived by a sharp understanding," Comgall warned, "and their knowledge was a cause of their ruin." Molua, however, suggested that learning would neither drag him to the Devil nor offend God.[84] In fact, a great many Irish monks put their hands to pen rather than to plow. Comgall's own monastery of Bennchor was a famous center of scholarship and scribery. The annals celebrated the careers of famous *fir léiginn*, "men of learning," and society, both monastic and secular, counted such men among its aristocracy. The bounty of scholarship produced by Ireland's monks is well known to historians, since the monks carried it to Britain and the Continent.[85] Yet travelers returning to Ireland brought back that persistent tradition of the church fathers that frowned upon secular book learning as a prideful waste of time, preferring hard labor or a quiet spell of contemplation.

80. Adomnán, 488–89.
81. PVSH 2:194–95.
82. Ibid., 177–78.
83. Ibid., 184–85.
84. HVSH, 136.
85. See chap. 1, n. 20, above; also Rolf Baumgarten, *Bibliography of Irish Linguistics and Literature 1942–71* (Dublin, 1986), 662–66.

For Molua, as for other scholars, scribes, and administrators, labor was not a necessity but an alternative to study and prayer. When one poet gave up his craft to enter the sacred enclosure, Molua took him to the woods and taught him how to chop thistles. The man was learned in words and rhyme but "he did not know how to work with his hands."[86] Molua's rule advised his monks to persist at hard labor, "for if you labor well you will be content, and you will endure steadily; and if you are steady, you will be holy."[87] But once they had settled down to the business of being steady and holy, monks were to relinquish the work of hands for prayer.[88]

Manual labor carried a penitential value for monks who had no practical need to work with their hands. The Irish agreed with Saint Benedict that "they are truly monks if they live by the labors of their hands."[89] Labor subdued temptation and bestowed grace. It helped to make a monk steady, pious, humble, and patient, at whatever age he learned to toil. Indeed, some turned to labor quite late in life. Moling, already an abbot and founder of monasteries, subdued his body and its temptations by digging a canal.[90] St. Flannán, after he had become a man of letters, learned humility and patience under the tutelage of Blathmac, who instructed him in plowing, sowing, reaping, grinding, sieving, and baking with his own hands.[91] On the other hand, Énda, later abbot of Ára, first prepared himself for the monastic life with lessons in labor. He began as an "athlete of Christ" who dug ditches and weeded the ground. Once this former war chief had learned the hard lessons of humility, he moved to less arduous work as the man in charge of meals and supplies.[92]

For the monks, then, labor was penance and penance was labor; the words and concepts became interchangeable. A brother at Bennchor announced that no monk was better than himself at labor (*ultra se plus laborentem*), by which he meant that no one excelled him in such acts of penitence as praying naked in an icy stream.[93] Devotees of Columcille venerated his psalter, the Cathach, and the monks at Ard Macha treasured the book left on their altar by an angel, but pilgrims to Monenna's shrine revered her hoe and her spade, as precious as any piece of sheep's skin.[94]

86. HVSH, 139.
87. Ibid., 143.
88. Ibid.
89. *Benedicti Regula,* sec. 48.
90. PVSH 2:193–94; see also 71–72.
91. HVSH, 282.
92. PVSH 2:62.
93. Ibid., 17.
94. USMLS, Conchubranus III, 428; Kenney, *Sources,* 369.

Some monks may have carried the equation of labor and penance too far. According to the *Vita tripartita*, the brothers at a farm in Trían Conchobair toiled obediently all day in the fields, neglecting their bodily needs and laboring without rest. When one died of thirst, the hagiographer interpreted it as a sign that the settlement would prosper and its fields would produce plenty in the years to come.[95] The ninth-century writer of the *Vita tripartita* expressed no disapproval of this sacrifice.

Hagiographers of later lives were less appreciative of the excesses of a severely penitential devotion to labor. One of Mochuda's hagiographers was fascinated by his saint's obsession with manual labor; in fact, Mochuda's reputation as a laborer was so well established that the hagiographer had many separate illustrations of it to choose from, and like a typical Irish writer of saints' lives, he used them all.[96] (The hagiographer also made it clear that ordinary monks and even other saints found virtue in a combination of labor and other ways to grace.) In one episode, Mochuda's poor monks labored with their hoes until local kings insisted on making donations of gold, silver, and other valuables; this saved the brothers from sweating in the fields, for they could now afford clients, equipment, and food supplies. Another time, Saint Fínán came to scold Mochuda for allowing his monks to do the work of animals; the monks "used to plow with hoes and feet the whole year long, and carried burdens on their own shoulders." Fínán went on a hunger strike until Mochuda relented and allowed his community to keep cattle and horses to help with the work.[97]

But the saint did not learn his lesson the first or second time. In a third episode of the same *vita*, Saint Lachtán also tricked Mochuda into agreeing to keep cattle. Knowing that the abbot would refuse a gift of thirty cows, a bull, and herdsmen to mind them, Lachtán hid the herd and appeared at Rathan feigning illness; this was, in effect, a demand for milk, the common drink for sick men. When Mochuda changed water to milk, the visitor changed it back to water. He declared good-humoredly to his host: "Our Father, Carthachus is a good monk, but his successors will not be able to make milk from water." Mochuda finally had to admit that his devotion to penitential labor did not suit everyone, and accepted the gift of cattle.[98]

These stories emphasized the spiritual value of manual labor and yet

95. VT, 236.
96. PVSH 1:188–89.
97. Ibid., 178, 188.
98. Ibid., 188.

indicated the limits of the ideal. Some work with the hands was beneficial to all monks but, like other forms of penitence, the saints were best at it. The hagiographers' frequent descriptions of monastic labor show that visitors to Mochóemóc were right to suspect some symbolism in his toil. For labor to have carried a spiritual value it could not have been required for monastic survival; the monks earned heavenly credit by denying themselves worldly pleasures, not by submitting to earthly necessities.

In fact, even if they had wanted to, monks of the larger communities could not have supported themselves, let alone all the dependents, guests, and servants of their populous settlements. As a result of the monks' success in attracting property and population to their settlements, their monasteries rapidly outgrew their abilities and desire for self-sufficiency. The practice of child recruitment meant that the brothers trained for other jobs from an early age; boys learned their letters and their psalms rather than how to raise rye in a bad season, or when to separate cows from their calves. Also, the monastic recruitment pool consisted of freemen and nobles, men from families more accustomed to ordering a day's work in the fields than using the spade themselves.

In spite of these changes, the saints of the *vitae* remained willing to work, thus manifesting the Christian ideal; but their hagiographers represented the saints' efforts in a strange way: Many saints proved less than useful around a farm. Saints were lords and employers of laborers and craftsmen who could do what they could not. Máedóc wanted to build a basilica, but did not have the *peritium artificem*, the training.[99] Abbán needed an *artifex* to build for him, so he restored sight to the blind Gobbán just long enough for the craftsman to complete the project.[100] Cainnech lacked the *artifices* and *operares* to make a threshing floor for his monks; his brothers could reap, but they had not the talent to build. Both Moling and Cianán employed *operarii* and Cianán also used *cementarii*, specialists in stone, to build a stone church.[101] Some holy abbots had no idea of the talent, technology, and hard work involved in producing a good crop. Máedóc plagued his farmers by giving away their oxen. His workers (*aratores*) knew that it was impossible to get the seed in the ground without the proper equipment, but the saint was more interested in charity than in wheat production.[102] Máedóc's whimsical charity was just another example of the theme of otherworldliness running quietly

99. HVSH, 244–45.
100. Ibid., 270–71; PBNE 1:188.
101. PVSH 2:187, 194.
102. HVSH, 240; PBNE 1:186.

through some saints' lives; his incomprehension of agricultural business showed that his mind lay beyond the *saeculum*.

No abbot or monk, however absorbed in prayer or study, was completely removed from the care of fields and animals. Irish society was too agrarian for that. The fact that monks of the *vitae* did not need to labor and did not know how to labor well was a sign of their special status and functions. While the hagiographers commemorated a time when saints toiled in the fields, they did not intend to remind their noble abbots that monks had once been less wealthy and less important to Irish society. Manual labor was a symbol for the monks who read and wrote the *vitae* while their clients and tenants hauled food and clothing to the enclosure's gates.

The Rules of Labor

The monks justified their division of labor and their clientage relations with a formal theory, hinted at in laws and hagiography but expressed most directly in written rules. Monks recorded most of the rules at the end of the eighth century or during the ninth; their writers usually attributed authorship of the rules to the saints, whose names validated the contents and indicated which monastery had generated the rule.[103] According to hagiographers, many saints and abbots made up rules. It seems that almost every house functioned according to a different one.[104]

Similar themes regarding the division of labor appeared in all the rules. Most of the texts laid out a schedule of labor and a management hierarchy, and outlined the duties of various monastic officers, monastic clients, and other allies of the monks. The rules regulated interactions between officers of the community and other monks, and between monks and lay members of the community. Some, such as the *Rule* of Mochuda, extended to lay communities beyond the enclosure, setting out behavioral guidelines for bishops and kings who interacted with the monks as well as for the monks themselves and their dependents.[105] Writers of the rules aimed to create a productive and supportive community in which the

---

103. Kenney, *Sources,* 813: "Rules, Monastic"; G. S. M. Walker, ed., *Sancti Columbani Opera* (Dublin, 1957), xlvi–lii.

104. Monks could wander from settlement to settlement seeking the rule and way of life they preferred. Brénainn, for example, sampled many and found none to his liking; he ended up combining several to create one of his own: PVSH 1:102–3.

105. Mac Eclaise, "The Rule of St. Carthage," IER 27 (1910), 514–17.

special jobs of the monks were most important to the community, but were meant to be performed in cooperation with the labor of others. Certain standard virtues recommended by the rules, such as humility and obedience, were the traits that enabled all members of a community to get along and work efficiently as a unit.

None of the rules copied Saint Benedict's insistence on manual labor as the work of God. Ailbe's *Rule,* for instance, allowed the monks one canonical hour for the minor domestic chores of sewing and washing, to be performed individually within their cells. The rest of their day was filled with psalms, prayers, and genuflections.[106] The *Rule of the Lord* insisted on extensive prayer to fill a brother's day, and implicitly delegated the most important manual labor to others. The rule advised monks to love their dependents—implying that the spiritual elite might otherwise despise or exploit their tenants and clients. This particular rule ordered monastic tenants to perform their duty of manual labor in good spirit— suggesting that such labor was their begrudged responsibility.[107] Ailbe's *Rule* also instructed the community's leader to deal fairly with his tenants, again implying that cooperation between monks and clients required some effort from both sides.[108]

Mochuda's *Rule* explained more explicitly the difference between those who toiled and those who did not. Those in orders were to pray and chant mass, while the learned (*oes legind*) were to preach; the novices were to perform domestic chores along with their studies; and the unlearned (*oes anechaid*), probably clients, were to take care of all the heavy work.[109] Saint Gerald's hagiographer, writing around 1100 or later, repeated this division of labor. Gerald separated his community into three groups. Two groups labored manually, farming to feed the community or building walls to enclose the sacred space; these were the duties that lawyers formally specified as clients' labor dues.[110] The other group was to devote itself to prayer, not just for itself, but *pro populo,* for the people under its spiritual direction.[111]

The rules, along with other texts, hinted at a sophisticated distribution of duties and power within the monastic community. As the settlement grew, the abbot could not attend personally to all aspects of its organiza-

106. J. O'Neill, ed., "The Rule of Ailbe of Emly," *Eriu* 3 (1907), 98–102.
107. J. Strachan, "An Old-Irish Metrical Rule," *Eriu* 1 (1904), 202.
108. Ibid., 196, 202; O'Neill, "Rule of Ailbe," 102.
109. Mac Eclaise, "Rule of St. Carthage," 510.
110. CIH 2:525.
111. PVSH 2:112.

tion and operation. An administrative structure emerged that was based on the division of specialized labor and influenced by the status hierarchy of the monastic *familia* itself. *Seniores* of the community took on jobs as officers supervising different groups of activities or people; eventually, in some communities, these offices became semihereditary. Management, like prayer, became a form of labor that distinguished the monastic elite from its dependents.

For example, the ninth-century *Rule* of Mochuda outlined the responsibilities of the bishop, abbot, priest, confessor, and resident ascetic (*céile dé*) of the community. Each of these officers had his own job. The abbot was the legal representative of the community as well as its judge within the enclosure walls; the priest delivered sacraments; the confessor was also a counselor and priest who helped control the behavior of monks and *manaig*.[112] One early eleventh-century poem gave a more detailed list of the officers of a sizable community:

> Psalm-singer, beginning student, historian, who
>   is not insignificant,
> instructor, teacher of ecclesiastical law, head teacher with
>   great knowledge.
>
> Bishop, priest and deacon, subdeacon, a noble course,
> lector, porter, swift exorcist, the excellent holy man
>   is renowned.
>
> Erenagh, his assistant, vice-abbot, cook, proper and right,
> counselor, steward, alternate vice-abbot. . .[113]

Other managerial roles and the men who filled them were clearly important in the monastic community. The *oeconimus*, or steward, was a particularly powerful figure; as the Latin name implies, he oversaw the daily finances of the settlement, kept track of production and resources, and delegated labor.[114] The hagiographers made clear that his authority was second only to that of the abbot; the annals called him *secnap* or *tánaise ap*, "vice-abbot." The cook (*cocus, coic*), was also an official with great responsibility and status, since he commanded the kitchens that

---

112. Mac Eclaise, "Rule of St. Carthage," 499–503.
113. Kuno Meyer, "Mitteilungen aus irischen Handschriften," ZCP 5 (1905), 498–99.
114. PVSH 1:cxviii, 153, 187–88; II, 144–45.

sustained the monks.[115] And the community's porter had the special duty of guarding the entrance to the saint's enclosure.[116]

But even more important were the men in charge of prayer and learning, and the superior officers who managed all these petty officers along with the other monks, the *manaig,* and the rest of the enclosure's inhabitants and dependents. The annalists used a confusion of titles for these monastic officers, many of whom were teachers, and all of whom were leaders of subgroups within the monastic community. Different men and women took charge of tenants, *céili dé,* nuns, male and female guests, students, and pilgrims.[117] Officers and their subgroups sometimes had endowments and clients of their own.[118]

The abbot often shared authority and duties with a manager and, in the largest communities, with a bishop. Sometimes these were the same man, other times one succeeded another as head of the community. Titles for monastic leaders varied from community to community, according to different annals. Abbots ruled monastic communities throughout the Middle Ages. Annalists called them *ap/abb/abbas* or, after political models, *princeps.* Starting in the ninth century, however, abbots used two more titles with increasing frequency: *comarbae,* "heir" of the community's patron saint, and *airchinnech,* "leader, superior" (from *airchenn,* meaning "head"). Frequently the man described by the *Annals of Ulster* as *airchinnech* appears in the later *Annals of the Four Masters* as *abb;* the *airchinnech* of the Four Masters is sometimes *princeps, secnap* ("secondary abbot"), or *comarbae* to the *Annals of Ulster.* In a few instances, the *airchinnech* was also a priest or a bishop.[119]

The lawyers added to the problem by suggesting that the *airchinnech* was sometimes a layman, in effect, a well-to-do *manach* or noble patron of the community. The legal writers of the *Heptads* frowned on any community in which an abbot tolerated a lay *airchinnech* as his aide. A glossator on the same legal text referred to a situation in which the abbot or bishop

---

115. PVSH 1:259–60; 2:15, 27–28, 99, 244–45.

116. Wasserschleben, *Collectio,* 25.

117. Aidan MacDonald, "Notes on Monastic Archaeology in the Annals of Ulster, 650–1050," in Ó Corráin, *Irish Antiquity,* 314–19.

118. HVSH, 138.

119. J. Barry, "The Appointment of Coarb and Erenagh," IER 93 (1960), 361–65; Barry, "The Status of Coarbs and Erenaghs," IER 94 (1960), 147–53. The annals provide a particularly illustrative example for the years 901–902. Láthrach Briúin had the misfortune to lose two of its leaders in those years: Tipraite mac Nuadat, called *aircinnech* by the *Annals of Ulster* and *abb* by the Four Masters; and Fogartach mac Flainn, called *princeps* by the *Annals of Ulster* and *abb* by the Four Masters. AU, 352; FM 1:554.

held authority over a layman in the office of *airchinnech:* "lay *airchin-nech* . . . that is, a church in which is an *airchinnech* of the local tribe who does not rebuke or reprove the abbot, who is of higher status, or the bishop."[120] The text calls for a reform of such a situation, for it declares that a lay *airchinnech* deserved no honor price, thus no social standing or legal powers, until he repented and accepted a tonsure. Yet commentators on the original text of the *Heptads* went on to state that an *airchinnech* could collect the honor-price due a cleric if he had hired a priest or bishop to fulfill the religious duties of his office. The same tract also makes provisions for a lay *airchinnech,* who collected the rents and dues of his church but kept them distinct from his personal property.[121]

Other texts suggested the ambiguous status of the *airchinnech* within the community. A life of Cóemgen described how shepherds who gave up their property for Glenn Dá Locha became the saint's *manaig* and eventually the family that produced the community's *airchennaig*.[122] Besides that single entry, interestingly, the hagiographers ignored the problem almost entirely. In one of the legends about Saint Cuimmíne Fota and his idiot protégé, Mac Dá Cherda, the two characters debated the dubious holy purpose of the *airchinnech,* slyly mocking his greed for donations:

> Cumaín: The cow which one gives at death
> In his last bequest?
> Comgán: Though the erenagh be grateful for it
> The patron-saint is not grateful.[123]

Another semireligious text cited a similar proverb. When the ninth-century king and bishop Cormac mac Cuilennáin ejected an *airchinnech* who was also a successful smith from his post at Ros Glais in Munster, the patron of the church, Saint Éimín, appeared to Cormac and recited:

> O Cormac mac Cuilennáin,
> The words are true:
> Although the *airchinnech* be bad
> The saint is good.[124]

---

120. CIH 1:2.
121. Ibid., 3. See the entire section on *airchennaig,* CIH 1:1–4; ALI 5:119–29; also CIH 2:648; ALI 5:55.
122. PBNE 1:127.
123. J. G. O'Keeffe, "Mac Dá Cherda and Cummaíne Foda," *Ériu* 5 (1911), 24–25.
124. C. Plummer, "Cáin Éimíne Báin," *Ériu* 4 (1910), 40.

Both of these texts suggest that *airchennaig* were often not monks in the strictest sense, but administrators of semireligious status. They also hint that some disgruntled ascetics would have preferred to leave the management of monastic settlements in more trustworthy, if possibly less professional, hands.

Unfortunately, the texts reveal no standard plan for the management of monasteries. In fact, it is unclear whether other legal tracts, such as the *Córus Béscnai* and *Cáin Lanamna*, envisioned the abbot or the *airchinnech* in control of estates and clientage relationships, while the *Críth Gablach* neglected abbots and *airchennaig* altogether and granted the bishop the highest status of all clerics.[125] Frequently the laws simply referred to the church (*eclais*), made up of the *grád necalsa*, as the legal corporation that made contracts for the monastic community. It may be that the whole problem of authority can be reduced to one of variety. Different kinds of ecclesiastical settlements had different kinds of leaders, and different social and spiritual functions. The only certainty is that after the eighth century, management of monastic property and clients frequently fell to an official other than the abbot, who may not have been a tonsured monk.[126]

The line between abbot and *airchinnech*, between monk and *manach*, was less clear than the hagiographers would have us believe. The elaborate and theoretical division of labor generated by monastic scholars shows just how important the concept, not the practice, of labor was in determining the identity of the religious elite. Their criticism of greedy *airchennaig* demonstrates how difficult it was for the monks to reconcile the many confusing lessons of labor with the practical demands of running productive monastic estates.

---

125. CIH 1:502–3, 525–26, commentary and gloss; Binchy, *Críth Gablach*, 24.

126. The problem of who had the job of controlling the monastic community, overseeing its properties and tenants, and ordering its rituals has been broached by many historians. Kenney thought *airchinnech* was just a post-Viking term for *abbas* (*Sources*, 12). Kathleen Hughes saw a degenerate post-Viking society allowing its churches to be coopted by secular lords greedy for the wealth of monastic communities; *airchennaig* managed church property and handed it on to their children, while a few clerics struggled to maintain some spiritual purity and some ritual schedule amidst the sorry business of crop yields and tenants' rents (*Church in Early Irish Society*, 157–72). The debate over the roles of bishops and abbots has been just as obsessive and confusing. Hughes and others thought that the frequency of bishops' obits in the pre-eighth-century annal entries, and subsequent disappearance in favor of abbots' obits, meant that Irish churches were originally episcopal and parochial in nature; later, monasticism absorbed all Christian life. But as Richard Sharpe has pointed out, bishops played a prominent role in the eighth-century canons, where they were allowed jurisdiction over abbots and the entire spiritual life of Christian communities: "Some Problems Concerning the Organization of the Church," 230–70.

Monastic Labor and Monastic Identity

Like the rules, the saints' lives also show that the monks recognized important distinctions between themselves and the lay people who lived around them. Hagiographers distinguished between *manach* and *muinter* and between "fratres et populi."[127] Everyone in the community, from writers of rules to the *manaig*, acknowledged this principle of organization.

At an earlier period than that of the *vitae*, all enthusiastic converts to Christianity had felt a similar need to signify their religious status. The penitentialists, determined to extend the Christian frontier, wanted to mark their flock by special behavior and dress, and thus keep their sheep distinct from pagan goats.[128] A few centuries after the penitentials were written, ordinary Christians no longer needed a special mark. Christian identity extended to most people, whether they sought it or not. People entered and exited life by the sacraments, flocked to the shrines of saints, and paid their ecclesiastical taxes, their *cána*. Some attached themselves even more securely to the centers of Christian ritual by contract and economic dependence.

The monks continued to set themselves apart from laics, but some genuine ascetics felt the need to distinguish themselves still further. In the early seventh century, Saint Columbán clearly felt himself different from the lay people whose life was "dwelt in, loved, and warranted by the stupid and the lost, disdained by men of sense, avoided by those that shall be saved."[129] Other monks, such as the *céili dé*, knew themselves to be superior to the men and women around them. They even chose to leave society altogether for small foundations filled with ascetics like themselves. In fact, according to the canonists of the eighth century, the Latin word for monk had a variant from the Greek: *unialis*, "alone." This was because, whether a hermit in the desert or a man of the world who rejected worldly things, he was alone; even if he lived among the iniquitous, he remained "in this life alone."[130] His aspiration was personal salvation, accomplished by rejecting both pleasures and toils of human life for spiritual concerns, and by avoiding all contact with the nonmonastic

---

127. PBNE 1:321; HVSH, 224.
128. See, e.g., restrictions on superstition, dress, oaths, conjugal relations, etc., in the "First Synod of St. Patrick," in Ludwig Bieler, ed., *The Irish Penitentials* (Dublin, 1975), 56–59.
129. Walker, *Sancti Columbani Opera*, 84–85.
130. Wasserschleben, *Collectio*, 147.

world. His identity and that of his brothers lay in his soul's aims, not in his hands' labor.

But most monks of the ninth century and later faced a different situation, one in which churchmen were well integrated into nonecclesiastical life. It had been appropriate for sixth-century holy men and women to abandon society altogether, but later monks, committed to a more sophisticated spiritual function, were dedicated to community life. Layfolk needed the monks, and the monks needed them, not just for their economic support but because the laity validated monastic existence. By being the ordinary unholy folk they were, laymen and women made it possible for monks to be especially holy. A monk could not flee society if society did not care whether he went or stayed, and he could not prove himself different from anyone who acted as he did. If he labored beside his peasant neighbors, how was he to demonstrate his vocation? The religious elite were the most important subgroup of the monastic community by virtue of the very existence of the larger community itself.

The monks sought many ways to make the differences between themselves and others visible and meaningful to all; their architecture, dress, and sexual behavior all helped the monks present themselves as the religious elite. Tonsures, for example, marked monks who strayed outside the enclosures.[131] Clothing also enabled a monk to mark himself as one of the spiritual elite among the secular of his community. To one hagiographer, typical monastic dress symbolized the religious function of the wearer. He described how a royal novice was content to appear "in a black hood, the color of sheep's wool, and in a short white tunic with a black border, and in plain shoes."[132] On feast days, the days of their most important spiritual labors, some brothers marked themselves like a more exclusive company, the angels, by wearing all white.[133] These snowy robes were hardly the working clothes of farmers and herders.

At home, such visible signs of monastic identity were more symbols than necessary markers. Everyone at a settlement like Cluain Iraird or Bennchor recognized the monastic elite from more obvious signs than their haircuts. In a small settlement, people knew each other so well that

131. Edward James, "Bede and the Tonsure Question," *Peritia* 3 (1984), 85–94. On tonsures, see Bede, HBE 5:21; Wasserschleben, *Collectio*, 211–23; E. J. Gwynn and W. Purton, "The Monastery of Tallaght," PRIA 29 C (1911), 137; VT, 188. See also the story of Óenu moccu Laigsi, a warrior who was persuaded to become a client of God through the ritual of tonsuring: FO, 50 ("Tecstar a folt annisin 7 ailitir srisin eclais").

132. HVSH, 204–5.

133. Adomnán, 488–89.

no one needed distinctive clothing to tell monks from farmers. The brothers' crude markers of dress and architecture reinforced other, less immediately obvious indicators of their spiritual functions and corporate identity. No matter that monks dwelt among the laity, gathered wealth, maintained families, and occasionally engaged in manual labor. The surest sign of the monk's identity was the confidence with which he performed his prayers and rituals. He knew that his spiritual labor was subsistence labor, and was just as vital for the survival of all as the sweaty toil of the *manaig* who fed him.

CHAPTER FIVE

Saints, Kings, and
Social Order

A<small>LTHOUGH</small> I<small>RISH MONKS PROVED ADEPT AT CREATING STABLE CLI-</small>
entage relationships, their local successes could not guarantee them
security in the world beyond the enclosure, or ensure the durability of
their communities. They had to be wary of encounters with anyone who
did not live near enough to be a neighbor, client, or lord. A monk who
crossed the boundary onto another lord's estates or another king's territory became subject to another man's jurisdiction and exposed himself to all
the legal disputes, blood feuds, and battles raging in that alien region. But
the monks did not have to leave the sacred space to find violence. Murderous strangers regularly marched up to the enclosure and stormed the
consecrated walls.

The annalists' lists of battles and dead warriors hardly approximates the
brutality that permeated the daily life of the monks, or the catastrophes
that probably seemed so common to the monks and their allies: the year's
food supply lost under the hooves of horses and the torches of raiders;
houses pulled down and furniture smashed; cows and pigs scattered and
stolen; family and friends assaulted, maimed, raped, and murdered. Not
every day brought ruin, but even ordinary transactions readily became
cruel and bloody. At treaty negotiations, princes broke oaths and attacked
each other and those nearby. Noblemen who needed but could not peace-
fully obtain wives kidnapped them. Legal disputes led to quarrels, assaults, and eventually generations of blood feud. With a familiarity unimaginable to us, death and destruction stalked the people of early Ireland
every day of their lives.

No law dictated the peace of all Ireland, no king could keep it, no police

[145]

existed to enforce it. Indeed, since the topography of Ireland compartmentalized the political landscape with hills and drumlins, bogs, rivers, and forests, the land itself helped prevent any sort of national authority that might enforce order. However, the Irish had traditionally settled their disputes through personal negotiation and contract. When feuding political leaders made a treaty, they exchanged hostages to maintain peace. When one farmer sold land to another, guarantors witnessed the exchange to prevent any cheating or subsequent argument over terms. Each side in a legal dispute employed a learned specialist, a judge or jurist (*breithem*); these professional men were responsible for understanding and recording law, for quoting it when consulted, but not for enforcing it. People depended upon pressure from neighbors, relatives, and lords to make each other honor contracts and other legal arrangements.[1] But as the elaborate system of legal sureties and guaranties and the violence recorded in the annals reveal, the community was not always able to keep its laws.

Formal laws did not operate above the community level. As we have seen, even kings could not enforce order between their own *túatha* (tribal territories) and others. The traditional judicial powers of an Irish king were less than those of any feudal lord of the Continent. He enforced decisions, but did not make them. He fought wars, but was not supposed to initiate them.[2] Warriors from prominent dynasties vied for leadership of larger provincial kingdoms, struggling constantly to keep client kings in their place and to force them to pay their dues.[3] But still no law governed the powers of kings, and no tradition forced clients and subjects to obey. Kings got nothing unless they had the power and created the authority

1. Neil McLeod, "Parallel and Paradox: Compensation in the Legal Systems of Celtic Ireland and Anglo-Saxon England," *Studia Celtica* 16/17 (1981–82), 64–66; Richard Sharpe, "Dispute Settlement in Medieval Ireland: A Preliminary Inquiry," in Wendy Davies and Paul Fouracre, eds., *The Settlement of Disputes in Early Medieval Europe* (Cambridge, 1986), 187; Simon Roberts, "The Study of Dispute: Anthropological Perspectives," in John Bossy, ed., *Disputes and Settlements: Law and Human Relations in the West* (Cambridge, 1983), 1–24. The topic of disputes and their settlements has a growing historiography; see the other articles in Bossy, *Disputes and Settlements*, and Davies and Fouracre, *Settlement of Disputes*.

2. D. A. Binchy, ed., *Críth Gablach* (Dublin, 1941), 20–21, 104–5; Donnchadh Ó Corráin, "Nationality and Kingship," in T. W. Moody, ed., *Nationality and the Pursuit of National Independence*, Irish Historical Studies 11 (Belfast, 1978), 1–35, esp. 16–18.

3. D. A. Binchy, "The Passing of the Old Order," in Dublin Institute for Advanced Studies, *Proceedings of the International Congress of Celtic Studies* (Dublin, 1962), 122–31; Binchy, *Celtic and Anglo-Saxon Kingship*, O'Donnell Lectures for 1967–68 (Oxford 1970), 31–46; F. J. Byrne, *Irish Kings and High Kings* (London, 1973), 46–47; Donnchadh Ó Corráin, *Ireland before the Normans* (Dublin, 1972), 28–32.

that allowed them to take it. But by doing this they often perpetuated the very violence that laws and royal authority might have quelled.

The monks were profoundly afraid of the disorder that besieged them. They rejected the inefficient laws and peacemaking methods of the laity. They developed their own rules for behavior and persuaded their friends and allies to impose peace upon the population. In particular, monks and royal allies worked together to reinforce the authority and jurisdiction of kings, and to extend royal power beyond the boundaries of the *túath*. The monks combatted personal violence and the limitations of personal law by relying on their own very personal relations with rulers who were friends and kinsmen. Then they persuaded their neighbors and other noble allies to accept a social order engineered by the saints and promoted by kings. The monks used their prayers and rituals to bless and protect those who supported their Christian order. They used the same power granted by the saints to threaten and curse those who violated order.

The monks, who often reserved their friendship for other elites, did not forsake the common laity in their program for peace. While they offered the protection of their religious rituals and their enclosed spaces to powerful rulers, they never neglected powerless hostages and slaves, debtors and rent-payers, criminals, and any loser in violent conflict with the mighty. They helped any whose kinfolk and secular patrons failed them. Just as they brokered peace treaties among princes, so they mediated in legal disputes, arguments over contracts, and other mundane disagreements. Sometimes the monks even supported clients against their own patrons; and occasionally, paradoxically, the monks even helped people break the very laws that they had worked so hard to create.

Peacemaking

The Irish monks had no comprehensive, organized program for peace. They often made their own jobs more difficult by allowing friendship or kinship or plain ambition, rather than ethical ideals, to guide their political maneuvers. For, predictably, the pervasive violence of early Irish society infected the monks themselves. Many holy men were as guilty of violence as their secular brothers and sisters, either directly or by supporting vicious warrior-kings.

The monks of Cluain Moccu Nóis were typical in this respect. Their ties of friendship and patronage remained just as important to them as any

Christian ideals of order. In 900, the abbot negotiated an amicable clientage arrangement between King Flann Sinna, the great patron of Cluain, and a former enemy, Cathal mac Conchobair, king of Connacht. In Flann's house, within the sacred enclosure of the monastery, the abbot formally placed the treaty "under the protection of the peace of the congregation of Ciarán."[4] But Flann's conciliation with Connacht did not make him a prince of peace, or prevent him from raiding in all other directions in the following years. In 904 he violated Cenannas by beheading the confederates of his rebellious son at the very oratory of Columcille. The following year he raided Osraige, and the next he "harried from Gabrán to Luimnech," the traditional boundaries of eastern Munster. In 910 he defeated Bréifne, and in 914 he went to Brega and southern Cianacht, profaning churches again. Such behavior continued until his death in 916.[5]

Yet the monks of Cluain continued to bless their friend Flann. He maintained his house at Cluain Moccu Nóis and paid for the high cross there, which his loyal monastic friends had inscribed: "Pray for King Flann, son of Máelsechlann and for Colmán who caused this cross to be made for King Flann."[6] The ruin spread by Flann meant less to the monks than the flow of gifts to Cluain and Flann's military protection of the settlement.

Many besides Flann raided holy places with the tacit approval of other monastic communities, and with no regard for the sanctity of the enclosures.[7] Ecclesiastical communities even battled each other. War parties burned monasteries because of the wealth contained within them, or because the inhabitants were allied with competing political factions. Sometimes raiders assaulted the monastic enclosures that lay in their path to the enemy, or that gave sanctuary to enemies. Other times attackers themselves came from competing monasteries. In fact, almost any excuse seems to have served. Ard Macha, despite the efforts of its monks at peaceable negotiation and their high and holy claims to religious leadership, was burned, raided, or otherwise violated at least fifty times between 800 and 1200. The annalists who recorded such depredations often

4. FM 1:554.
5. AU, 354, 358, 360, 364.
6. Françoise Henry, "Around an Inscription: The Cross of the Scriptures at Clonmacnois," in Henry, *Studies in Early Christian and Medieval Irish Art* (London, 1985), 3:369–79.
7. A. T. Lucas, "Irish-Norse Relations: Time for a Reappraisal?" JCHAS 71 (1966), 62–75; Lucas, "The Plundering and Burning of Churches in Ireland, 7th to 16th Century," in E. Rynne, ed., *North Munster Studies* (Limerick, 1967), 172–229.

saved space in their manuscripts by noting simply, as in 1016, "Dún Lethglaise was totally burned. Cluain Moccu Nóis and Cluain Ferta and Cenannas were burned."[8]

Still, many monks saw the advantage of political calm over the chaos that always threatened them. The monks' safety and that of their dependents, the prosperity of all, and, not least important, obedience to the dictates of Christ—all these could be satisfied if only the monks' allies fought for peace rather than blood and booty. The monks of Cluain may have supported Flann Sinna with this very idea in mind; perhaps Flann appeared a stronger king, and thus more competent to impose order by force, than the men whom he destroyed.[9]

For their own sakes and also for some greater good, the religious elite of Ireland became professional political mediators. The monks gained the confidence of feuding princes precisely because they were so intimately related to them by ties of blood and friendship.[10] They were not outsiders, like the saintly negotiators of Byzantium described by Peter Brown, but insiders thoroughly involved in local and provincial politics. The abbots of Ard Macha, as sons, brothers, and in-laws to kings, besides being the alleged keepers of the relics of Pátraic, Peter, and Paul, were highly regarded negotiators. Similarly, abbots of Cluain Moccu Nóis carried more political weight than other communities in Mide and Connacht during the periods when they enjoyed close alliances with the aggressive kings of their territory, such as Flann Sinna.[11]

Not just the most prominent monastic leaders, but monks of many communities negotiated between armies. *Vitae* and annals suggest that the brothers of all sizable monastic communities performed similar functions at various levels of the political hierarchy. In fact, lay people expected the monks to work at peacemaking. The laws ruled that the *deorad dé* (a term meaning literally "pilgrim of God" but referring to any cleric) had

---

8. AU, 452. Many of the burnings of monasteries mentioned in the annals were probably accidental; it is difficult to detect the cause of burning in many entries.

9. J. M. Wallace-Hadrill, *Early Germanic Kinship in England and on the Continent* (Oxford, 1971), 49.

10. Patrick J. Geary, "Vivre en conflit dans une France sans état: Typologie des mécanismes de règlement des conflits (1050–1200)," *Annales, E.S.C.* 41 (September–October 1986), 1118–23; Stephen D. White, "Feuding and Peace-Making in the Touraine around the Year 1100," *Traditio* 42 (1986), 195–263.

11. J. Ryan, *Clonmacnois: A Historical Summary* (1973); Pádraig O Riain, ed., *Corpus Genealogiarum Sanctorum Hiberniae* (Dublin, 1985), 4, 63, 81, et passim; Peter Brown, "The Rise and Function of the Holy Man in Late Antiquity," *Journal of Roman Studies* 61 (1971), 80–101.

the special ability to insure treaties, negotiations, and contracts.[12] The monks themselves saw political negotiations as both their obligation and their right. Máedóc's Irish *vita* claimed the right for his *comarbae* to broker peace for the Uí Briúin whenever they needed it, in exchange for extensive dues.[13]

To laymen, the most useful service of monastic mediators was their provision of a safe place in which to negotiate. Often, as we have seen, monasteries sat conveniently at politically neutral borders. The worst enemies could conclude a sensitive treaty in the sacred enclosure knowing that the saint, provoked by the ritual curse of the monks, would punish its violators.[14] A *rígdál*, royal parley, took place at Ráith Áeda Meic Bricc in 859 between the kings of Temair and Osraige. The abbot of Ard Macha and the successor of Finnian at Cluain Iraird made "peace and amity between the men of Ireland," presumably performing rituals with relics to sanctify the treaty. At a similar parley in 1093, the monks of Lis Mór and the Patrician delegates to Munster persuaded Diarmait ua Briain to quit his fight for the kingship and accept the rule of his brother Muirchertach; or, as the annalist put it, Diarmait "came into the house of Muirchertach, his brother, and they made peace and a covenant in Caisel and in Lis Mór upon the relics of Ireland around the Bachall Ísu [Pátraic's staff] in the witness of Ua Énnae [bishop of Caisel] and the nobles of Munster."[15]

These are but two of the many entries from the annals in which monks offered their enclosures, their relics, and their ritual services to warriors seeking an alternative to violence. These negotiations took place in Munster monasteries, where no single ecclesiastical community seemed more efficient than the rest at creating detente among kings. Every community used its saint's influence to push for peace.

The situation was different farther north, where one monastery enjoyed vastly more prestige and influence than the rest. Although every monastic community took part in the political process, kings and princes sought out the monks of Pátraic, Ireland's most revered saint, for the weightiest negotiations. In Ulster, the senior monks of Ard Macha seem to have conducted most of the negotiations recorded in the annals, including some treaties involving the major political leaders of all Ireland.[16] As early

---

12. D. A. Binchy, "Irish Law Tracts Re-edited: I. Coibnes Uisci Thairidne," *Ériu* 17 (1955), 66–68.

13. PBNE 1:202; see also HVSH, 99–100; PVSH 2:45–47; Adomnán, 362.

14. AU, 284; FM 1:440; Byrne, *Irish Kings*, 221.

15. AU, 190; FM 2:1074; Denis Murphy, ed., *The Annals of Clonmacnois* (Dublin, 1896), 198; Seán mac Airt, ed., *The Annals of Inisfallen* (Dublin, 1951), 246; see also FM 2:1092.

16. Charles Doherty, "The Use of Relics in Early Ireland," in Proinséas Ní Chatháin and M. Richter, eds., *Ireland and Europe* (Stuttgart, 1984), 100–101.

as 804, the abbot there used his status as successor to Pátraic and guardian of the saints' relics to head a "congressio senadorum nepotum Neill," a gathering of the southern and northern Uí Néill war leaders at Dún Cuair.[17] In 851, the abbots of Ard Macha and Cluain Iraird joined forces to help the Uí Néill and Ulaid make peace.[18] Again and again in the following centuries the abbots took up *bachall* (bishop's staff) and bell to negotiate and force peace upon provincial leaders. In 1005, 1007, and 1010, the abbot helped Brian Bóroma, self-proclaimed king of Ireland, who had earlier cemented his friendship with the monks of Ard Macha with donations of gold, take hostages of the Uí Néill at Ard Macha rather than allowing the king to loose his armies upon the north.[19] The abbots of Ard Macha were busy politicking during the next century or so, up to 1126, when "a storm of great war" fell upon Ireland, "so that it was necessary for the *comarbae* of Pátraic to be a year and a month abroad from Ard Macha pacifying the men of Ireland and imposing good conduct upon every one, both laic and cleric."[20]

Peace was hard to make and harder to keep, even for holy men and women. While the monks concluded many treaties, they were not always able to enforce them. Warriors frequently broke their oaths, creating exactly the sort of lawless situation feared by the monks. According to the hagiographers, the saints had encountered the same problem in their day. The kings and chieftains of the *vitae* were often ornery when saints disrupted their feuds, yet saintly negotiators triumphed in the end, at least in hagiography. The saints always accomplished a peace, and what the saints had done with miracles, monastic diplomats hoped to accomplish through formal invocation of the saints and ritual use of relics.

The hagiographers intended to bolster the negotiating powers of their abbots with these tales of treaties honored and aggressors punished.[21] Ciarán of Saigir, the "sower of peace and calmer of quarrels," resorted to miracles when conventional mediation failed to prevent a battle just outside his sacred walls. After the king of Munster declared Ciarán's efforts at negotiation crazy (*deliramenta*), the saint summoned the elements, tearing out trees by the roots and replanting them across the plain of battle. He caused the river that separated the opponents to boil over its banks.

17. AU, 258.
18. Ibid., 310.
19. Mac Airt, *Annals of Inisfallen*, 176, 178, 180; AU, 440; see also AU, 532, 538, 548.
20. AU, 570, 552, 554, 560, 564.
21. H. Platelle, "Crime et châtiment à Marchiennes: Étude sur la conception et le fonctionnement de la justice d'après les miracles de saint Rictrude (XIIe s.)," *Sacris Erudiri* 24 (1980), 156–202.

Terrified, the hosts raised their trembling shields and retreated. The Uí Néill went home and the Munstermen went to Saigir, where Ciarán treated them to a hearty meal.[22]

Abbán was an even more spectacular impresario of peacemaking, who used highly dramatic tactics on warmongering kings. Once, two tribal leaders camped at Achad Fobair, on the verge of committing bloodshed. The saint prayed to God that the warriors should not fight, and was rewarded with a miracle of slapstick: Both armies were propelled backward and pinned motionless until they agreed to make peace.[23] Abbán did not perform for free; for the forced peace, the kings gave thanks to God and donations to Abbán.

The monastic heirs of the saints claimed these same peacemaking powers. Abbán handed down his powers to his successors at Mag Arnaide, as an episode at the conclusion of his *vita* demonstrated. After his death, local kings armed to fight over the saints' bones, hoping to claim his relics for the churches they patronized. Abbán's monks clamored to their *érlam* (patron) in death because his peacemaking activities in life had successfully prevented conflict.[24]

No annalists noted that monks of the Viking period pulled out trees or raised water levels, but the monks did invoke the powers of their patron saints in order to oppose violent kings and nobles. The monks' most impressive technique was the formal direction of the vengeance of the saints upon malefactors. When kings and nobles disrupted the peace, the monks resorted to what they did best; they prayed, they cursed, and they appealed to their patrons to punish the criminals.[25] Not only hagiographers but also annalists published the results of monastic threats and curses, which were no doubt related to warriors and their kings.

The monks of Cluain Moccu Nóis left an unusually thorough record of their prayers to their saintly protector and his responses to their pleas. The annals reveal a series of raids and other violations at Cluain, as at other monasteries. But Cluain took advantage of its resident annalists to make sure that other potential warmongers knew of Ciarán's judgment upon such crimes.[26] For instance, in 846 Feidlimid mac Crimthainn raided Mide and Connacht, including Termonn Ciaráin; this was to be the last in

22. HVSH, 350–51; PVSH 1:225; PBNE 1:108.
23. HVSH, 270; see also PBNE 1:10.
24. HVSH, 273–74.
25. Lester K. Little, "La morphologie des malédictions monastiques," *Annales, E.S.C.* 34 (1979), 43–60.
26. John V. Kelleher, "The Táin and the Annals," *Ériu* 22 (1971), 117, 125–26.

a lifetime of distinctly ungodly depredations committed by the bishop-king of Munster. The annalists wrote with righteous satisfaction: "Ciarán, however, went after him to Munster and thrust his *bachall* in him so that he wounded him in the gut, and so that eventually he died."[27] Feidlimid, described as "King of Munster, a scribe and anchorite, and the best of the Irish" died the next year but, as the Four Masters reminded their readers, "because of a gut wound through the miracles of God and Ciarán."[28]

Feidlimid was only one of many disorderly rulers to suffer the fury of Ciarán. The monks at Tulach Garba, another of Ciarán's foundations, fasted against Áed ua Coinfhiacla, the king of Tethba, in 1043, presumably for raids and other disruptive crimes. The monks solemnly struck a bell called Bernán Ciaráin with Pátraic's own staff, the Bachall Ísu, borrowed from Ard Macha. With the weight of two mighty saints and their monks thrown against him, the king got what he deserved, for "in the place at which he turned his back on the clerics, in that place his head was cut off before the month's end by Muircheartach ua Maeleachlainn."[29] Again in 1112 Cluain Moccu Nóis's prayers brought about the demise of other noble attackers, including the abbot of another monastery.[30]

Other communities, heartened by hagiographic stories of saintly peacekeeping, used the same methods of prayer, fasting, and ritual deployment of relics to vent their saints' anger upon those who disrupted society and violated monastic communities. In 866 a Viking leader of Luimnech, Earl Tomrar, made an abortive raid on Cluain Ferta Brenainn; but thanks to God and Brénainn, no doubt invoked by Cluain Ferta's monks, Tomrar died of insanity within a year.[31] Ard Macha gave the credit to Pátraic when its political allies avenged the destruction of monastic property or the profanation of relics; in 1102, when the Ulaid killed Echrí ua Aitidh of the Uí Echach, a glossator added: "I.e., in the fifth month after outraging Patrick."[32] But, as an annalist showed in an entry for 1122, the saints did not manifest their anger unless the monks invoked them. When the abbot of Imlech and the king of Áine were attacked in the middle of the community's enclosure, both escaped "through the grace of Ailbe and the church [*na hecailsi*]." The man who stormed the abbot's house was caught and

---

27. FM 1:470; modified translation.
28. Ibid., 472.
29. FM 2:842–44; AU, 480.
30. W. M. Hennessy, ed., *Chronicum Scotorum* (London, 1866), 314.
31. Joan Radner, ed., *The Fragmentary Annals of Ireland* (Dublin, 1978), 122–23; Mac Airt, *Annals of Inisfallen*, 132.
32. AU, 385.

beheaded within a month of the crime only because the *eclais,* the monks of Imlech, knew how to direct their saint's power.[33]

The hagiographers corroborated the message of the annals, making a formal record of the vengeance of saints upon nobles who broke the public peace. In the fifth century, Pátraic had written of his fear of local rulers and his negotiations for his own safety while traveling and preaching. Yet two hundred years later lay people had already come to believe in the power of Pátraic, Columcille, Brigit, and other saints to exact an eye for an eye, thanks partly to the efforts of the hagiographers.[34] Less laconic than the annals, the *vitae* elaborated on the process of saintly vengeance and its meaning. Adomnán, for example, wrote vividly and tragically of how a young woman fled from a vicious nobleman to cower under the cloaks of Columcille and Gemmán. Her pursuer thrust his spear through the clerics' clothing, killing the woman. Columcille pronounced sentence—and immediately the murderer dropped dead. According to Adomnán, the warrior had committed two offenses: murder of a woman and insult to the religious men who protected her. It remains unclear which offense prompted the death sentence.[35]

Hagiographers regularly recounted in detail how the saints caused the mightiest warriors to sicken, to lose their possessions or kinfolk, to suffer dishonor or defeat in battle, and even to die because they had broken the rules of churchmen. One of the most colorful of such episodes, mentioned earlier, led to the famous cursing of Temair. The story may represent a struggle over the concept of sanctuary, as James Kenney has suggested, but it also meant much more to the early Irish.[36] Two moral and legal orders were in conflict in the story, two approaches to peace and social harmony. The hagiographer who wrote about them recognized an almost equal validity to both, but also understood that only one allowed for control by monks.

It all began with a dispute between the kings of Temair and Connacht after Diarmait mac Cerbaill, the king of Temair who had "made peace throughout Ireland," tried to impose dues on Áed Guaire. Enraged, Áed

---

33. Ibid., 568–69.

34. A. B. E. Hood, ed. and trans., *St. Patrick: His Writings and Muirchu's Life* (London, 1978), 33; Ludwig Bieler, ed., *Patrician Texts in the Book of Armagh* (Dublin, 1979), 82–96, 136, 139–40, 150; Migne, PL 72:790.

35. Adomnán, 382–84. See also a chronicler's account of how Adomnán himself punished noble sinners: Radner, *Fragmentary Annals,* 46–49.

36. Kenney, *Sources,* 392. See the "secular" version in Standish O'Grady, ed., *Silva Gadelica* (London, 1892), 1:72–82, 2:76–88.

killed the steward sent to collect the dues and then took refuge with Saint Ruadán. But Diarmait violated Ruadán's sanctuary and dragged Áed to Temair. The conflict escalated from a personal clientage dispute over dues to a battle between clerics and king over two interpretations of justice. Ruadán summoned all the saints of Ireland to gather around Diarmait's fort at Temair, besieging the closed gates with nonstop maledictions, the clamor of psalms, and the racket of ritually rung bells; the saints even struck the son of Diarmait dead, but later revived him. The exhausted king finally appeared at his gates at dawn. He defended his attempts to collect his rightful dues and to punish the man who had killed his steward: "I defend the justice of the state [*iustitiam reipuplice*], so that there may be peace everywhere; you encourage evil, defend it. God shall deprive you of heirs; for in all Ireland your *paruchia* will be first to fail and dwindle away."[37] Ruadán responded rather lamely that Diarmait's kingdom would fail before any others, and that his heirs would never reign. The two then indulged in an exchange of fierce and colorful curses, complete with references to barnyard excrement and including Ruadán's famous pronouncement that Temair would be without a king for centuries. The scene ended when Diarmait released Áed Guaire to the saints in exchange for a payment of horses (which later disappeared into the sea, leaving him with nothing).

The real importance of the story lies not in the saints' curse on Temair but in Diarmait's defense of his *iustitiam reipuplice* and his final statement to Ruadán. The king complained to the saint: "You have defended injustice, I defend truth. You have confounded my rule; but God loves you more. So go on, and take your man, and give me some payment for him."[38] The hagiographer was almost as sensitive to Diarmait's claims as to Ruadán's victory. Diarmait had tried to impose strong royal authority but not, unfortunately for him, a Christian authority.

Ultimately the religious elite believed that only they, whom God loved best, could dictate law and order. They wanted secular leaders to enforce the peace that they had engineered; they also wanted to mediate disputes when law broke down, and to be paid dues for arranging everything. The monks' spokesmen, the hagiographers, demonstrated how this could be accomplished with their didactic tales of the saints. Kings who offended the saints and hindered their endeavors were punished. Áed mac Bricc's hagiographer wrote of the saint's efforts to control rulers: "Indeed, kings

37. HVSH, 165.
38. Ibid.; PBNE 1:321–25.

were always enemies to him, but by divine power they were forced to obey him."[39]

Ecclesiastical Law and Royal Authority

The stories of the saints and ecclesiastical laws suggest that monks worked to increase the authority and jurisdiction of virtuous kings as part of their social program. As F. J. Byrne has argued, the early medieval concept of kingship developed as much in monasteries as in royal *ráths*.[40] The monks believed that even well-behaved Christian kings could not obtain extralegal power without the aid of the saints and their keepers.

The hagiographers described many friendships between wise, fatherly saints and humble, obedient kings. Finnian's hagiographer, for example, recounted how the saint sent to ask the king of Leinster, Muiredach mac Óengusa, for permission to enter his land. Thrilled at the request, the king not only granted his permission but offered to carry Finnian over the boundary on his own back. After his ride, Finnian blessed Muiredach for his humility, guaranteeing him a place in heaven and promising that his descendants would never be subject to other kings. The saint was pleased that the king had offered him a *locus* in Leinster, and that both Muiredach and his queen had prostrated themselves at his feet; he promised the couple that they would bear a line of kings, including Brandub mac Echach, the legendary king of Leinster (d. 605).[41] This happy exchange between saint and king symbolized the saint's foundation of Achad Aball (Aghowle, county Wicklow), but it may also have represented connections between Finnian's churches and the Uí Cheinselaig dynasty of Leinster in the twelfth century; the mention of Brandub was significant, because he was the last Uí Cheinselaig king to rule Leinster until Diarmait mac Máel na mBó took control in 1046.[42] The episode was probably an acknowledgment of royal patronage, since the church standing at Aghowle today was built in the twelfth century.[43]

---

39. HVSH, 178.

40. Byrne, *Irish Kings*, 244–74; Donnchadh Ó Corráin, "Nationality and Kingship in Pre-Norman Ireland," in T. W. Moody, ed., *Nationality and the Pursuit of Independence, Historical Studies 11* (Belfast, 1978), 22–24. Cf. Wendy Davies, "Clerics as Rulers," in N. P. Brooks, ed., *Latin and the Vernacular Languages in Early Medieval Europe* (Leicester, 1982), 81–98.

41. HVSH, 99.

42. AU, 480, for Diarmait's first appearance in the annals; Ó Corráin, *Ireland before the Normans*, 133–37.

43. H. G. Leask, *Irish Churches and Monastic Buildings*, vol. 1 (Dundalk, 1955), 85.

Such allegorical episodes fill the *vitae*. The saints' interactions with kings of the sixth and seventh centuries almost always symbolize political relationships of the ninth, tenth, eleventh, or twelfth centuries; or rather, the episodes suggest the sort of relationships that monks thought *ought* to exist between themselves and local kings. Pátraic's conversion of Lóegaire ua Néill referred to Uí Néill support of Ard Macha and the monastery's efforts to promote the kingship of Temair.[44] The many lives of Brigit charted a shift in Cell Dara's political position. The earliest hagiographers may have seen Cell Dara as an Uí Dúnlainge-backed candidate for the leadership of all Ireland's churches. In later *vitae*, Brigit's church had clearly become a subordinate ally of Ard Macha and its Mide patrons, in order to protect itself from the further aggression of northern clerics.[45] Many more complicated, more obscure references to alliances between monasteries and secular leadership clutter the *vitae,* as well as numerous references to enmities and broken treaties.[46]

But beyond the political intricacies, these literary relationships reveal a common hagiographic theme: kings needed monastic support as much as monasteries needed royal patronage. Hagiographers promoted the idea that kings were not the clever, manipulative, powerful warriors who appeared in the annals and secular legends. They were both bad and good, mean and generous, but they were never as intelligent as the saints. Monks wanted to persuade rulers and their clients that it was impossible to succeed in politics without the help of ecclesiastics. Kings who refused to obey the saints were fools and objects of fun; royal stupidity helped the saints to bring down obstructive kings. Mochuda's hagiographer mocked even the joint rulers of Temair, who were so afraid to approach the saint's sanctuary and expel him from Rathan that they made other monks do the dirty work.[47] The theme of the kingly fool found its best expression in Suibne Geilt, the king who insulted St. Rónán and as a result suffered the saint's curse, went made in battle, grew feathers, and flew about Ireland chanting nature poetry until Moling took him in at Tech Moling. There

44. Byrne, *Irish Kings,* 50, 82, 117, 124–25, 220, 255–56, 268; T. Ó Fiaich, "The Church of Armagh under Lay Control," *Seanchas Ard Mhacha* 5 (1969), 75–127.

45. Kim McCone, "Brigit in the Seventh Century: A Saint with Three Lives?" *Peritia* 1 (1982), 107–45.

46. Seán Ó Coileáin, "The Saint and the King," in Pádraig de Brun et al., eds., *Folia Gadelica* (Cork, 1983), 36–46; Kathleen Hughes, "The Historical Value of the Lives of St. Finnian of Clonard," *English Historical Review* 272 (July 1954), 353–72; Charles Doherty, "The Historical Value of the Medieval Lives of Máedóc of Ferns" (master's thesis, University College, Dublin, 1971).

47. PBNE 1:303–4.

Suibne met a graceless end, dying on a dung heap at the hands of a serf.[48]

In the *vitae*, even decent kings were bunglers who needed the saints and monks to guide them. Óengus mac Nadfraích, king of Munster, was so impressed by the ritual pomp of his baptism and subsequent ordination that when Pátraic accidentally thrust his *bachall* through his foot, Óengus thought it part of the ceremony.[49] This same king obediently climbed to the top of the hill of Caisel, the political capital of Munster, with Saint Énda. He genuflected when told to do so, believing himself about to be rebaptized. Actually, Énda wanted to bless Óengus's vision so that the king could see as far as Ára, off the west coast, and could grant the island *locus* to the saint.[50] A good and simple Christian ruler, Óengus did as he was told.

The best example of a mutually supportive arrangement between a clever cleric and a somewhat thick king was the friendship between Saint Máedóc and Brandub mac Echach of Leinster. Brandub gave Máedóc land and donations; he visited the saint often, protecting the community at Ferna Mór. He even offered once to rid Máedóc of an unruly monk the kingly way, by killing him.[51] Máedóc accepted the king's friendship and subsequently helped Brandub in battle, saved him from hell with an out-of-body experience, and buried him in the sacred ground at Ferna Mór.[52] Máedóc's hagiographer could not show the saint saving Brandub from assassination, since the murder was already a strong historical tradition; but, lest readers of hagiography think this failure a slur on the saint's power, Máedóc fasted for a year to revive the king, so that Brandub could be given the choice of returning to temporal life or gaining eternal life.[53]

Kings such as Brandub entrusted themselves to monks who knew better. They put their souls, their success in battle, their children, and the futures of their kingdoms in the hands of the saints.[54] The moral of these kingly stories was as simple as the kings themselves: Holy men made kings. Kings gave extensive donations and endowments to monastic communities and protected them from other warriors. In return, they secured places in heaven, prosperity for their kingdoms, military victories, the royal succession of their heirs, and, most important, acceptance of royal

48. J. G. O'Keeffe, ed., *Buile Suibhne* (London, 1910).
49. VT, 196.
50. PVSH 2:66.
51. HVSH, 242; PBNE 1:226.
52. HVSH, 238–39, 243–44; PBNE 1:185–86, 216–17, 230–31.
53. PBNE 1:188, 231–32.
54. HVSH, 156–57.

authority and jurisdiction within their territories. Rulers learned that they needed monastic patronage because they could not rule without it, because their heirs would not succeed them without it, because they would not reach heaven without it. All the saints' rough dealing with contrary kings proved that. Conall Derg claimed a divine right to rule without Molaise's help, but the saint deprived his heirs of kingship because Conall refused to convert and would not become Molaise's ally.[55] On the other hand, it may have taken Brandub mac Echach's descendants five hundred years to regain the kingship of Leinster, but by the time Máedóc's twelfth-century Irish *vita* was written they were back in power again; twelfth-century Uí Cheinselaig kings enjoyed much more extensive jurisdiction and authority than their seventh-century ancestor, thanks to the help of Máedóc and his own successors at Ferna Mor.[56]

From as early as the seventh century, the language of monastic texts on kings and kingship betrayed the monks' ambitions for their royal allies.[57] Muirchú, in his life of Pátraic, referred to Temair as the seat of kings of Ireland. Adomnán called Diarmait mac Cerbaill, an Uí Néill king, "king of all Ireland ordained by God" (*totius Scotiae regnatorem a deo ordinatum*).[58] Beginning in the eighth century, clerics systematically laid down the rights and obligations of kings in formal ecclesiastical laws. Canonists ordered that kings be anointed by priests.[59] Irish clergymen obviously learned the trick of using religious ritual to reinforce their influence on politics long before the Carolingians and bishops of Rome. Kings appreciated the value of ritual installation. In 993, for example, Áed Oirdnide ("the Ordained") was consecrated four years after he had secured the kingship of Cruachán.[60]

Monastic support brought the kings more than ritual affirmation of power already gained. The monks generated an alternative legal system that allowed kings to judge and punish criminals, especially adulterers,

---

55. PVSH 2:134–35.

56. A. P. Smyth, *Celtic Leinster* (Blackrock, 1982), 59–67; Ó Corráin, *Ireland before the Normans*, 133–37. See also PVSH 1:174.

57. Wallace-Hadrill, *Early Germanic Kingship*, 47–71; František Graus, *Volk, Herrscher und Heiliger im Reich der Merowinger: Studien zur Hagiographie der Merowingerzeit* (Prague, 1965), 303–437.

58. L. Bieler, ed., *Patrician Texts in the Book of Armagh* (Dublin, 1979), 74; Adomnán, 280; Byrne, *Irish Kings*, 254–55; Liam de Paor, *The Peoples of Ireland* (South Bend, Ind., 1986), 74, 76.

59. Wasserschleben, *Collectio*, 76.

60. Ibid., Byrne, *Irish Kings*, 256; PBNE 1:203–4; AU, 424. See also Michael J. Enright, "Royal Succession and Abbatial Prerogative in Adomnán's Vita Columbae," *Peritia* 4 (1985), 83–103.

perjurers, and parricides. These were powers of judgment far beyond those accorded kings by traditional secular law; but adultery, perjury, and parricide carried more profound moral connotations than ordinary murders, assaults, and thefts. These crimes were serious sins, which no amount of civil negotiation could absolve. As sins, they were subject to the laws of the Church. Although the canonists and penitentialists maintained the rights of abbots and bishops to judge many cases, they included the king among those who could carry out public punishments of sinful crimes.[61] They designed the rituals of judgment and punishment specifically to display the authority of kings and the ecclesiastical laws that they upheld. But punishments were to take place only at the gates of the monastic community, a place where people gathered to trade and to socialize, not at royal *ráths*.[62] Canonists further enhanced the social status of kings when they ordered that royal authority was to be accepted as God-given; they were warning nobles who tried to better their own positions by snatching the kingship away from a legitimate ally of churchmen.

Kings paid for their increased authority and status with good behavior. Once in office, a Christian king was to follow strict rules of conduct. He was not, for example, to indulge in polygamy, as churchmen referred to the Irish practice of secondary marriage or formal concubinage by contract.[63] For the iniquitous king "disturbs the public peace," leading naturally to such disasters as war, death, tempests, and barrenness upon the land.[64] A virtuous king dispensed justice, protected widows and children, punished adulterers and thieves, disdained actors and other riffraff, executed parricides and perjurers, took council with his elders, defended his territory, and, more important, protected churches, ignored superstitions, paid his alms, put his faith in God, and insisted on proper observance of prayers. Such a king exemplified *justitia*. And, as the canonists observed, "king's justice is the people's peace."[65] A just and Christian rule meant safe borders, a healthy and happy people, prosperity, and good weather. It created exactly the sort of Christian order cherished by the monks—

61. Wasserschleben, *Collectio*, 63–73; Ó Corráin, "Nationality and Kingship," 23–24.
62. Wasserschleben, *Collectio*, 63, 85.
63. Ibid., 78. Another version of the text exists in Pseudo-Cyprianus, *De XII Abusivis Saeculi*, ed. S. Hellmann, Texte und Untersuchungen zur Geschichte der altchristlichen Literatur 3, ser. 4 (Leipzig, 1910).
64. Wasserschleben, *Collectio*, 77; Ó Corráin, "Nationality and Kingship," 16–17; Migne, PL 4:887–88.
65. Wasserschleben, *Collectio*, 77.

including military protection for ecclesiastical communities and a steady flow of royal donations from fruitful farms.[66]

Kings also owed more tangible dues in return for such extensive canonical and saintly support. Demands for donations and endowments were extremely prominent in the saints' lives. Monks also insisted that kings uphold ecclesiastical law and protect monastic allies and property, and the monks themselves. Kings had to defend churches and their dependents, and show allegiance to Christian doctrine. Although they collected heavy dues from subjects, according to the canons, they were not to levy the same on churches or on the poor protected by churchmen. Under a chapter entitled "That dues are not to be levied upon a church," canonists quoted their highest authorities, such as Augustine, Ambrose, Jerome, and Christ himself: "Therefore the sons of the King are free in every kingdom."[67] If they made outrageous demands upon monks or failed in their duties, kings became enemies of the monastic order. The canonists quoted Pope Gregory I concerning bad kings: "It is certainly stupid if we seek to please those whom we know do not please God."[68] The monks would not hesitate to back a good king against a disobedient one. The price of increased authority was high, but kings were willing to pay it.

Alternative Laws

The monks manipulated kings and laws for an admirable purpose: to bring about a peace that would profit everyone, man and woman, noble and slave, monk and laic. For the monks, proper social order included a rigid social hierarchy, with kings at the top. Irish political theorists were no different from their Continental peers in their firm belief that the nobler a person, the more rights he or she had, both legally and morally.

Nonetheless, the monks also insisted that kings and laws protect every Christian soul, even those without high status or extensive legal rights. By

---

66. Ibid., 77–78. Merovingian, Breton, and Welsh saints struggled for Christian order too; see Wallace-Hadrill, *Early Germanic Kingship*, 55–59; James E. Doan, "A Structural Approach to Celtic Saints' Lives" in P. Ford, ed., *Celtic Folklore and Christianity* (Santa Barbara, Calif., 1975), 16–28. See also pre-Christian traditions of the just rules in Fergus Kelly, ed., *Audacht Morainn* (Dublin, 1976), and the "mirror for princes" contained in the sage story edited by Myles Dillon, *Serglige Con Culainn* (Dublin, 1975).

67. Wasserschleben, *Collectio*, 78–79.

68. Ibid., 82.

working to limit the warlike behavior of kings and promoting a Christian concept of kingship, the monks helped people live and work productively without fear of economic devastation or death. If kings stayed at home and punished criminals instead of raiding the herds of neighboring territories, everyone could sleep better at night. The canonists correctly equated the king's justice with public peace.

Yet, inevitably in a society where a few profited from the labor of many, this liberal monastic agenda occasionally clashed with the interests of the secular elite.[69] The indirect benefits of monastic alliances with friendly, peacekeeping kings did not always bring enough protection to farmers and laborers in contest with their lords. Church laws did not cover the civil conflicts that crowded daily life, which might always erupt into violence, and which the elite always won. Contract disputes, ruptured clientage relations, rents, alleged thefts: these were the province of secular law and custom, which decreed that justice favored the free and noble and, further, that elites might legally achieve their justice through violence. When his property was enticing or his behavior troublesome, a peasant's life came cheap to a nobleman, who had only to pay a very low honor-price to the victim's lord or kin in order to vindicate assault or murder. Even the dense network of blood and clientage ties could not stave off this kind of injustice.[70]

But the monks could and did help those who slipped through the networks of clientage and kinship. Churchmen and women worked outside the laws to help these peasant allies, sometimes against the very relatives or lords who were supposed to support them, in two ways. First, monks joined kings in proclaiming special extralocal laws to protect the powerless against the powerful. Second, following the saints' example, the monks used their prominent position in the community to supplant the patrons or kinfolk of helpless people. They offered themselves as substitute lords of kinsmen to those whose social ties failed them. The monks relied on their own patrons, the saints, to help provide protection and support to others in need. The monks' efforts were part of their larger program of social order, for they aimed in these legislative and personal ways to extend the saints' guardianship not just to kings, but to all Christians.

It was this essentially altruistic concern for Christians of all classes that formed the monks' ambiguous attitude toward the laws. They were happy

69. Wallace-Hadrill, *Early Germanic Kingship,* 62–69.
70. Paul Fouracre, "'Placita' and the Settlement of Disputes in Later Merovingian Francia," in Davies and Fouracre, *Settlement of Disputes,* 23–43.

to use existing laws to secure their own property, dues, and rents. Indeed, monks may well have written some of the legal tracts, as we have seen. But beginning in the seventh century the monks issued extraordinary laws called *cána,* unlike the customary laws kept by trained jurists. Kings and monks together formally enacted and proclaimed a *cáin,* and usually caused it to be written down. *Cána* extended across political boundaries, sometimes to all Ireland; local kings, backed by the saints and by the curses of the monks, enforced them.

As with monastic rules, the monks attributed authorship of *cána* to the saints, which lent the laws added authority.[71] A description of the contents of some *cána* appears in the ninth-century *Félire Óenguso,* which mentions four: the *Cáin Pátraic,* which prohibited the slaying of clerics; the *Cáin Dar Í,* against cattle raiding; the *Cáin Adamnáin,* against killing women; and the *Cáin Domnaig,* against laboring on Sunday.[72] The texts of three of these *cána* remain, the most extensive and earliest of which is the *Cáin Adamnáin.*

Adomnán's seventh-century law clearly illustrates the monks' purpose in promulgating *cána.* It consisted of four sections. The narrative framework of the text was written about 900, showing its popularity two hundred years after the law's first enactment. The introduction told the story of Adomnán's suffering at the hands of his mother, who pitied the plight of women in her day because they were enslaved by men; men forced women to stand in deep pits holding the wooden cooking stakes upon which meat roasted, and thrashed women and sent them into battle to kill each other for the sake of men's warlike ambitions. Adomnán was at first unwilling to release women from bondage, so his mother tortured her son for years, even imprisoning him in a coffin. Finally, an angel came down to help her persuade Adomnán to make a law that would protect women from abuse.

Following this strange narrative, a list of clerical and law guarantors lent historical validity to the law and provided the spiritual sanctions to ensure its operation. A third section consisted of a Latin version of the law, applying its protection to women only. The final section, written in formal legal terms, forbade the violation of church property and violence against

71. DIL, 95–96; M. A. O'Brien, "Etymologies and Notes . . . 4. O.Ir. *cáin,* Slav. *kazně,*" *Celtica* 3 (1956), 172–73.

72. FO, 210; W. Stokes and J. Strachan, eds., *Thesaurus Paleohibernicus,* vol. 2 (Cambridge, 1903), 306; Kathleen Hughes, "The Church and the World in Early Christian Ireland," *Irish Historical Studies* 13 (1962–63), 103.

church tenants, clerics, women, and children; it also described the process by which the law was to be enforced, with pledges and sureties, and penalties for those who broke it. This last, according to Kathleen Hughes, was the original version of the *cáin*.[73]

The assumption behind the ninth-century narrative of *Cáin Adamnáin* was that good but weak Christians, such as women and clerics, needed protection beyond that provided by society and its laws. Everyone, including Adomnán, God's angelic messenger, and Ireland's secular rulers, had to be forced to protect women. The sadistic fantasy of enslaved women and Adomnán's torture suggested that the situation had been worse two centuries earlier; but violence was still rampant, and Irish society needed more than the traditional legal controls. The *cáin*'s authors could not eliminate assault and murder, but they did seek to limit them.

The law also assumed that monks and secular nobility were equally obliged to prevent violence by enforcing the *cáin*. The list of the law's seventh-century guarantors included such notables as the kings of all the major kingdoms and the prominent clergy of both south and north; except for a few anachronistic names added in textual transmission, the list is probably authentic.[74] It is unlikely that all of these leaders gathered in a synod to enact the *Cáin Adamnáin*, but it is clear that, at least as early as 700, monks and kings had begun to take specific measures to protect the powerless.

The author of the last part of the *Cáin Adamnáin* conceived of a regular process by which the law was to be enforced. Messengers were to proclaim the *cáin* to the gathered inhabitants of an area, after which a representative (*rechtaire*) of Adomnán's churches would collect dues from the beneficiaries of the *cáin*. Women owed gifts of clothing, food, and domestic animals in return for protection. These dues were separate from secular dues of clientage, the law carefully pointed out, and they were also not to be levied on churches or church clients; thus, although the *cáin* existed separately from traditional laws of clientage it did not conflict with them.[75] Adomnán's churches also appointed a professional negotiator (*breithem*) in each area to adjudicate disputes over dues and over violations of the *cáin*. He was to apply a long list of formal legal fines and

73. W. Stokes, ed., *Cáin Adamnáin* (Oxford, 1905); Hughes, "Church and the World," 101–2.

74. Kenney, *Sources,* 246; Máirín ní Dhonnchada, "The Guarantor List of Cáin Adamnáin, 697," *Peritia* 1 (1982), 178–215.

75. Stokes, *Cáin Adamnáin,* 20.

penalties found in the text when making his decisions. Three guarantors (*secnap, coic, ferthigis:* secondary abbot, cook, steward) from the major monastic community in the area were to witness and uphold the *breithem*'s decisions.

Cáin Adamnáin in its ninth-century form represented the ideal of monks and ruling nobility working together to promote social stability by protecting those who could not protect themselves. Ultimately, all regional and provincial leaders took joint responsibility for the law's enforcement. Yet the *cáin*'s authors could imagine instances when the law failed; "then the holy men of the churches of Ireland prayed." The monks, in response, prayed to a whole host of saints, invoked the natural elements, and proclaimed psalms of malediction and three *gairi mallacht* or curses upon anyone who transgressed the law.[76]

Political leaders, both clerical and secular, actually put the *cána* into practice. Nine different saints' laws appeared in the annals, enforced at least thirty-three times between the first appearance of Adomnan's law and the year 842.[77] Although *Cáin Adamnáin* extended to all of Ireland's helpless, *cána* were usually regional laws. In 793, Artrach mac Cathail proclaimed Ailbe's law in Munster, significantly, at the same time he was ordained king.[78] In 814, according to the *Annals of Ulster,* "Ciarán's law was exalted at Cruachain by Muirgus [mac Tomaltaigh, king of Connacht]."[79] Officials from Ard Macha enacted Pátraic's law against the murder of clerics many times in the eighth and ninth centuries, often assisted by kings of Mide and Connacht.[80]

Kings and monks frequently promulgated *cána* during the hundred years from 750 to 850, but then abruptly ceased.[81] Possibly the Viking attacks disrupted the ritual promotion of public order and also prevented people from paying dues for *cána*. But monastic efforts to protect the weak in exchange for material support took other forms after 850. Abbots and bishops continued to make local circuits or *cúarta* (sg. *cúairt*) of the territories under their spiritual care. They carried their relics with them,

---

76. Ibid., 12. Cf. Daniel Melia, "Law and the Shaman-saint," in Ford, *Celtic Folklore and Christianity,* 113–28. Melia argues that shamanistic methods by which Adomnán acquired power, according to the textual introduction to *Cáin Adamnáin,* also contributed to the saint's ability to enforce the *cáin.*

77. Hughes, "Church and the World," 102.

78. AU, 248.

79. Ibid., 270.

80. Ibid., 190, 238, 254, 262, 266, 274, 278, 282, 294, 342; Doherty, "Use of Relics," 96.

81. Hughes, *Church in Early Irish Society,* 152.

displaying them publicly and allowing the assembled audience to see and perhaps touch the saints' bones, then claiming dues. Abbots of Ard Macha, for example, went on provincial circuits in 947, 960, 973, 986, 993, and at least thirteen more times up to 1120.[82] The laws described the obligation of lay people to pay for such *cúarta:* "The wage of a reliquary, i.e., pay for protection to the relic i.e., which is earned by the relics that are carried about i.e., of tithes and first fruits and alms."[83]

But circuits were not simply business trips to gather rents. A circuit in 986, as described in the Annals of Tigernach, demonstrated that the *cúarta* continued the tradition of *cána,* and that the monks intended them to promote public order. Máelsechnaill, the king of Temair, carried Pátraic's shrine off to Mide during his feud with Ciarchaille mac Cairelláin, king of northern Brega. After the two leaders had made peace, Máelsechnaill paid his dues to St. Pátraic by allowing Pátraic's *comarbae* to make a *cúairt* of all the ecclesiastical and secular communities of Mide; the abbot collected penalty fees, regular dues, and free hospitality as the fine for Máelsechnaill's kidnapping of the shrine and his violation of the peace.[84] The collaboration of monks and kings, to their mutual profit and the benefit of all, also continued after the *cána* disappeared. When the abbot of Ard Macha ordained Áed mac Domnaill as king of Ailech in 993, for example, the abbot made a full circuit of northern Uí Néill territories; thus, Áed gained Christian sanction for his rule while the monks of Ard Macha strengthened their position as public defenders, and at the same time collected dues from all those who acknowledged their authority.[85]

The lay public believed that these abbatial *cúarta* did indeed preserve them from harm, and that their dues were well spent. Even in the midst of natural disaster, the inhabitants of Connacht had faith in the power of Pátraic to preserve order, and also to save them from famine and plague. After a severe winter and spring in 1115 famine spread throughout Ireland and lasted through 1116, causing epidemics in that year. Yet the abbot of Ard Macha made a circuit of Connacht in 1116 and brought away all the due that he demanded.[86] The efficacy of *cúarta* and *cána* had long been established by the twelfth century, as had the practice of making material thanks to the saints for their protective services.

---

82. AU, 392, 402, 410, 424, 436, 444, 458, 486, 504, 526, 528, 546, 550, 558, 560, 564.
83. CIH 1:40; ALI 5:226; cited in Doherty, "Use of Relics," 97.
84. FM 2:718.
85. AU, 424.
86. Ibid., 556–68; Hughes, *Church in Early Irish Society,* 168–69.

Alternative Patrons

The monks worked outside traditional secular law and custom when they proclaimed *cána* and *cúarta*. They also ignored the laws when they offered themselves as mediators and alternative patrons to those in distress. The *vitae* catalogue the sorts of extralegal help that people could expect from the saints and their representatives, the monks. In general, the monks moved between rulers and subjects, lords and clients, neighbors, and even blood relatives, to protect people from lawless lords and unjust laws. In particular, they subverted the laws of hostage exchange and slavery, and protected criminals from punishment.

Their actions were legally illogical. After all, the monks sought social order, and kings traded hostages in order to prevent war; slavery was part of the hierarchical social system approved by the monks, who held slaves themselves; and criminals violated the very order endorsed by the monks. The logic of the monks was not legal but moral: they protected good Christians of every legal status, including hostages, slaves, and criminals, with individual social ties, as well as with the proclamation of *cána* and political alliance. They aimed not to weaken the social order or hinder peace, but to bolster peace and order by correcting flaws in the social structure and the legal system. The monks resisted the hostage system elaborated in the laws because it simply did not work well. For centuries, kings had been exchanging hostages in order to prevent armed conflict; they reasoned that a man whose son or brother was kept prisoner in a neighboring kingdom would not dare to attack, for fear that his enemy would kill his kinsman. As the laws put it: "He is no king who has no hostage in chains."[87] Yet nothing stopped war leaders from killing their own hostages and sacrificing their men held elsewhere when they wanted to resume hostilities.

The monks worked to undermine the hostage system from an early period, or at least tried to incorporate it into their own style of peacemaking by sanctioning the exchange of hostages with relics and rituals. In the sixth or seventh century, when monks still kept themselves apart from the pagan world, the penitentialists had tried to prevent monks and priests from interfering in the hostage system. Monks were not to use their own funds to redeem hostages.[88] But some monks felt otherwise, and the

87. Byrne, *Irish Kings*, 31.
88. Ludwig Bieler, ed., *The Irish Penitentials* (Dublin, 1975), 54, 58, 84.

saints set contrary examples by using both fair means and low tricks to secure the release of legally held political prisoners.

The hagiographers provided a manual for subverting the hostage system. Some saints gave ransom money to hostages who begged for it, performing miracles to find gold when they did not have any handy.[89] When money did not work, the saints used other methods. Fínán made a king's son mute until the ruler released a hostage.[90] Other saints merely dissolved the chains binding hostages and led them to safety, or raised their staves to terrify kings and protect the hostages.[91]

The saints were determined to protect helpless Christians caught by an imperfect system, despite the possible benefits that a successful exchange of hostages might bring. Samthann, for instance, was far more sympathetic to the entreaties of a widow whose only son was a captive of the king of Tethba than to the fact that such a hostage supposedly prevented war between Tethba and Connacht. Samthann sent her prioress to seek the release of the man and to accomplish his freedom in her name, forcibly if necessary.[92] Yet the saints consulted their own criteria in deciding which hostages to free, for not every captive enjoyed their patronage. It seems that the peace and order that generally benefited all could occasionally harm a few; when it did, the saints sometimes instructed that the few be given priority.

The hagiographers felt the same antagonism toward slavery, which, like hostage taking, they considered unchristian. Many of the saints freed *ancillae*, female slaves (though in view of the monks' disapproval of polygamy and formalized concubinage, these women in the *vitae* may have been secondary wives rather than actual slaves).[93] Not all slaves were emancipated. In the *vitae*, the saints' decision to free a slave resulted from appeals by the victims themselves. Fintan of Dún Bleisce freed men whose burden of labor consisted of preparing the daily baths of a pagan king; the slaves hated hauling the jars of water and prayed to Fintan to release them.[94] Brénainn, *pátrún na pían* (patron of sufferings), helped a poor man who begged him: "Have pity on me, and help me out of the servitude which I suffer at the hands of the king, for he has ruined us and my children." Brénainn struck the sod upon which he stood with his staff and caused a

---

89. HVSH, 139–40; PBNE 1:106.
90. HVSH, 158–59; see also PBNE 1:187.
91. Adomnán, 230–32; HVSH, 128; PVSH 2:180–81, 225, 256.
92. PVSH 2:256.
93. HVSH, 178, 212; Adomnán, 398–404.
94. HVSH, 115.

pound of refined gold to spring out of it, which he gave to the man to pay off his lord and buy his release from service.[95]

The slave's dilemma was very similar to that of some clients or tenants described in the *vitae* who could not collect enough for their annual rents. According to secular law, a man who could not pay his rent was liable to have his property seized.[96] The hagiographers expressed their disapproval of the nobility's legalistic oppression of laborers and tenants by suggesting that the gap between slavery and clientship was slight in the saints' eyes. Máedóc's Latin life showed how the saint aided a certain pauper whose lord exacted a heavy rent. The tenant came to Máedóc, who gave him barley, for a poverty-sworn saint never had wealth lying about; but the barley turned to gold, which the tenant then handed to his lord. The lord was so impressed that he freed the pauper of his obligations and returned the gold to Máedóc.[97] Saint Áed performed a similar service for a man who owed a herd of pigs to his landlord, a *magus* or druid. The pigs supplied by Áed fulfilled the client's dues but later disappeared, leaving the greedy landlord with nothing.[98]

The hagiographers did not voice a general condemnation of the clientship system; indeed, the saints' assistance to needy clients actually signified monastic support of clientage. The *vitae* consistently proclaimed the saints' rights to dues on the property held by their successors. Máedóc, who paid the pauper's rent, cursed with hell the client who neglected his dues to Ferna Mór.[99] When a clientage relationship appeared tenuous because one partner failed in his obligations, the saints stepped in to supply what was needed and to prevent the destruction of the relationship.

Although they had various reasons for helping poor farmers, the saints showed their monks how to enhance their own position when they ignored the rigidity of the secular legal structure and helped out other men's clients and slaves. Their altruistic services brought returns both from farmers who were late with their rent and from landlords whose dues were otherwise unlikely to be rendered. Máedóc, after all, got a legitimate donation of gold from the rent-collecting king, when originally he had nothing but barley. The monks' services as middlemen indicate an extralegal patronage relationship between themselves and the rent-payers. Even

95. PBNE 1:87, 2:84.
96. CIH 2:434–36.
97. HVSH, 244; PVN 1:188.
98. HVSH, 175–76.
99. PBNE 1:203.

in secular law, clients were allowed to have more than one lord; the laws also recognized the tendency of ecclesiastical communities to seduce clients away from other lords.[100]

According to the hagiographers, the monks could also profit when they extended their extralegal protection to criminals. However, their services to killers and thieves brought not material but spiritual and political rewards to the saints and their monastic successors. In the *vitae*, the saints were the last resort for a killer who would not face his penalty and whose kinfolk could not afford the fines or blood feuds that would pacify the victims of the crime.[101] Further, when it suited them, the saints even hindered the due process of king's law, the very law of judgment and capital punishment urged by the canonists and penitentialists. The parents of a fratricide appealed to Áed mac Bricc to save him, even though the man had been legally judged by the king of Connacht and condemned to death.[102] Saint Íte also saved a fratricide, ordering the king of Uí Conaill to free the criminal because his *infelix mater* (unhappy mother) grieved for the only son she had left. The king released his prisoner to Íte but warned that his crimes were upon her head. Íte serenely predicted that the killer would perform voluntary penance to expiate his sin.[103]

Ostensibly, the saints saved men from secular justice because they felt sorry for the malefactors. It was out of *trócaire* (pity) that Máedóc brought about the release of a man on his way to be judged by the king of Leinster.[104]

Their almost arbitrary defenses of some criminals demonstrated the ability of the religious elite to rise above human laws altogether and to exercise a higher, more personal form of justice based on Christian forgiveness. They expected criminals rescued from the judgment of kings to repent, perform penances, and possibly even become monks to expiate their sins. As we have seen, many of the *athláig* who were moved to become permanent members of monastic communities figured in the *vitae* as reformed murderers and thieves.[105] The eighth-century canons also suggest that monks sheltered criminal sinners. Canonists described elaborate laws of sanctuary offered by the enclosing walls of ecclesiastical com-

100. CIH 2:433, ll. 25–29.
101. HVSH, 351; PVSH 1:225–26.
102. HVSH, 176.
103. PVSH 2:128.
104. PBNE 1:238–29.
105. Kathleen Hughes and Ann Hamlin, *Celtic Monasticism: The Modern Traveller to the Early Irish Church* (New York, 1977), 15; Wasserschleben, *Collectio*, 94–98.

munities.[106] The annalists showed that guilty men fled to the security of the sacred space, although often only to find themselves cornered there by others with no regard for holy law.[107]

The saints were not indiscriminate in their mercy, and neither were the monks. Sometimes, when the law did not properly punish offenders, the saints did. Comgall exacted the death penalty from a thief who stole cattle from some of his nun friends.[108] Mochóemóc punished the killer of a legally held hostage who enjoyed the saint's protective blessing.[109] Men who were clearly guilty enjoyed the protection of monks, while those who escaped legal prosecution suffered saintly persecution. And the same prince who raided one monastery, calling down the curses of its holy patron, might well have been the blessed benefactor of another monastic community and its saint.

The monks did not condemn the criminal legal system, any more than they rejected clientship. They merely altered it to work according to the alternative moral system of the saints, so vividly illustrated in the *vitae*. Religious men, like God himself, could save or condemn according to their own mysterious criteria. A view into the souls of criminals, granted only to saints and their monks, helped them make the decision; so did the partiality caused by kinship ties, friendships, clientage relationships, and other alliances. Only men and women dedicated to God knew which criminals would repent under their patronage, which must be punished with death brought by ritual curse, and which were better left to king's law. Saints of the Viking period *vitae* no longer made the mistakes of Adomnán's Columcille, who allowed another monk to bring Áed Dub, killer of Diarmait mac Cerbaill, into sanctuary. Columcille merely prophesied the bad end of Áed Dub; later hagiographers would have seen to it that their saints punished the killer or forced him to repent.[110]

The monks of early Ireland did far more than take native law and make it more flexible.[111] They created an extralegal ethical system of their own, enforced by their obedient allies and controlled exclusively by themselves. They tolerated most of the daily business of customary and formal written law. In matters of landholding and clientship they were content to abide by secular law, especially when it worked to their benefit. But when they

106. Wasserschleben, *Collectio,* 94–98.
107. AU, 340, 572.
108. PVSH 2:19.
109. Ibid., 172–73.
110. Adomnán, 278–82.
111. Hughes, *Church in Early Irish Society,* 153.

disapproved of legal custom, they instituted themselves as judges and turned kings into enforcers. When the social relationships governed by law failed to function property, they inserted themselves as mediators and substitute patrons to the helpless.

Monks thus filled the gaps in existing social structures by offering to protect good Christians from the savagery of daily life when others could or would not. And to a limited extent this extralegal program for peace worked. The monks were able to extend the authority of secular rulers, who were formerly bound by laws of negotiation and contract, and to make the world a little less perilous for peasants, laborers, and themselves.

CHAPTER SIX

Spirituales Medici

ALMOST FROM THE ARRIVAL OF CHRISTIANITY IN IRELAND, MONKS took on the duties of doctors of body and soul. Irish saints of the sixth and seventh centuries performed an astonishing number of miraculous cures; their monastic successors, described by St. Columbán as *spirituales medici*, inherited the saints' medical skills along with their relics. Only the professional devotees of a saint could perform miraculous cures for the laity. According to the hagiographers, lay people were happy to compensate the monks for such services. And because of the medieval notion that external illness reflected inner decay, the monks were able to use their curative powers to reinforce the links between disease and disorder and between health and social equilibrium. When massive pandemics threatened the Christians of Ireland, only to be warded off by the prayers of the monks and the powers of the saints, the monks further established themselves as guardians of the social and political order that they set out in laws, *cána*, and *vitae*.

Saints everywhere performed healing miracles. From Ard Macha to Rome, the prayers and postures of healing were among the most popular rituals conducted by Christian monks. Lay people valued baptism and, perhaps even more, formal Christian burial, but the weekly mass and the calendar of feast days did not have the immediacy of a prayer for the wounded or a blessing over a sightless eye. Hagiographers assured Christians that only monastic cures brought the relief of a patient's physical diseases, psychological distress, and spiritual pains.

The restorative touch of the saints, extended by the hands of the monks, carried profound religious meaning for the healthy Christians of early

Ireland. The community that witnessed the cure and the family that helped to pay for it also participated in the healing experience. Because observers bore the same burden of sin that had brought on the patient's infections, they shared the patient's redeeming encounter with God and his saints. Healing thus reinforced social networks, monastic authority, and ecclesiastical values.

Secular and Religious Healers

The early Irish suffered from dropsy, gout, urinary infection, headache, and nosebleed, among other minor afflictions.[1] While the hagiographers mentioned all of these illnesses and symptoms, they rarely provided more specific descriptions of cases. Their diagnoses were vague, clearly the work of men untutored in professional medicine. While the saints sometimes cured people of ordinary maladies, basic health care was not the business of monks. For these ailments, as for all medical problems, the patient and his or her family performed initial triage; they decided, for example, to address a saint directly with specially formulated prayers, asking for the personal attention of a specialist in headaches, thorn pricks, or other ills. These prayers, called *loricae* or "shields," begged the saints' preventive help in staving off diseases and disasters.[2] A sufferer and his or her family may also have chosen to treat illnesses themselves. The secular laws suggest that patients often convalesced at home or in the homes of others but under the care of their own kin.[3]

When personal prayer and home remedies failed to bring relief, the Irish consulted secular physicians, *léigi* (sg. *liaig*). No pre-Norman medical literature survives, but a few legal tracts show that the Irish called in physicians to operate on victims of accidents and assaults, probably to set bones and treat wounds. The legal material reveals few details of medical practice, for the lawyers were more concerned with assigning responsibility for injury, and thus determining who would pay for the doctor's services and the patient's upkeep, than with the physician's training. According to the laws, physicians served as legal consultants on the question

---

1. HVSH, 379, 383, 393; PVSH 1:192; 2:20, 47, 132; Adomnán, 336–38, 364.

2. Kenney, *Sources*, 270–72, 218, 720–30; L. Gougaud, "Étude sur les loricae et sur les prières qui s'en rapprochent," *Bulletin d'ancienne littérature et d'archéologie chrétiennes* 1 (1911), 265–81; 2 (1912), 33–41, 101–27.

3. D. A. Binchy, ed., "Bretha Crólige" and "Sick-Maintenance in Irish Law," *Ériu* 12 (1934–1938), 1–77, 78–134.

of whether injured patients would or would not die; apparently doctors sometimes guessed incorrectly, and were fined heavily for doing so.[4]

Yet patients and their kin must have been generally satisfied with the care provided by *léigi*, for the laws also indicated that doctors were professional men of high social status.[5] *Léigi* were apparently successful at some delicate surgery. Skulls found in Collierstown, county Meath, show that medieval medical men knew how to treat head injuries with trepanation; at least some patients survived this process of boring a hole in the skull, and lived to die of other causes.[6] Doctors also practiced some postoperative care, serving as nutritionists and herbalists and possibly drawing on the skills of folk healers to create a homely body of knowledge about restorative diets. They believed in the value of eating honey, garlic, and celery, and ordered patients to avoid salt. They knew which herbs to gather in which seasons, and how to use them for medical purposes. The laws even declare that "it is for this most of all that the garden has been made, the care of sickness."[7]

Still, for some ailments, private supplication brought no relief and physicians were unable to provide remedies. In such cases patients had no alternative but to seek the help of the monks and ask the saints for a cure. Monks did not compete with physicians, but encouraged and even employed them, as their hagiographers suggested in the *vitae*. In the early version of Saint Ruadán's *vita*, a boy who wanted to be a doctor began his career by traveling to the saint's community of Lothra, to seek his blessing.[8] Déclán's hagiographer made it clear that there was a difference between religious and lay healers. One of Déclán's monks jokingly offered to heal the leg of a brother in the names of God and the saint, and was astonished to find that his cure worked. Déclán decreed that the monk and his descendants would change careers to become successful doctors. The hagiographer implied that Déclán's community supported a family of doctors in his own day.[9]

---

4. Binchy, "Bretha Crólige," 12–15, 52–53. Wendy Davies has suggested that *léigi* were merely dieticians and legal consultants, and that pre-Christian Ireland had no native tradition of professional healing: "The Place of Healing in Early Irish Society," in Donnchadh Ó Corráin et al., eds., *Sages, Saints and Storytellers* (Maynooth, 1989), 43–55.

5. CIH 6:2328: "Daernemead tra . . . saeir . . . & gobaind . . . & umaide . . . & cearda . . . &leigi . . . & Breitheamain . . . & druidh . . . & aes cacha dana olchena."

6. John F. Fleetwood, *The History of Medicine in Ireland* (Dublin, 1957; rpt. 1983), 15.

7. Binchy, "Bretha Crólige," 20–23, 36–37, 40–41, Robin Flower, "Popular Science in Medieval Ireland," *Ériu* 9 (1921–23), 61–67.

8. HVSH, 162; see also PBNE 1:319–20.

9. PVSH 2:53.

Lay patients, monks, and doctors all agreed that the functions of religious healers differed from those of professional *léigi*. Secular physicians
attended cases in which the injury and its cure were singular phenomena,
and in which the patient either became completely well or died soon after
the trauma. Religious healers, on the other hand, ministered to chronic
and degenerative afflictions. As the ninth-century *Vita tripartita* of Pátraic
put it, God had given to the *doctores*, his saints, "the power of curing the
ill, raising the dead, transforming lepers, expelling demons, causing the
blind to see, healing the mute and deaf, and so forth."[10] The saints trans-
ferred this power, immanent in their relics, to the monks.

Significantly, as the hagiographers realized, all of these common but
incurable afflictions directly affected the sufferer's social status and membership in the local community. Long-term physical disabilities, for instance, kept people from performing ordinary jobs and from attending
social gatherings. The early Irish found little use for disabled people in
their pastoral and agriculturally based subsistence economy. The disabled
offered no increase in prestige to a kin-group in the status-oriented societies of barbarian Europe; in fact, they were a burden and shame to
families of fighters and farmers. As Peter Brown has shown of Gallo-
Roman society, people feared the defects that prevented others from hearing and seeing what went on in the Christian world.[11] Only holy men and
women could cure that fear. According to hagiographers, resocializing the
victims of isolation presented no problems for the healer-saints of Ireland.
And, as with peacemaking and other sorts of protection, what the saints
had accomplished in life, they continued to do through their monastic
agents.

Paralysis, blindness, deafness, and muteness were all common in the
vitae, and their saintly cures routine. Molua, for example, cured a man
made immobile by disease simply because he could find no other way to
move the invalid from one place to another.[12] Blindness was frequently
and easily reparable by the saints. Cóemgen cured an artisan of his own
community who had accidentally gouged his eyes while working; Comgall's saliva, dripped in the eyes of a blind man, instantly returned his
vision.[13] Almost endless examples show that deafness and muteness offered no greater challenge to the saints; Cainnech, for instance, cured a

10. VT, 172.
11. Peter Brown, "Relics and Social Status in the Age of Gregory of Tours," in his *Society
and the Holy in Late Antiquity* (Berkeley and Los Angeles, 1982), 244.
12. HVSH, 135; see also HVSH, 355; PBNE 1:189.
13. PVSH 1:241, 2:6.

deaf and mute child left by his parents with the nuns of Cluain Siscnam.[14] Déclán's hagiographer declined to make a full catalogue of such miracles lest, as he put it, "the reader or listeners . . . be depressed with tedium."[15]

The dismay of the early Irish at physical disabilities caused them to fear severe defects in physical appearance. Ugliness was almost as great a debility as a game leg or bad eyesight, especially among the nobility. In the *Vita tripartita*, Pátraic indirectly cured a *mac ndall cláireinech*, a "blind flat-faced boy," when the boy washed his face in water from the well where Pátraic had been baptized.[16] Possibly this hideous defect derived not from some fateful combination of genes, diet, and medical ignorance, but from literary imagination and scribal error; the earliest reference to *cláireinech* or *cláraineeh*, "flat-faced," may have been meant originally as *clairínech*, "cripple."[17] But other, less dubious cases of extraordinary ugliness also point to the Irish revulsion at physical deformity. Áed Dub, the tribal king of the Uí Briúin, heard of Máedóc's reputation as a healer and sought him out in order to obtain a cosmetic cure. The king used a legal technique traditionally employed by powerless men and women against their social superiors: he fasted until Máedóc felt compelled to help him. As a result, the saint transformed Áed Dub (the black) into Áed Finn (the white or fair).[18] Another king, Rónán mac Áeda ua Branáin, considered physical appearance so important that he expelled his queenly wife and their new son and heir because the baby was so loathsomely ugly.[19]

Rónán's son, Áed Dub, and the table-faced boy did not merely offend aesthetically with their features. An elaborate tradition, detailed in legends and poems, had long decreed that physical deformity of any kind, whether disabling or cosmetic, could prevent a man from ruling. Moral and political weakness manifested itself in physical defects. The Irish would not tolerate any feeble, Merovingian-style monarchs who lounged in their horse carts. No warrior was willing to risk following a limping, nearsighted king; no farmer accepted the rule of a man who was an object of scorn and disgust because of his looks. Those who limped or squinted might even lose their rightful inheritance.[20]

14. HVSH, 192–93.
15. PVSH 2:57–58.
16. VT, 8.
17. DIL, 119. See also FO, 222–24; AU, 170.
18. PBNE 1:201–2.
19. PVSH 2:18.
20. VT, 132. For more on the traditions of blemished and unblemished kings, see D. A. Binchy, *Celtic and Anglo-Saxon Kingship* (Oxford, 1970), 10; Binchy, "Bretha Déin Chécht," *Ériu* 20 (1966), 24, 28–30, 34, 42, 44.

The numerous disabled and deformed people in the *vitae* probably did not accurately reflect the number of physically disabled in Irish villages of the ninth century and later. Gerald of Wales reported that he saw an astonishing number of deformed men and women in twelfth-century Ireland, and attributed this to the moral inferiority of the Irish.[21] But beyond the odd annalistic reference to a nobleman who lost an eye in battle and gained the nickname *cáech* (one-eyed), these sorts of people did not appear frequently in the pre-Norman sources.

The lack of specific detail in hagiographic descriptions of paralyzed, mute, deaf, blind, and ugly folk suggests that writers were drawing literary motifs from the New Testament. The disabled were frequently among Christ's patients, and the saints, Irish, British, and Continental, performed almost every cure found in Scripture.[22] The Irish hagiographers were not above using saga motifs, either, as when Máedóc healed a dumb, one-footed, one-armed, one-eyed prince; even one of the most ominous monsters of pagan folklore was an easy patient to a great saint.[23] Yet the hagiographers did not plagiarize randomly; they borrowed only symbols, motifs, and episodes that emphasized the ability of the miracle workers to preserve the community by transforming disabled, immoral outcasts into virtuous, sociable Christians.[24]

Other cases brought to holy healers, such as infertility, carried an equally devastating social stigma, and their cure returned patients to a normal, respectable social life. Nothing was more shameful to a man or woman of high status than the inability to have children. In medieval Welsh tradition, barrenness brought a mighty queen to her knees; childless Irish men and women faced the only slightly less degrading penalty of divorce.[25] Fortunately, besides making the defective whole and the ugly fair, saints could cure sterility and impotence. When a husband and wife were unsuccessful in their attempts to have children, they actively sought the help of the saints by consulting the monks. Máedóc's parents came to Druim

---

21. Gerald of Wales, *The History and Topography of Ireland*, trans. John J. O'Meara (London, 1982), 117–18.

22. Bede, HBE, 3:2, 9, 11–13; 4:10, 14, 31–32; 5:2–6; also his life of Saint Cuthbert, passim; J. Sieber, *Early Byzantine Urban Saints* (Oxford 1977), chap. 5, "Physical Illness and the Healing of the Soul," 82–96.

23. PBNE 1:185.

24. Brown, "Relics and Social Status in the Age of Gregory of Tours," 244. See also Victor Turner, "A Ndembu Doctor in Practice," in Turner, *The Forest of Symbols* (Ithaca, N.Y., 1967), 359–93.

25. Gwynn Jones and Thomas Jones, trans., *The Mabinogion* (London, 1984), 17–19; CIH 1:4–5, 47–48; 2:387–88.

Lethan so that the monks there, encouraged by donations, might pray for them and beg God to give them a child. The Lord obliged, as the couple realized when each had a charming vision: the father-to-be saw a star enter his wife's mouth and she saw a moon enter his.[26]

The saints guarded their prenatal patients from the moment of conception to the birth of the heir. Both male and female saints gained reputations as protectors of pregnant women. Saint Íte, a woman who "succoured many grievous diseases," often helped at birthings.[27] Mochuda relieved a woman of labor pains by handing her an apple to eat, reversing the Old Testament motif.[28] Several of the saints were careful not to cause their mothers any pain as they were born, thus indicating to devotees their power to prevent the distress of other childbearers.[29] These and other saints gave women good reason to approach them, via their monks, for succor in the midst of the perils of childbirth.

Ensuring the safe entry of noble babies into the world, and even bringing them back to it after death, was a specialty of the healer-saints. An appeal to the saints for medical miracles could save an endangered line of succession. The saints performed many resuscitations after the model of Christ, raising decapitated monks and nuns, and even horses and pigs, but they revived many more children, especially only children, than they did farm animals.[30] Adomnán's seventh-century life of Columcille set the hagiographic pattern with the story of how Columcille brought the son of a well-to-do Pict back from "the border between life and death." In an episode more moving than the often bland miracles of later *vitae*, Columcille knelt beside the boy's bier during the funeral rites. Pagan magicians taunted the saint as he prayed, wept, and triumphantly raised the boy to life.[31]

The hagiographers let it be known that the saints cured people from all classes, but were as particularly anxious to protect children of high status as they were to cure the ugliness of their noble fathers. Still, the lower classes also occasionally benefited from the saints' general concern for children. A farmer's wife came wailing to Pátraic that her son had been

---

26. PBNE 1:183, 190; HVSH, 234. See also PVSH 2:54–55, 135.
27. FO, 36; see also PVSH 2:166.
28. PVSH 1:190; see also PVSH 1:4–5.
29. PBNE 1:125–26; PVSH 2:107; see also HVSH, 134, 143.
30. Clerics and animals: PVSH 1:183–84, 201; PBNE 1:107. Children: PVSH 1:181; PBNE 1:184, 185, 191–92; see also PBNE 1:14, 35; HVSH, 391–92, 393; see also HVSH, 212, 337–38, 355.
31. Adomnán, 396–98.

dismembered by pigs, and the saint quickly reassembled the boy.[32] But, except for a few references to poor children, when the hagiographers made special mention of the social status of young patients, they emphasized the saints' care for the nobility.

Christians who heard stories of the saints and saw relics in action learned that only supernatural patronage brought relief from the illnesses of exclusion and ensured the smooth transfer of power from one noble generation to another. No doubt many monks felt the genuine compassion of healers for the patients who sought their help. Yet the religious elite also had a stake in supporting the stability of the social hierarchy, since they sat near the top of it. Disability, illness, and disease destabilized communities and thus, like unruly kings, were enemies of the monks. By assuming the saintly role of healer, the monks sought not only to conform the afflicted but to heal the community of its disorders by asserting control over the composition of the community, its behavior, and its leadership. The saints held such power over the community and were able to pass it on to the monks primarily because of their exclusive control of access to the spiritual world.

Saints, monks, doctors, and lay folk equated outward decay with inward spiritual flaws. Because of their position as intercessors with the sacred, saints and monks were masters of that element in the body which was not physical.[33] Irish doctors conceived of twelve parts of the body as "doors to the soul"; such areas as the temple, the Adam's apple, and the navel were considered the portals out of which, when opened by a wound, the thinking, breathing spirit of a person might escape.[34] Both Irish and Continental monks made the same connection between maladies of body and soul. Columbán, among other authors of penitential tracts, equated sin with disease, and penance with medicine. "For doctors of the body also compound their medicine in diverse kinds," he wrote. "Thus they heal wounds in one manner, sicknesses in another, boils in another, bruises in another, festering sores in another, eye diseases in another, fractures in another, burns in another. So also should spiritual doctors treat with diverse kinds of cures the wounds of souls, their sicknesses, [offenses], pains, ailments, and infirmities."[35]

Monks and their patients believed that demons brought disease to sinners. When Christians contemplated evil, demons stormed the gates to

32. VT, 198.
33. Even secular physicians retained a vestige of priestly status: Binchy, "Bretha Déin Chécht," 6–7.
34. Ibid., 24–25, 51–52.
35. Ludwig Bieler, ed., *The Irish Penitentials* (Dublin, 1975), 98–99; see also 84, 108.

their souls and attacked their bodies. Columcille used prayers to drive off demons carrying iron spits, but they flew on to Eth (Tiree), striking monks there with plague.[36] Berach initiated a practice at Glenn Dá Locha that continued to his hagiographer's day: monks circled the sacred enclosure ringing bells to prevent demons and plague from entering the sacred space.[37] But wily demons evaded the saints; they could so vex a man that he would try to tear himself to pieces, forgetting the body's function as a temple of God.[38] Yet demons brought diseases into the temple only when they found a way into the body already opened to them.

The hagiographers showed that the saints had treated infections of mind and soul in the same way as physical ills. Ciarán fed blackberries to a queen to cure her of an adulterous love from which she was wasting away.[39] Moling tried to cure a mad boy with a prayer and a hot bath.[40] Many more saints healed the rot of madness and possession. The vocabulary of exorcism in the *vitae* borrowed from medicine. Hagiographers used the same words to describe the saints' efforts to save the lunatic as they used for cures of deaf, dumb, and disabled people. Mochuda healed a possessed man, afterward described in the *vitae* as *sanus*.[41]

Like physical disabilities, insanity and possession kept a person from maintaining normal social relationships and prevented his or her full membership in the Christian community. A demented wife in Mac Caírthinn's community was left chained in a secret corner while her husband slept with another woman. After the saint had cured her madness she rejoined her husband, who presumably rejected his lover, and all relationships returned to equilibrium.[42] Causes and effects of spiritual, physical, and social infection were the same and so the means to cure them were identical. The very nature of illness turned holy healers into doctors of the inside and the outside.

The Healing Process

The moral definition of certain illnesses influenced the process through which patients sought cures and monks healed. Because illness spread

36. Adomnán, 480–81.
37. PBNE 1:29.
38. HVSH, 381.
39. Ibid., 350; PBNE 1:107–8. See also PVSH 2:184–85, where rustic Saint Mochua cures the scholarly Saint Colmán Ela of memory loss.
40. HVSH, 206, 355.
41. PVSH 1:179.
42. HVSH, 346.

outward from the soul, patients had to achieve the proper spiritual condition before the saints or their representatives would consider attempting to cure them. First, the patient had to make a decision to seek out a religious healer, usually approaching the saint in a holy place, such as a shrine or church. Next the patient explained the nature of his or her illness to the monks, acknowledging the spiritual weakness that brought it on, then humbly awaited the judgment of the saint, which, if favorable, led to healing. The monks contacted the saints on the patient's behalf, finally accomplishing a cure with specific rituals involving relics and prayers to the saint.[43]

The entire process was ineffective, however, if the patient failed to achieve a state of inner awareness. As Columcille pointed out, only *credentes,* believers, could be cured.[44] A patient who came to a healer without the proper penitential attitude brought himself trouble, such as the king who tried to test Máedóc's medical powers by pretending to be deaf and blind. As soon as he had his servants carry him into Máedóc's presence on a litter, the saint denounced him: "You held your kingdom and lordship," he said, "until you tried to conceal the gifts which God has given you. And since you have lied, you will be as they said until your death."[45]

Yet it was not easy for a sick person to perform the necessary spiritual preparation and become a patient, admitting illness and the need to be healed, since it meant the likely loss of status. The patients themselves have left no personal histories of their descent into illness and, if they were good Christians, their ascent back to health. But other sources show that the patient's position in society became more precarious as his or her illness became public. Kinfolk and other allies determined among themselves just how much to invest in the sick, and whether they would profit more by caring for the victim or by finding a substitute for him or her. Munnu, for example, cured a man who subsequently took the job of another whom the saint allowed to die a natural death.[46] The early Irish sometimes abandoned the replaceable and less valuable members of their society, such as weak infants and the mad and terminal incurables, such as lepers. Even its wounded warriors were only compensated with free health care after a predetermined number of days and the judgment of a professional that the patient would survive.[47] Anyone who contracted a serious

43. Seiber, *Early Byzantine Urban Saints,* 82–96. See also Pierre-André Sigal, *L'homme et le miracle dans la France médiévale (XIe–XIIe siècle)* (Paris, 1985), 29–45.

44. Adomnán, 340.

45. PBNE 1:211.

46. HVSH, 208.

47. Binchy, "Bretha Crólige," 1–77. See also Binchy, "Sick-Maintenance in Irish Law," 82.

disease or suffered a disabling accident faded from the community, drawing back to the place where those born with defects already dwelt.

On the borderline between safe society and a hostile world, many of these marginal characters traveled to monastic communities, where, on another boundary between temporal and eternal worlds, they sought cures. In the presence of God, the saints, and the rest of the community, the monks might rescue a patient from both illness and social death. Hagiographers suggested that ailing outcasts from all classes still came publicly to the saints at their monasteries. A nobleman of Éile journeyed to Saigir, bringing with him his dead son for Ciarán to raise. Ciarán obliged by performing a cross-vigil, that is, by chanting prayers while stretching his arms out rigidly in the form of a cross; the posture was strenuous, but monks could perform it almost as easily as saints. Ciarán's prayer revived the boy and the saint received in return good publicity and extensive endowments.[48]

Outside their sacred enclosures, saints cured before crowds. Mochuda performed a miraculous cure for the household of Cuanu mac Caílchíne, whose daughter had a shriveled hand. Mochuda held out an apple to the child, who automatically reached for it with her useless hand, to the astonishment of all present except Mochuda himself. Such public display benefited the saint while it healed, awed, and humbled the patient and often, as in this case, the audience. Cuanu repaid Mochuda for this particular healing with a subsidiary house of nuns, while the admiring crowd contributed to the saint's reputation as a healer and miracle worker.[49]

The saints supposedly preferred to keep such miracles out of the public eye, out of modesty, but the hagiographers were determined that the marvelous healing techniques of the saints be set down for posterity. Once a leper was too ashamed to approach Saint Comgall openly, but he followed the saint, wiping up holy saliva from where Comgall had drooled on the pavement after a three-day fast. The leper mixed it with water and cured himself. Although Comgall told him to keep the cure a secret, the patient told everyone.[50] Comgall's hagiographer could not resist telling, either; his monastic colleagues were likely to gain business by promoting Comgall's powers. After all, it was not the healer but the patient seeking help who felt the shame of disease or disability; worse, the sufferer was forced to acknowledge his or her defect and beg intercessory help from the monks.

48. PBNE 1:106.
49. PVSH 1:184–85.
50. PVSH 2:7–8.

Although the saints preferred their noble clients to ailing peasants, according to the hagiographers, the nobility and the lowest slave shared the same ambiguous status while awaiting healing inside the monastic enclosure. In Glenn Dá Locha, and probably at other communities, the laity formally shed all social standing and legal rights once they had entered the gates of the enclosure.[51] Even outside the monastic community, in a public gathering, the patient existed in front of the crowd rather than in its midst. The community knew the state of the patient's soul and even his or her true social status by watching to see how the patient interacted with monastic healers. Would the saint acknowledge that the patient had already achieved genuine humility? Would the saint extend the redemptive healing touch? Or would the saint reject the sinful patient and cast him or her back into the depths of moral infection? The decision to heal lay with those who could read the patient's soul and grant him or her access to the saints, and thus to God, the ultimate physician.

The saints could do more than refuse to heal; if provoked, they could even inflict disease and injury upon a deserving patient, like the king who tried to trick Máedóc. In hagiographic examples the monks threatened to imitate the saints by punishing those who refused to recognize their powers, not just to heal but also to keep peace and offer other sorts of protection. Cóemgen's Irish *vita* described four specific diseases—tumors, scrofula, anthrax, and madness—that would afflict anyone who violated Glenn Dá Locha.[52] Other saints went to extremes when kings refused to pay dues, violated sacred space, or broke the peace of God, as many annalistic entries show. The saints could raise patients from the dead, but the monks could condemn landlords and kings and their lineages to illness and extinction.[53] The definition of illness was sometimes as much a political definition as a moral one for the monks, their allies, and their enemies.

Once they had decided to heal deserving patients, the actual techniques of the monks varied. Some brothers cultivated a practical knowledge of medicine; the hagiographers often mentioned the use of milk as a cure for internal disorders, and monks kept gardens in which they presumably grew the herbs valued by *léigi*.[54] But for the shameful illnesses in which they specialized, the monks relied on the ritual use of relics, usually in

51. PBNE 1:161.
52. Ibid., 109.
53. HVSH, 128, 143; PVSH 1:228; 2:18, 134–35; PVNE 1:202, 203, 247–48, 285–86.
54. For the therapeutic use of milk: HVSH, 129, 191; PVSH 1:188, 2:13; PBNE 1:114. For gardens in monasteries: PVSH 1:95–96; 2:9, 77.

sacred places. Thus they healed while they publicly reinforced their saintly inheritance. As Máedóc's hagiographer wrote in the twelfth century, "Although Máedóc passed to heaven he did not cease from his miracles on earth. For by the earth (of his sepulchre), by his clothing, and by his relics were healed blind and deaf and lame and all other diseases."[55]

In the trained hands of the monks, the bones and clothing of the saints worked medical wonders. The *vitae* offered a guide to the use of such relics for healing. Ruadán, for instance, had brought a corpse back to life when he placed its head in his cowl; Columcille's hemline had cured those who touched it.[56] Episodes in the *vitae* showed the saints reluctantly handing on these techniques, along with their clothing, to disciples. Munnu's guest-master stole the saint's cloak and covered a patient with it, so that she immediately arose in perfect health; Molua's *oeconimus* did the same for a plowman.[57] No doubt these episodes substantiated the monks' claims that they could continue to heal with the saints' clothes.

More potent than clothing were the saints' very bones; thus the monks derived their authority to heal from the same source as their power to intercede with God and to sanctify space. At the house-shaped shrines of some saints, such as Saint Crónán, patients fondled the moldering bones in hopes of a cure. But to reach the saint the patients had to gain the monks' permission to enter the sacred space; given their jealous protection of sacred space, the monks probably strictly guided patients' approach.[58] Patients sought to touch some saints' bones more often than others; they revered Saint Martin and his bones, whether in the shrine at Tours or brought home from Gaul, because of his impressive reputation as a healer in his own lifetime.[59] The monks of other saints made more modest and specialized use of their bones, for example, to cure simple headache. Even today, certain cemetery shrines carry placards indicating that a patient can expect relief from a particular illness at the grave of the holy man or woman buried there.[60] Still other saints' bones carried such extensive

55. PBNE 1:189.
56. Ibid., 327; Adomnán, 340.
57. HVSH, 206, 143.
58. Peter Brown, *The Cult of the Saints: Its Rise and Function in Latin Christianity* (Chicago, 1981), 86–105; Ronald C. Finucane, *Miracles and Pilgrims: Popular Beliefs in Medieval England* (Totowa, N.J., 1977), 25–38, 83–99.
59. HVSH 109, 226–27; PVSH 2:60, 136, 254, 263; Clare Stancliffe, *St. Martin and His Hagiographer: History and Miracle in Sulpicius Severus* (Oxford, 1983), 149–249; Aline Rousselle, "Du sanctuaire au thaumaturge: Le guérison en Gaule en IVe siècle," *Annales, E.S.C.* 31 (1976), 1085–1107.
60. HVSH, 173.

guarantees of restored health that abbots were able to take them on circuits, carting elaborate reliquaries from community to community and providing a touch of the bones to diverse patients in return for material dues.[61]

When the bones or rags of the saints were not available, the monks found other ways to transmit the healing power of relics. Water that had bathed the saint's remains helped many sick Christians back into the fold. Columcille himself healed a broken hip by inscribing a blessing on vellum and placing it in a box; when the box was dipped in water, and the water sprinkled on the patient's hip, she was cured.[62] The same method worked with blessed bread, salt, or pebbles dipped in water.[63] Lay people were familiar with this curative method. When Columcille sent a disciple from Í to Ireland with a bit of blessed bread to dunk in water and cure the plague, people flocked to meet the monk, well understanding his purpose.[64]

Later *vitae* also showed that the saints need not have personally blessed or applied the water, so long as the water had somehow touched the saint or, the implication was, the saint's relics. Moling refused to revive a dead child, so its mother wrapped it in her cloak and set it adrift in the river, that perilous boundary between life and death. The infant floated back to shore alive and unharmed, preserved and healed by the water that the saint himself had merely happened to touch.[65] More normally, monks administered the healing water. The monks of Cluain Moccu Nóis brought water blessed by Saint Íte to cure their abbot; Saint Éimín Bán's monks gathered water in his bell to protect patients against any and all diseases.[66] And Déclán left a stone called the *petra Declani* to his monks. His mother had been sitting on it at the time of his birth, and the head of the emerging saint made an impression in the stone, turning it into a bullaun. At the hagiographer's time, the bullaun rested beside the door to the forecourt of Déclán's community, where people came to be healed by the rainwater that filled it.[67]

Blessed water signified cleanliness of body and soul, for its application brought a second baptism to patients. Columcille had both healed and

61. Doherty, "Use of Relics," 96–97.
62. Adomnán, 336–38.
63. Ibid., 338–40, 402.
64. Ibid., 330–36.
65. HVSH, 355.
66. PVSH 2:129–30; Eric Poppe, "A Middle Irish Poem on St. Éimín's Bell," *Celtica* 17 (1985), 65.
67. PVSH 2:35–36.

converted by blessing an evil, disease-giving well controlled by druids; instead of dealing out leprosy and blindness, the Christianized well restored health.[68] Perhaps the episode recorded a pre-Christian healing ritual co-opted by Columcille. But after the early days of Christianity, competitive methods of religious healing with water faded with other pagan practices into semi-religious folk tradition. A spring near Cell Sléibe healed invalids in the twelfth century because Monenna had been accustomed to stand in its icy waters up to her breasts, chanting the psalter, five centuries earlier.[69] Holy fonts and bullauns dedicated to saints remain scattered about the ruined monastic sites of Ireland today, further demonstrating the enduring religious meaning of wells and their curative functions.[70]

Rewards for Healing

Like baptism, a monastic cure marked a patient's permanent conversion. The monks used their healing rituals to create lasting relationships with lay Christians who lived beyond the enclosure. When the monks healed an ailing lay person, they expected the grateful patient to pay a fee, usually in the form of a donation of material goods. But patients also felt greater, less tangible obligations to their protector which the patients of a secular physician never experienced. Possibly for fear of relapse, possibly because the process of inner healing wrought such profound effects, their responsibility to maintain a state of humility extended beyond the period of the cure itself. They felt prolonged behavioral constraints and the need to maintain a certain penitent frame of mind. Moreover, healers and patients could easily extend their relationship when gratitude led patients to become devoted and regular donors to the saint, or when they made repeated requests to the saint's representatives for help with some lingering ailment. To be a patient of the saint was to become a client and a marginal member of the monastic community. When the sick person was already a tenant, a client, or kin of the monks, the role of patient added one more strand to the social web that bound him or her to the saint.

The monks were eager to persuade any patient of the saint to form a permanent clientage relationship, as the *vitae* showed. Many of the de-

---

68. PBNE 1:189; see also Ludwig Bieler, ed., *Patrician Texts on the Book of Armagh* (Dublin, 1979), 142–46, 152–53.
69. USMLS, Conchubranus I, 268; PVSH 1:198.
70. Patrick Logan, *The Holy Wells of Ireland* (Gerrards Cross, 1980), especially 69–88.

mands placed upon patients, as described by hagiographers, sound suspiciously like the dues of formal legal clientage. When patients neglected the obligatory gifts of thanks they were liable to punishment, just as when they missed payments of rents to ecclesiastical landlords. The saints and their monks had a responsibility to heal the lay people who approached them, while those whom they cured were equally obliged to provide material support for holy men and women. The monks relied upon this income almost as much as the dues of their formal clients.

Hagiographers often used the story of a miraculous cure to justify endowments. Munnu got the field upon which he founded Achad Liacc just for curing a rich man's cattle.[71] Others received forts, mills, arable, and monastic settlements for their cures of human patients.[72] The monks, anxious to increase their holdings, tried to encourage further endowments with their hagiographic reports of cures. No other interaction between saints or monks and lay folk occasioned such generous donations.

The monks admitted that payments for healing services were not simple gifts. In the *vitae*, the endowments of kings or nobles symbolized their commitment to enduring relationships with local monastic communities. The patient had already admitted his or her spiritual inferiority by falling ill in the first place. The lay patient's gift to the healer reversed this imbalance in status. The monks then took plenty of opportunities to extend additional healing services, protective blessings, baptisms and burials, and any other requested intercessory services to their lay allies. Monks demanded and received more dues for these services. They asked their clients to supply monasteries with the physical protection and material sustenance that they themselves could not. The monks and their patients could not terminate a relationship while one still owed the other dues or services, nor could they continue a long-term relationship under inequitable terms of exchange. Healers and patients thus constantly augmented their roles, offering each other the dues, gifts, and services of healing, clientage, and tenancy, kinship, and political alliances.

The monks recognized the obligatory nature of the exchanges. Often the original cures provided by saints in the *vitae* were for ailments or disasters that they themselves had inflicted on kings reluctant to enter into permanent relationships. For example, Coirpre, a *"rex iniqus"* (*sic*) acquaintance of Mochuda, saw a third of his army, his wife, and his only son struck dead by lighting. Fearing God's wrath for sins unspecified by the

71. HVSH, 200.
72. Ibid., 128, 143, 166, 392; PVSH 1:184–85, 228; 2:48–49, 113–14; PBNE 1:26–27.

hagiographer, the king went humbly to Mochuda and begged the saint to ease the divine anger. He offered the service of himself and his successors forever should Mochuda raise his wife and child by prayer. Mochuda agreed, but only because the king had been taught awe for God and his religious professionals. The relationship probably represented the tie between Mochuda's community of Lis Mór and local secular patrons of Mochuda's monks, although no details in the *vita* specified which community or noble kin-group was meant.[73] The obligation of the king to begin and to continue in an acceptable exchange relationship with neighboring monks, as well as his acceptance of their spiritual guidance, was evident to the hagiographer. In other *vitae,* people cured or revived by the saints actually gave their lives in thanks and became monks, nuns, clients, or tenants of monastic communities.[74]

Monks felt as great an obligation to heal as lay folk felt to pay for their cures. Saint Brénainn acknowledged such responsibility when he revived a dead man who offered him a gift of land. Brénainn refused payment because he wanted to continue his travels rather than settle in the area: had he accepted the endowment, the saint would have become caught in a cycle of exchanges and never would have found the Isle of the Blessed.[75] On the other hand, a king told Saint Gerald quite bluntly that the saint would gain no land and no honor in his territory unless he raised the king's dead daughter and, what is more, turned her into a son.[76] Less enthusiastic about travel than Brénainn, Gerald performed the double miracle and gained an endowment. Without providing the expected cure and care for the king's royal line, monks had no place and no status.

Everyone in a Christian community took part in the long-term healer-patient relationship. Some witnessed, some helped repay the saint. Even the patient's eventual death did not relieve the debt for the cure; the obligations of those made well by the saints fell upon their descendants. Máedóc raised the son of Coirpre mac Echach; in exchange, the patient's father donated his own service plus that of the healed son and of their descendants forever. Even Coirpre's own clients had to help repay the saint for the cure; every household in the nine *tríchait cét* or cantreds of Airgialla owed a regular monetary due to Máedóc for saving their future lord.[77] Ultimately, sin and disease contaminated everyone; everyone

73. HVSH, 337–38.
74. Ibid., 212, 337–38; PBNE 1:35, 128, 178–79, 184.
75. PBNE 1:48.
76. PVSH 2:109–10.
77. PBNE 1:197–98.

needed to be healed and to pay for the healing. When a nobleman anxiously awaited the safe entry of his child into the world, or when his wife endured pain in her game leg, many people in the patient's social network were liable to participate in the lengthy process of seeking, gaining, and paying for a cure.

For brief moments during the arduous business of healing—the visit to the saint's shrine, viewing or touching relics, undergoing the ritual, hearing the prayers of the monks, and the offer of gifts and dues appropriate to monastic services—the patient and his or her allies approached the potentially miraculous. They shared the sacred space and access to the deity that the monks enjoyed daily, and that only the regular clients and most pious and important allies of the monks gained on a regular basis. Beyond baptism and burial, a trip to the shrine to cure a limp or to ensure a safe pregnancy was probably the most common type of ritual contact with God experienced by the majority of Christians in early medieval Europe. Healing was not simply a functionalist process designed to relieve the patient's pain and increase the monks' property; it was an authentic spiritual encounter.

Some, such as the incurably diseased or disabled, even became semiprofessional religious personnel themselves. They symbolized the sickness that afflicted all, and carried the danger away with them when ejected from the secular community. Lepers, for example, roamed the roads of the *vitae,* wandering everywhere, accepted nowhere except in the sacred space of monastic communities. At Rathan they lived with Saint Mochuda; when Mochuda left the settlement, he took them with him to the monastery of Lis Mór, where they remained "with honor."[78] Similar references to lepers living in other communities showed that they held a privileged position among the monks.[79] When lepers made outrageous demands upon saints and lay folk, both strove to supply what the invalids wanted. They gave the lepers oxen, clothing, and food; Colmán Ela and a humble queen of the Déise even licked their scabby faces and noses.[80]

And as sick people became almost holy, so religious professionals sought to play the patient's role to prove their own holiness. When Máedóc visited Tech Munnu, he healed the resident monk so that they might share a meal with him in the refectory; but when the meal was done, Abbot Munnu politely requested that his brothers be made sick

78. PVSH 1:193–94.
79. HVSH, 238, 358; PBNE 1:216.
80. PVSH 1:38; 2:80–81, 254; PBNE 1:325, 326.

once again, because virtues could best be perfected in the physically weak.[81]

The diseased, the disabled, the sterile, and the mad were in a position to gain spiritually from their physical distress. Although they suffered a temporary loss of status, patients also profited socially in the long run. Rejected by the healthy community, the patient touched what lay beyond: the boundaries of society, the monastery, God. By seeking a cure, the afflicted entered into a series of exchanges with the religious elite that brought their associates into that spiritual relationship, to the ultimate benefit and support of all.

Plague or Peace

In the seventh century, Justinian's plague came to Ireland. According to the *cáin* or law of Éimín Bán, the kings of Leinster approached Saint Éimín as patients and penitents, offering to sacrifice themselves to the monastic life in order to prevent widespread death. Evil had invaded every soul and the result was plague; for as Bran ua Fáeláin put it, "We have been under God's displeasure hitherto in everything we have engaged upon. It is right now that we should for the terms of our lives be praying together against the plague."[82] When they consulted Éimín, the professional prayer-maker and healer took over. He, in turn, prayed to God in an all-night fasting session, and announced his decision the next morning: One monk would die for each chief of Leinster. Such desperate measures were necessary to stave off the plague, to protect society, and to prevent dishonor to the religious professionals who had agreed to heal the Christians of Leinster.

Éimín Bán would not accept lands or material goods for his healing services, as he told Bran, "lest (anyone) say that it was as a bargain we prayed God to protect you."[83] But he did accept two considerable favors from Bran and the nobles. First and most important, the chiefs were to fear God, love him, and behave like proper Christian rulers. Second, they were to free Éimín's community of Ros Glais and its dependencies of all secular dues and rents, and to enforce legal decisions favorable to the community. They were also to protect the monastery and its lands from

81. PBNE 1:218–19.
82. O. J. Bergin et al., eds., *Anecdota from Irish Manuscripts*, vol. 1 (Dublin, 1907), 40; Charles Plummer, trans., "Cáin Éimíne Báin," *Ériu* 4 (1910), 41.
83. Bergin, *Anecdota from Irish Manuscripts*, 1:42; Plummer, "Cáin Eimíne Báin," 43.

violation. If Bran ever neglected his half of the bargain, Éimín's monks—
the ones who were left—swore to use his bell in a ritual curse against the
king, signaling the end of the saint's healing, blessing, and protection.
And in return for the king's services, Éimín promised Bran that his line
would prosper and its members would be buried in the saint's cemetery.[84]

All the humble king and his chiefs asked was preventive medicine; all
the saint demanded in return was a guarantee of the social order endorsed
by the monks. Significantly, the entire arrangement was recorded in a *cáin*,
a law usually set down jointly by clerics and kings to protect the helpless
and promote general order. Thus was the monk's function as *pius medicus*
intimately linked to his role as peacemaker. Simply by being the men who
owned the relics, and thus controlled access to the saints and to God, the
monks were able to offer themselves as doctors of the body, healers of the
soul, and protectors of society. As masters of inner health and outer order,
they were the only ones able to preserve both, as well as maintaining the
conceptual link between them. Epidemics such as plague provided the
most severe test of their powers ever faced by the holy healers. According
to the *Cáin Éimíne Báin,* the monks passed the test and claimed a legiti-
macy for their healing services that would last for centuries.

When plague threatened the inhabitants of all Ireland again in 1096, a
retribution for the legendary Irish complicity in the death of Saint John
the Baptist, the only solution was public prayer, fasting, and extensive
offerings. An excerpt from the *Annals of the Four Masters* for that year
illustrates well the plight of lay folk and monks:

> The festival of John fell on Friday this year; the men of Ireland were seized
> with great fear in consequence and the resolution adopted by the clergy of
> Ireland, with the successor of Patrick [at their head], to protect them against
> the pestilence which had been predicted to them at a remote period, was to
> command all in general to observe abstinence, from Wednesday till Sunday,
> every month, and to fast [on one meal] every day till the end of a year, except
> on Sundays, solemnities, and great festivals; and they also made alms and
> many offering to God.[85]

Should the members of the lay community refuse either to consult their
own consciences or to reward their professional healers, the dire results
were well publicized. As the introduction to the *Senchus Mór* collection of

84. Plummer, "Cáin Éimíne Báin," 45.
85. FM 1:952.

laws warned, the neglect of regular ecclesiastical dues and tithes led to plague, war, and the dissolution of fundamental social ties.[86]

When health and order were threatened, the monks restored them, for a price: material dues and, more important, acceptance of their roles as creators and guardians of the Christian community. The monks preferred to heal nobles and royalty, preserving the health of the upper classes in order to maintain the status quo; but their ultimate, admirable aim was to involve every Christian in the lengthy process of healing and purification. For lay folk, the disease-infected, accident-ridden, violent world about them often offered no alternative but to accept the monastic invitation to a lifelong exchange relationship. But the benefits and obligations were mutual. Monks were dependent upon the fears and needs of their patients and allies. When the cure did not work or the peace did not hold, the monks were liable to be left, as Saint Gerald almost was, with no land, no honor, and no protection.

86. Binchy, CIH 2:350–52; ALI 1:51.

CHAPTER SEVEN

The Politics of
Hospitality

IRISH MONKS RELIED ON MEMBERS OF THEIR OWN FAMILIAE FOR companionship, counting on tenants, clients, and noble allies to protect and maintain them. But occasionally monks also sought contact with other communities of their own kind. Monks came together to exchange blessings and curses, gifts and favors, but above all hospitality. In an age when effective communication always took place face to face, the practice of hospitality provided both the context and the vocabulary for contact among the religious elite.

At least, this was how hagiographers expressed the ties between monastic communities. One claimed that the Irish "strove to provide hospitality more than any other nation."[1] All of them depicted saints and monks journeying on an endless round of visits to each other. Sometimes characters in the *vitae* came together for nothing more than a friendly encounter, a good chat, or a shared meal.[2] More often monastic travelers in these episodes arrived loaded with the baggage of ulterior motives, and the monks who welcomed them were also ready to play a complicated game of guests and hosts.

A late life of Columcille, extant only in a sixteenth-century manuscript but derived from earlier sources, told a story of one such meaningful visit. Columcille went to see Saint Molaise of Daim Inis who, for reasons unexplained, disliked his guest. Molaise sent Columcille to a dormitory for the night, leaving him nothing to eat but salt pork, even though it was

1. HVSH, 256.
2. PVSH 1:146, 2:11.

[194]

a fast day according to the church calendar. If Columcille refused to eat he brought insult and disgrace to his host; if he ate the pork, he broke the period of abstinence. So the polite guest ate just a little of the meat. Meanwhile, Molaise himself dined on eggs and bread. In the morning, both saints went to church for the hours and mass. Molaise asked his guest why he had eaten meat in a period of fasting. "It would be improper for me," said Columcille, "to refuse whatever meat you sent, for fear of shaming you if I went without food in your house, since I did not know whether you had anything else but meat for me." Columcille suggested that they put eggs and pork on the altar and pray to God to reveal whether either of them had broken the fast. When they did so, a cock arose out of one of the eggs and began to crow loudly and embarrassingly, while the salt pork turned into an acorn. This showed, as the hagiographer suggested, that God decided in favor of Columcille against Molaise and saved him from the other's enmity.[3]

None of this surprised the hagiographer, who took for granted the miracle of crowing eggs and acorns, as well as Molaise's hostility toward Columcille. This hagiographer, like all of the others, assumed that saints and their communities of monks were sometimes friendly, sometimes in conflict. Saints performed rituals for each other, instructed and advised each other, and offered each other choice *loca* on which to build enclosures. They also competed for donations, cursed each other's clients, and contested with miracles.[4] The hagiographers used these stories of personal encounters between individual saints and monks to describe the entire dynamic cycle of feud and alliance among monastic communities.[5]

3. Manus O'Donnell, *Betha Colaim Chille*, ed. A. O'Kelleher and G. Schoepperle (Urbana, Ill., 1918), 118–21.

4. Friendship, services, instruction, *loca*: HVSH, 100, 101, 107–8, 111, 118–19, 124, 125, 140, 153, 198, 256, 353, 364, 409; PBNE 1:247–48, 2:240–41; PVSH 1:67–68, 161, 198, 199, 214, 268, 358. For a competitive miracles contest caused by a religious debate: HVSH, 207.

5. Historians have suggested a pattern for the alliances and antagonisms of monastic communities. They have argued for monastic *paruchiae*, or networks of communities, spread across Ireland. The monks of each community in a *paruchia* obeyed their own abbot, but together many *familiae* made up a larger *familia, paruchia, muinter,* league, or federation—depending upon the historian's presentation of the network—under the leadership of a mother monastery. Most often, the bones of the patron saint lay at the mother house, and that was also where the *comarbae* or heir of the saint ruled as abbot. The monks of the lesser communities in the *paruchia* owed allegiance and dues to the leader; in return, they received the protection of the saint and some reflection of the prestige of the mother community. *Paruchiae* were the closest that the rural Irish could come to a national church organization, for without cities there could be no episcopal sees, and without sees there could be no dioceses, as even the British had. See Kenney, *Sources,* 292–99; Kathleen Hughes, *The Church in Early Irish Society* (London, 1966), 57–90; Donnchadh Ó Corráin, "Early Irish Churches:

Analysis of how the hagiographers told these stories, rather than the stories' actual contents, helps explain monastic networks. For instance, Pátraic, Columcille, Brigit, and a few others were strong characters in all *vitae;* this suggests that hagiographers acknowledged these saints as spiritual authorities and that the communities of these saints remained more powerful than others. But the hagiographers were less explicit about how the second-string communities related to even smaller, less prominent communities, or how exactly the monks of these monasteries actually interacted. To discover that, we must probe the narrative structure of saintly interactions more deeply, for the hagiographers expressed all kinds of relations between saints and their communities with the vocabulary of hospitality.

The Obligations of Hospitality

Hospitality has long been a legal obligation and a social duty in Ireland. Secular jurists formalized their own rich vocabulary of guests and hosts, from which the hagiographers freely borrowed.

The eighth-century tract *Críth Gablach* set forth the traveler's rights of hospitality at the house of a specially appointed class of freeman, the *briugu*. This well-to-do farmer had to feed and shelter anyone off the road, no matter how many times the guest demanded hospitality of him.[6] Such legally mandated hospitality included both the entertainment of stray guests and the formal feasting of overlords. Native lawyers used the concept to express many of the dues and obligations between patrons and clients, both secular and ecclesiastical. The legal text *Córus Béscnai,* for

---

Some Aspects of Organisation," in Ó Córrain, ed., *Irish Antiquity* (Cork, 1980), 327–41.

A few scholars have suggested that a variety of ecclesiastical establishments may have existed that did not fit into this neat hierarchical scheme; by and large, however, the *paruchiae* still dominate historiography. See Richard Sharpe, "Some Problems Concerning the Organization of the Church in Early Medieval Ireland," *Peritia* 3 (1984), 230–70; see also Vincent Hurley's description of different kinds of ecclesiastical settlements in the southwest of Ireland, "Additions to the Map of Monastic Ireland: The Southwest," JCHAS 85 (1980), 52–65.

The hagiographers themselves presented a more ambiguous picture of ecclesiastical organization, although they mentioned the existence of networks, which they sometimes called *paruchiae*. See, e.g., Ludwig Bieler, ed., *Patrician Texts in the Book of Armagh* (Dublin, 1979), 123–67; also 167–91; PVSH 2:7.

6. Fergus Kelly, *A Guide to Early Irish Law* (Dublin, 1988), 36–38; E. Mac Neill, "The Ancient Law of Status or Franchise," PRIA 36 C (1923), 276; Katherine Simms, "Guesting and Feasting in Gaelic Ireland," JRSAI 108 (1978), 68–69.

instance, describes clientage exchanges in terms of "fled deoda fled doéna fled demanda," the godly feast, the human feast, and the demon feast. The first category included the feasts that monastic lords gave for their clients, and vice versa; the second described different feasts provided by secular lords and their clients; and the third described the formal entertainment of itinerants, including druids, satirists, prostitutes, and professional farters. As in other barbarian societies, where wealth consisted of land and animals but rarely money, the provision of shelter and sustenance became a convenient way to pay all kinds of dues.[7]

But hospitality meant more than just obligatory feasting and guesting: It lay at the core of a code of honorable behavior. The composers of saga considered inhospitality a serious taboo; the "six sons of Dishonour" included "Niggardliness and Refusal and Denial, Hardness and Rigour and Rapacity."[8] They understood that only those who gave hospitality received it when they themselves needed it. Hospitality assured travelers food, shelter from wind and rain, and protection, but also obligated them to entertain wayfarers who knocked on their own doors. The system functioned to protect all against the hostilities of the wilderness through which they passed. At the same time, the exchange of food, shelter, and plain good company reinforced existing social ties and created new alliances.

In their own theoretical statements about hospitality, monastic scholars modified legal concepts to include a moral imperative. According to the monks, every guest represented Christ; penitentialists laid down severe penalties for those who refused hospitality to traveling clerics.[9] The hagiographers used the examples of the saints to teach the importance of hospitality to monks and lay people alike. Adomnán wrote didactic episodes in which guests frequently disturbed Columcille while he sat writing or reading in his little hut by the gate of Í. Even though they caused work and trouble for the monks, Columcille always insisted that visitors be rowed over to his island. Whether a guest lacked *subtilis sensus* or was a *hospes molestus,* he still deserved what the monks could provide.[10]

Many other examples existed to teach Christians that hospitality was

7. CIH 2:524–26; Simms, "Guesting and Feasting," 67–100; Kelly, *Guide to Early Irish Law,* 139–40.

8. Whitely Stokes, "The Wooing of Luaine and Death of Athirne," *Révue Celtique* 24 (1903), 281; Simms, "Guesting and Feasting," 68.

9. Kuno Meyer, "The Duties of a Husbandman," *Ériu* 2 (1905), 172–73; Simms, "Guesting and Feasting," 68; Ludwig Bieler, ed., *The Irish Penitentials* (Dublin, 1975), 172.

10. Adomnán, 258, 270–72, 296–98.

both a virtue and an obligation.[11] Cóemgen abandoned his ascetic retreat to build Glenn Dá Locha; he built it on the accessible floor of the valley specifically for the purpose of feeding "companies and strangers and guests and pilgrims." Glenn Dá Locha became a place "where no one was refused entertainment / For the grace of the lord is there."[12] Máedóc's twelfth-century hagiographer knew that his saint provided the most effective lesson of all, for Máedóc was seven times more hospitable even than Columcille. He was endowed with the best of virtues: "hospitality unstinted for everyone."[13] He was able to carry out his hospitable impulses thanks to abundant donations to his churches. The saint passed his prosperity and the virtue of hospitality to successive *comarbai*.[14] Monks who could not match his boundless hospitality received the saint's censure, for he "gave refusal to the inhospitable, / Such as no one ever gave before."[15]

To emphasize the importance of hospitality, the hagiographers used both the negative lesson of inhospitality and the virtuous example of the saints.[16] No genuine saint actually neglected his or her duties of hospitality, but others of the religious elite dared to do so and were punished for it. Ruadán's cook spilled the milk every day for a week and was at his wit's end about the waste when Ruadán revealed the problem: the cook had been showing disrespect to guests and paupers by not feeding them properly, prompting demons to smash his milk buckets with iron hammers.[17] Hagiographers also stressed the shortcomings of lay people in order to teach hospitality. Ciarán of Cluain Moccu Nóis met a man on the road who had stopped at the house of the saint's mother but had received no hospitality there. Enraged, the saint charged into his mother's kitchen and hurled all the food onto the ground, reviling her for her lack of charity.[18] The practice of hospitality came of virtue and bestowed saintliness; its neglect caused harm, even disaster.[19]

But the hagiographers admitted that hospitality could also bring disadvantages to those who practiced it and accepted it, as well as those who neglected it. Because its provision was obligatory, hosts suffered the rude and sometimes excessive demands of guests. Anyone who enjoyed a repu-

11. PVSH 2:133; HVSH, 143.
12. PBNE 1:131, 125.
13. Ibid., 279–82; cf. 194.
14. Ibid., 261–64.
15. Ibid., 200; 2:194.
16. PVSH 1:194.
17. PBNE 1:318–19.
18. PVSH 1:204.
19. Adomnán, 366–68.

tation as a reliable host was liable to be eaten out of house and home by unscrupulous visitors.[20] When paupers or lepers arrived at monastery gates and demanded luxury, even the saints hastened to obey.[21] But guests faced potential dangers, too, from hosts who betrayed the trust so integral to successful hospitality. Writers of Irish saga repeated the motif of warriors lured to a feast only to have their hosts trap them in the banqueting house and attempt to burn them to death.[22] Both hosts and guests could abuse hospitality for their own ends. In the famous twelfth-century tale "Fled Bricrenn" (The Feast of Bricriu), the title character invited the champions of his province to a feast simply in order to foment competition and disrupt amiable relationships between the Ulstermen and women. He was repaid for his trouble by ruin and disgrace, but not before he had insulted and infuriated all of his noble guests.[23]

While the obligations and dangers of hospitality were the same for lay folk and monks, monastic hospitality differed from traditional secular hospitality in several important ways. In the first place, its practice was obligatory for all Christians, especially the religious elite. But while providing for travelers and paupers was a duty, monks claimed that their communities were exempt (in Irish, *saer*) from many of the legal dues of hospitality imposed upon lay people.[24] Hagiographers objected to guesting inflicted by secular lords on monastic communities. According to Molua's hagiographer, when Brandub mac Echach had the nerve to demand dinner for four hundred warriors on a Sunday, Molua was so outraged that he caused the king to choke on his food until the Sabbath was over. Brandub ended up offering gifts to the saint, instead of the other way around.[25] Fínán's hagiographer told how nine dubious pilgrims arrived at Cenn Éitig to demand food. The monks were at mass and could not be disturbed, so the nine knocked the meager offerings of the porter

20. Simms, "Guesting and Feasting," 69; Whitely Stokes, "Esnada Tige Buchet," *Révue Celtique* 25 (1904), 21. See also Seán Ó Coileáin, ed. and trans., "Ceisneamh Inghine Ghuil," Houghton Library MS 3 (1970), manuscript translation in the collection of the Robinson Library, Harvard University, esp. 8–9; D. A. Binchy, ed., *Críth Gablach* (Dublin, 1941), 24; Simms, "Guesting and Feasting," 74.

21. HVSH, 115; PVSH 1:38; 2:80–81, 254; PBNE 1:178–79.

22. Eleanor Knott, ed., *Togail Bruidne Da Derga* (Dublin, 1975); synopsis in Myles Dillon, *Early Irish Literature* (Chicago, 1948), 25–31.

23. George Henderson, ed., *Fled Bricrenn* (London, 1899); synopsis in Dillon, *Early Irish Literature*, 19–24.

24. Wasserschleben, *Collectio,* 78–79; Gearóid Mac Niocaill, ed., *Notitiae as Leabhar Cheanannais 1033–1161* (Cló Moirainn, 1961), 34–36; AU, 258; Seán Mac Airt, ed., *The Annals of Inisfallen* (Dublin, 1951), 108.

25. HVSH, 142.

from his hands. The saint gained revenge when all nine died before the day was out. The hagiographer wished to teach a harsh lesson to those who might demand hospitality dues of Fínán's successors.[26]

The legal complexities were more explicitly evident in a later life of Máedóc. By the twelfth century, secular leaders had come to ignore many of the traditional bans on demanding legal hospitality from clerics, although monks continued to claim exemption, as the *vitae* showed. During the abbacy of Conchobar mac Máelbrigte ua Faircellaig at the community of Druim Lethan, the king of Bréifne came with thirteen nobles and more than three hundred fighting men to seek hospitality. Although such provision was "a hard bargain" and "ignoble" for the *comarbae*, he fed and sheltered them for three nights. But when the king, Fergal ua Rúairc, insisted that Drium Lethan maintain two hundred of his men for a year, the *comarbae* refused, on the ground that it was improper to quarter men on a monastic community; such obligatory long-term hospitality was not required of monks for soldiers. Ua Rúairc responded by taking all the community's cattle, but Máedóc and his heir eventually punished the criminals: the saint deprived Ua Rúairc of his kingship and prevented his sons from succeeding to office.[27] As the hagiographer warned, "Maircc dan comharsa naomh garcc": "Woe to him whose neighbor is an angry saint."[28]

Monks continued to escape other customary controls on hospitality between the ninth and twelfth centuries. Traditionally, to refuse shelter and entertainment to wayfarers of the learned and artisan classes brought great dishonor. Men of the *áes dána* could ruin the reputation of an inhospitable household with the satire they noised abroad. But the saints were impervious to the demands of artists and craftsmen; most hagiographers portrayed these travelers as parasites and sinners.[29] Cóemgen dealt with ornery, rejected musicians by turning their instruments to stone.[30] Pátraic tried to accommodate some *áes cerda*, artistic folk, but the monks with whom he was staying refused to provide a crumb of food for such people.[31] The people of the "demon feast," as the *Córus Béscnai* put

26. Ibid., 154–55.
27. PBNE 1:287–89, 2:278–81. Note that Máedóc's hagiographer condemned Ua Rúiarc for forcing hospitality from the monks, but praised him less than truthfully as king of Temair and even implied that Ua Rúairc resided at Temair.
28. PBNE 1:286; 2:278; see also 1:315, 2:306–7.
29. HVSH, 117.
30. PBNE 1:129; cf. 1:163.
31. VT, 202. But see O'Donnell, *Betha Colaim Chille*, 70–71 (sec. 80), where Columcille treats poets with some generosity.

it, deserved no refection within consecrated walls. Such episodes described an unchanging monastic attitude toward the most ancient of customary hospitality dues when levied on religious communities. Neither traditional demands nor traditional enforcements affected monks. They alone chose the people for whom they would provide food and shelter.

The monks also chose their hosts, avoiding the hospitality of lay people when they could, because such outsiders did not understand the protocol of monastic hospitality. Rarely did lay folk welcome their monastic guests properly.[32] Some hid inside their houses hoping that visiting monks would become discouraged and go away. Columcille's visit to his later ally, Brude, found him knocking on locked doors. He made the sign of the cross, the gates swung open, and the guest strolled in to meet his astonished host.[33] When monks dispensed hospitality or accepted it from lay people, they did so on their own exclusive terms. The few laymen who provided acceptable hospitality were highly devout, observing religious taboos and behaving like monks. Hagiographers portrayed them as Christians who built chapels in their farm enclosures and demonstrated such unmistakable piety that miracles took place in their homes.[34] But in general, sheltering with the laity was more trouble than pleasure for monastic travelers in the *vitae;* such stays proved full of dangers and insults. Even outside their enclosures, the religious elite remained aware of the social split between themselves and their lay associates. It was better for a monk to sleep in the open and go hungry than risk compromising his professional status by staying with ordinary sinners.

When monks agreed to host lay guests at their monasteries, the travelers had to assume the semisacred status of pilgrims, patients, or clients. Lay guests usually stayed within the monastic enclosure, but always in a building set apart for them, the *hospitium* or *tech n-oíged*. The guesthouse was a particularly prominent building in the monks' settlements, set apart from the sacred centers and from more profane spaces, sometimes even within its own special enclosure. At Ard Macha the guesthouse had a separate *lis n-oíged* or enclosure.[35] At the community of Luchen and Odran, the *eleemosinarium* and *hospitium* actually stood outside the enclosure.[36] The guesthouse was not just a roof over the heads of travelers. It symbolized monastic charity and the social cooperation that lay behind all hospitality.

32. PVSH 2:50–51.
33. Adomnán, 408; see also HVSH, 129; PBNE 1:27–28.
34. PVSH 2:133–34, 169.
35. AU, 450; see also 432.
36. PVSH 1:209.

It also bestowed spiritual benefits on the monks and their guests, thus justifying a certain amount of importance in the architectural layout. Just to build a guesthouse was a religious act, as Brénainn demonstrated when he raised a *tech n-oíged* in Dub Dáire "in honor of his Lord."[37] To some, the site of the guesthouse was more important than the location of the brothers' own quarters. Molua led his senior monks onto their new property at Cluain Ferta and asked them blandly where he should build the abbot's house; when the monks selected the choicest site, Molua announced that the guesthouse would stand there. When the brothers chose the best-looking fields, Molua took them to endow the *hospitium*.[38]

Inside the guesthouse, people of all sorts mixed under the sacred protection of the monks and their saints.[39] The distinction between travelers needing temporary support and the chronic migrant poor disappeared in the house whose overseer was "the man who had the care of guests and paupers."[40] The *hospitium*, isolated from both the secular world and the hosts' own living spaces, temporarily conferred a certain marginality on all who entered it.

Just as lay folk had to practice near-monastic piety to receive ecclesiastics as guests, so they had to assume semimonastic status in the guesthouse. But churchmen and women preferred to give and receive hospitality among their own kind. The exclusiveness of monastic hospitality suggests that it had purposes other than the simple provision of shelter and charity.

Rituals of Hospitality

Monks used the exchanges of hospitality among themselves primarily to act out and affirm their place in the hierarchy of monastic communities. Important *familiae* with prestigious patrons played hosts and guests to maintain positions of power; weaker and poorer monks used hospitality to press demands on more powerful communities. In the *vitae*, the major characters in hospitable exchanges, as well as the exchanges themselves, had a symbolic function. But hospitality involved more than ritualistic role playing. In real life, hospitality must have been both event and symbol for the monks who gave it, took it, and witnessed it.

37. PBNE 1:81; 2:79.
38. HVSH, 138.
39. Ibid., 135.
40. Ibid., 216.

Set apart intentionally from traditional, legal practices, monastic hospitality observed its own rules. Hospitality inside the enclosure usually consisted of formal welcome, the offer of shelter and a bath, participation in Christian rituals, and eating. Hagiographers used each of these steps in the process of hospitality to describe relationships among saints and among their communities. Within this context, the rituals surrounding eating became the focus of interactions among members of different monastic communities.

The formal greetings with which monks welcomed their brothers revealed that some guests were not as prestigious as others. Adomnán wrote that when Columcille visited his community at Dermag the monks came running from the surrounding fields to fetch all their brothers. They assembled with their abbot, Ailither, outside the walls of their enclosure to greet the saint with awe and joy, as they would an angel. They bowed their faces to the earth and then crowded around to kiss him. But the welcome was reserved for the elite; the monks sheltered Columcille with branches to keep off the lay rabble as they led the saint inside the walls. They all proceeded to the church, singing hymns of jubilation.[41] No such elaborate reception awaited the deacon Nessán when he visited Ailbe. The saint's *minister hospitum* conducted the cleric to the guesthouse immediately, without any offer of ritual washing or a meeting with the abbot himself. Ailbe remained at prayer for hours until the guest-master came to remind him of his guest's presence.[42] Whatever the specific purposes of these hagiographic episodes the differences between the treatment of Columcille by his own subordinates and the welcome accorded Nessán by a famous abbot derived from their differences in status.

The hagiographers made it clear that monks should calculate the style of their hospitality to fit the rank of the guest and his or her community. For instance, the monks of Clúain Moccu Nóis prepared such a banquet for Columcille's visit that its fame spread throughout the neighborhood. But as a monk boasted to the visitor, that banquet was hardly comparable to a fantastic feast that the monks had thrown many years previously, complete with wine imported from Gaul.[43]

Columcille and others, such as Pátraic, Brigit, and Ciarán, gained and lost status as the leading guests of the *vitae*. Sometimes Brigit was the

41. Adomnán, 214–16.
42. HVSH, 129–30.
43. PVSH 1:214. Plummer notes that the episode was clearly conflated from two originals, one in which Ciarán turned water to wine, and one in which wine was bought from merchants.

honored guest of a community, sometimes Pátraic, sometimes another saint. It depended upon all the complex relationships of the hagiographer and his community to the communities at Cell Dara, Ard Macha, Cluain Moccu Nóis, and elsewhere. But visits from these major ecclesiastical figures were always more significant occasions for celebration than those of unknown monks. Like modern society hostesses, abbots and abbesses gained status from such famous visitors. Since the hagiographers also endowed their heroes with the traditional power of the host over the guest, based on the guest's obligation to repay hospitality, important guests enhanced the status of hosts in two ways: Hosts gained by receiving major saints as guests, and by placing such guests temporarily in a position inferior to their own.

Monks could use the formal process of welcome to make a more refined statement about the differences in status between guest and host. Gestures of greeting carried subtle but familiar connotations for hagiographers and their readers. The lavish welcome accorded Columcille by the monks at Dermag, with their humble bows to the ground, signified his Christlike command over them. But a simple kiss represented equitable affection between host and guest. When either host or guest refused the kiss, he or she threatened the amicable relationship. A nun wrongly accused of theft in a community that hosted Íte refused to offer a kiss to the saint, for fear of Íte's reaction; but Íte reassured the woman of their friendship and affirmed her innocence.[44] With the kiss, host and guest demonstrated mutual trust.

Ritual bathing also carried a clear message about the relationships between monks. Although the order of the various elements of welcome sometimes differed by community, bathing was among the first concerns of guest and host, for both practical and political reasons. According to his Latin *vita*, when Bairre arrived at the enclosure of Colingus, a cleric much senior to himself, the host's guest-master greeted him: "Loose your shoes from your feet so that they may be washed with water, and then bathe." Bairre objected, wanting to greet his host. But Colingus ordered Bairre to be bathed and to return home; he himself would visit in seven days' time to take the humbler role of guest to Bairre's host.[45] In the Irish life of Bairre, the saint journeyed to visit Eolang, who prepared a bath and food for his guest. Bairre wanted to talk first and bathe second, but his host insisted on a different order of things.[46] Whatever the practical

44. PVSH 2:125–26.
45. PVSH 1:72–73.
46. PBNE 1:18–19; see also PVSH 1:116–17.

comforts of the tub, the offer of a bath implied a need for purification. Eolang made this clear by refusing to speak to Bairre before the saint had washed the filth of the *saeculum* from his body. Only after a monk had made himself fit for the sacred space could he indulge in discussion and relaxation with his hosts. Until then he temporarily lost full membership in the religious elite, and with it the right to socialize with his brothers. Guest and host conducted elaborate negotiations over the timing of the bath, over who won the ritual honor of washing whose feet, and other details of the tub. These bargains revealed an awareness of status differences and the need to act them out.

Participation of host and guest in formal Christian rituals also offered the monks a chance to acknowledge the hierarchy among those present. When four saints visited Columcille, the guests, Comgall, Cainnech, Brénainn, and Cormac, politely picked their host to sing the mass. Entering the church after the Gospel reading, Brénainn knew that they had chosen correctly when a fireball and a column of fire arose from Columcille's head. Such a sign could only mean that their host was the most holy among the assembled saints.[47] In other *vitae,* saints sometimes visited each other with the primary purpose of co-participation in Christian rituals. They negotiated the status of host and guest with their choice of a leader for the ritual. But the competition did not always yield an obvious result.

When saints visited dependent communities or their monastic subordinates in order to perform sacraments or other rituals for them, the status of guest and host remained stable. In fact, hagiographers used these anecdotes to reaffirm the inequitable tie between two monasteries. For example, when Ciarán made his yearly Christmas visit to Ros mBendchuir to say mass for his foster mother, no one questioned their relationship. Although Ciarán had once been subordinate to his nanny, he was now an adult male, an important founder of monasteries, and a miracle worker; he was doing the old nun a favor. He even traveled impossible distances in incredible time to honor the woman who had raised him.[48] His hagiographer signaled a similar relationship between Saigir and Ros mBendchuir; whatever the political connections between the two houses, neither doubted which house was more prestigious.

However, other monks of seemingly equal status used their roles in formal rituals to renegotiate their relationships. A charming incident in

47. Adomnán, 500.
48. PVSH 1:226–27.

Mochóemóc's *vita* began with Cainnech, that absentminded saint, forgetting a promise to visit Mochóemóc. He remembered at the last minute, began running, and accomplished a day's journey in miraculous time. Mochóemóc suggested that Cainnech say mass while he himself performed the host's duties, such as ordering a bath and gathering the brothers for dinner. Cainnech humbly refused the privilege, in effect denying further obligation to his host. But at dinner a miracle put Cainnech in his proper place: the bread bled until Cainnech agreed to sing mass.[49] Mochóemóc gained status from this interaction, because he controlled the assignment of ritual roles and because God confirmed his choice with a rather threatening miracle. If Mochóemóc's status had been uncertain to readers before this anecdote, the saint's negotiations with Cainnech established the exact status of the actors and the houses that they represented.

At times, the hagiographers used their descriptions of rituals to claim the greater sanctity of host over guest and over the rest of his or her fellow saints. A visiting hermit, Critán, verified Comgall's precedence among the saints when he watched angels attend him during the paschal Eucharist.[50] But guests also turned tables on hosts, depending on whose *vita* contained the episode. Often in such stories the host was spiritually or physically weaker than the guest, and needed his or her help. According to Mochóemóc's hagiographer, when the saint called on Comgall only the guest was able to interpret his host's dream of demons. Then Mochóemóc ordered an exorcism that Comgall could not accomplish for himself.[51] Other saintly guests came for a last visit to their saintly brothers and sisters about to die; the protocol of who visited and buried whom was another marker of relative status of the saints and their communities.[52] When Colmán Ela's end approached, all the saints in the neighborhood came to do him honor as guests at his deathbed.[53]

The complicated relations between visiting saints and their hosts show that monks considered themselves to be participants in a constantly renegotiated network of relationships rather than part of a static hierarchy of communities. Characters in the *vitae* used gestures of greeting, purification, and co-participation in Christian rituals to represent their positions in relation to other monks and nuns. No doubt hagiographic relationships of guest and host mirrored interactions among monks of the

49. PVSH 2:177; see also PVSH 1:141–42.
50. PVSH 2:9.
51. Ibid., 167–68.
52. Ibid., 120.
53. HVSH, 224.

ninth to twelfth centuries. These literary relationships demonstrated that all communities participated in a network of social relations, with some houses at the center and some at the periphery; but some monastic communities were not satisfied with their places in the network, while others supported the status quo. The malcontents did not sit passively in their unimportant communities, paying obeisance and dues to the great saints and their abbatial heirs. They worked to improve the position of their own communities in the hierarchy. To achieve this, they resorted to the politics of food.

The Politics of Food

In hagiographic accounts, one element of formal hospitality was most useful for a community actively seeking to improve its place in the network: eating. Eating or not eating together dominated hospitable interactions; no other activity was as important in the game of monastic hospitality. The offer, acceptance or rejection, and consumption of food and drink provided monks of different communities with many opportunities for renegotiating their relationships with each other and for trying to alter those relationships. The hagiographers described in detail how saints and other monks used the politics of food to ally with, compete with, and manipulate each other.

Only control of the production and distribution of food allowed control of its consumption. Those who obtained a surplus were able to accept some foods and reject others; and only the wealthy and powerful gained a surplus in the Irish subsistence economy. At certain times, everyone necessarily fasted. The economy lacked the sophistication to cope with environmental emergencies such as bad harvests, when peasant, monk, and lord all went hungry. But in good times, secular leaders exercised their privilege to eat luxury foods, favoring roasted meats and imported drink. Monks and nuns, on the other hand, traditionally asserted their identity by rejecting certain foods, thus practicing an abstinence that marked them as defectors from the indulgent classes.

At the very least, then, food and its consumption or rejection provided the monks with another means of identifying themselves as better than and apart from the laity, whether at home or in public. Within the monastery, the monks ate together but without other company, except occasional important guests. When outsiders joined the monks at their table, it was often an occasion for relaxing monastic discipline and eating like lay

[207]

people.[54] However, guests were usually monks or nuns from other communities who appreciated the attempt to eat only spiritually acceptable foods. Rulemakers attempted to establish a standard diet for all monks and their guests. In the sixth century, Columbán laid out strict guidelines as to what his followers should eat, and when. He counseled a sparse diet, for he saw food as necessary only because "we must go forward daily, toil daily, and daily read."[55]

In later centuries, the monks defined their special diet negatively: they specified foods that they would not eat and meals that they missed. Some of their dietary restrictions grew from earlier rules for all Christians, from the days when laymen and women needed to differentiate their food from that of pagans. Seventh and eighth-century canons reflected Christian taboos derived mostly from Leviticus, possibly influenced by observation of heathen custom. Horseflesh was forbidden, as was anything upon which dogs had been feeding, or that had been contaminated by animals or birds.[56] Carrion, or anything that fed on carrion or that had tasted human flesh, was also taboo. Drinking blood, sperm, or urine was intolerable.[57]

Meat was the most important item missing from the monastic diet. Haunches of beef and sides of pork were the basis of a noble warriors' feast, but the monks insisted that they themselves ate only bread, vegetables, and dairy products. Archaeological evidence shows, however, that monks were known to consume a variety of meats. At Í, for example, the monks fed very well on mutton, beef, goat, pork, domestic fowl of several kinds, fish, shellfish, dolphins, whales, and seals; since many of the last were old, very young, wounded, or beached, it seems that anything the monks could catch was fair game for their table.[58] But, according to hagiographers, other monastic leaders found meat so abhorrent that when they faced a plate of mutton or bacon for dinner, they miraculously changed the meat into bread, fish, or other more suitable dishes.[59]

Monks set themselves apart further by classing with these forbidden foods anything touched by an ordinary lay person; thus, commensality, or

---

54. Ibid., 197; Adomnán, 258–60, 488–50.
55. G. S. M. Walker, ed., *Sancti Columbani Opera* (Dublin, 1957), 125–27.
56. Bieler, *Penitentials,* 160–63.
57. Ibid., 160–63, 216.
58. R. Reece, "Recent Work on Iona," *Scottish Archaeological Forum* 5 (1973), 42–44; PBNE 1:105–6; Aline Rousselle, "Abstinence et continence dans les monastères. . . ," in *Hommage à André Dupont* (Montpellier, 1974), 239–54.
59. HVSH, 213; PBNE 1:326; PVSH 1:299–30.

avoidance of it, also helped churchmen and women define themselves. Penitentialists frowned on eating in the same house as a laic.[60] Certainly, a lay person was not to feed him or herself near sacred spaces, a crime that brought heavy penances to the secular offender.[61] In fact, even gifts of provisions from outsiders were untouchable in the eyes of some monks. Cóemgen, for instance, kept a sharp eye on some local women who tried to give alms of soft cheeses, the sensual "wet food" of the laity, to his monks laboring in a back pasture. Genuine Christian ascetics restricted themselves to raw foods; Cóemgen delivered the hungry monks of Glenn Dá Locha from the temptation of processed food by turning the cheeses into stones.[62]

Monks were also not supposed to eat as much as lay folk. The gluttony that caused a monk to steal food was a grievous offense that could result in his ejection from his community.[63] Excessive eating and drinking were serious sins, and penalties for overindulgence were much harsher for monks and nuns than for ordinary men and women.[64] Fasting, the refusal of a noncleric's meals, was a regular feature of the monastic ritual program. As penance, the monks denied themselves food when they acted too much like laymen. For example, the penitentials imposed fasts as punishment when monks lusted after virgins or after each other.[65]

In spite of such formal prohibitions, the brothers did not starve, by any means. Stories of Egyptian fathers who fled on the meager fruits of the desert found few parallels in Irish literature. Even hermits in the woods consumed a bounty of fruits and nuts.[66] Perhaps the early penitentials lost force in later centuries. As Ryan pointed out, the *vitae* showed monks taking an absolute delight in drinking.[67] Monenna's community of nuns at Cell Sléibe considered it a great miracle when the saint's successor, Derlaisre, turned water to beer in honor of an episcopal visit. As Conchubranus primly put it, guest and hostesses "were rendered so merry that if the bishop had not stopped them almost all would have become drunk."[68]

60. Bieler, *Penitentials,* 162.
61. Ibid., 104.
62. PBNE I:166; Bieler, *Penitentials,* 184; Wasserschleben, *Collectio,* 34; Rouselle, "Abstinence et continence"; John Ryan, *Irish Monasticism: Origins and Early Development* (Dublin, 1931), 391.
63. Bieler, *Penitentials,* 112; HVSH, 360.
64. Ibid., 110–12.
65. Ibid., 112–14, 126–28.
66. Gerard Murphy, *Early Irish Lyrics* (Oxford, 1956), 14.
67. Ryan, *Irish Monasticism,* 38.
68. USMLS, Conchubranus III, 448–49.

Although some saints argued over the relative merits, or demerits, of beer, the monks regularly drank it with meals.[69]

Some saints held out for a harsh and nonalcoholic diet.[70] These monks' regulation of their diet sprang not merely from the need for self-definition, but also from a basic ascetic impulse: the denial of self and body. The refusal to eat certain foods, at certain times, with certain people brought spiritual purity to fleshbound holy men and women. The Neoplatonic concept lurking behind early Christian asceticism revealed itself in the fasts of Irish saints. One of Cóemgen's most impressive displays of sanctity was his diet of water and grasses. Comgall was so firm in his rejection of hunger and body that he imposed fasts upon himself and his surviving monks even after several of them starved to death. Their triumph over the body was also a triumph over the disorderly *saeculum*, with its lay sinners and multivarious temptations.[71]

The saints were ascetic paradigms for monks who strove to conquer their own bodies with self-imposed fasts. Just as feeding—on the Eucharist, on restricted diets, on Christian feast days—allowed the monks to identify themselves collectively as Christians and as the religious elite, so fasting enabled them to achieve personal grace. And just as their battles against political disorder and bad kings helped bring peace to Irish society, so their fight against hunger induced God to send prosperity and abundance to the rest of society. Fasting and feeding were part of the same process in barbarian Europe; when one person ate less, someone else could eat more.[72]

In the monastic communities of early Ireland, the fast of the monks produced food for their guests. In the specific context of hospitality, the monks' ascetic ideals influenced their notions of commensality and collective identity. Sometimes this allowed them to open their larders and hearts to brothers from other communities. But often, according to the hagiographers, the monks' regulation of their diets became a sophisticated tactic in interpersonal and intercommunity relations. Monks competed with their bellies in hospitable contests of fasting and feeding.

69. Gwynn and Purton, "Monastery of Tallaght," 129–30.

70. Ibid., 129, 132, 135; HVSH, 147.

71. HVSH, 364; PBNE 1:156; PVSH 2:119. For a female equivalent, see PVSH 2:6–7, 10–11. See also Caroline Bynum, *Holy Feast and Holy Fast: The Religious Significance of Food to Medieval Women* (Berkeley and Los Angeles, 1982), 31–40. Here Bynum elegantly outlines the fundamental Christian connection between the asceticism of the few and the prosperity of the many, which is assumed in my own argument.

72. Bynum, *Holy Feast and Holy Fast*, 31–40.

The hagiographers never described fasting hosts without including feasting guests in the same episode. The poet who so praised Máedóc for being more hospitable than Columcille also lauded the saint for fasting each night until everyone else in the community had eaten.[73] Although the saint provided bountiful hospitality for all, he gave himself only one small measure of grain each day.[74] Fasting was an inherently holy act, but the hagiographers suggested that the faster acquired greater sanctity when others around him or her ate their fill. Moling ate nothing unless he had guests: "The most holy priest Moling used to await pilgrims, that they might eat with him. In fact, the holy bishop always wanted to dine with them in imitation of Christ. And he used to fast every day except Sundays and high feast days, until sunset, unless guests or pilgrims arrived."[75] Abundance was the natural result of Moling's abstinence; only the charitable hunger of an ascetic could persuade God to help feed the needy warfarer. The fasting host gained both status and grace by supplying his or her guests with sustenance. In such a situation, the host not only controlled his or her own consumption, but also assumed some control over the guest whom he or she fed as well.

The hagiographers described more extreme cases in which monastic hosts prepared feasts for their guests while their own communities suffered chronic hunger. Again and again in the lives, the monastery's *oeconimus* asked his abbot a question like the one Máedóc's monk put to him: "Today we have only a small jar of milk and a bit of butter. Is it to be distributed among the brothers or the guests?"[76] In this particular episode, Máedóc's community, like many in the *vitae*, fasted because it had no choice; the land upon which the monks lived, and which so grudgingly yielded a living to them, added a dangerously regular hunger to their lives. Máedóc's communities at Druim Lethan and Ferna Mór were successful enough to feel hunger pangs only rarely, in times of general distress. But the situation appeared often enough in the saints' lives to suggest that small communities frequently lacked sufficient food. Yet, in spite of such hardship—in fact, because of it—the hungry hosts never ceased to provide for their guests.

Poverty-stricken abbots relied on God's recognition of their own ascetic devotion when confronted by hungry visitors. Comgall solved the prob-

73. PBNE 1:279–80.
74. Ibid., 282–83.
75. PVSH 2:197.
76. HVSH, 243.

lem of what to serve Columcille by praying for fish, which obligingly followed an angel to shore and presented themselves as dinner.[77] Crónán faced a harried cellarer, frantic over the arrival of Mochóemóc and 120 of his companions when the community had only a little flour, a small jar of butter, and a little venison. Crónán blessed the dishes and ordered his monks to prepare for their guests. With God's aid, enough food appeared to feed all the guests and the entire host community, so that the brothers spent the greater part of the night eating and making merry. When a new recruit complained that the early morning offices were obviously going to be neglected, Crónán scolded him: "Brother, Christ is sheltered in the person of the guest. Indeed, we are obliged to rejoice and feast at the coming of Christ. But if you had not complained, angels of God would have prayed in our places this night."[78] Crónán's community could feast with their guests and even neglect a monk's first duty, prayer, while they played host to other churchmen; but afterward, they awakened to the regular duties of another hungry day.

The problem of what to eat also revealed the greater sanctity of the host and his or her power over guests. Saints often turned unacceptable foods into respectable suppers for discriminating visitors. For instance, Ciarán encountered the old problem of how to find food for visiting saints and their retinues, when the two Brénainns came to call. All he had in the monastery was a little pork fat, hardly saintly fare. He turned the fat to manna and water to wine to satisfy his guests. When an *athláech* dared complain about feeding ecclesiastical visitors food that was formerly meat, the saint responded, "not from revenge but from prophecy," that the convert would shed his monastic robes, eat meat, and wind up in hell, after being decapitated.[79] The obligations of hospitality for both guest and host were more important than ordinary dietary restrictions. If other adult recruits or nuns objected to eating meat with guests, even if there was no other food in the community, God or the saints severely punished them.[80]

In the hagiographic context of monastic hospitality, guests could not use the same techniques as their hosts to demonstrate their abundance of grace and protect themselves against manipulation. Since their hosts' fasts actually provided for guests, but never the other way around, guests could

77. PVSH 2:16; see also HVSH, 345, 398; PVSH 2:79, 255.
78. HVSH, 278.
79. Ibid., 352–53.
80. Ibid., 143, 367; PVSH 1:229–30.

not fully control their own consumption or their own bodies. Indeed, the only choice guests had was whether to visit in the first place. But since monastic business forced monks to visit one another, the acceptance of hospitality became an obvious necessity.

Still, monks and nuns found gifts of thanks an appropriate way to satisfy an obligation to a host and even to reassert their status in the game of hospitality. Columcille left gifts at Berach's community after stopping there, including a multitude of blessings and a gospel written by himself; such a relic was valuable to the community because it added to their spiritual prestige and brought in pilgrims.[81] Cainnech came closest to providing for his hosts while playing the guest: he preached and prophesied at Bennchor that Comgall's community there would no longer have cause to sorrow, but would thenceforth prosper.[82]

Visitors who neglected a gift of thanks were guilty of a social blunder and faced a continued obligation to their hosts. This left them in an uncomfortably inferior social and spiritual position to their hosts. Sometimes God helped unprepared guests out of such a mess. Saint Daig stayed with the sons of Luigne and the nun Riceille, but when mealtime arrived he realized that he had no gift to present; he prayed to God and was relieved to see gold fall from heaven. He gave it to his hosts to buy a field.[83] Gifts to their hosts allowed guests some defenses against hosts' use of hospitality in the status struggle. Yet ultimately the monk who produced and offered the food while rejecting it himself controlled the relationship.

Troscud

The fast for spiritual gains, called in Irish *aíne* (from Latin *ieiunium*), was similar to another kind of fast, called *troscud* in the laws, in which one person fasted directly against another. Monastic leaders used this competitive fasting technique directly against other monks and nuns, against laics, and even against God himself. The saints and their monks drew on both these traditions of fasting when they needed to shift their position from weaker to stronger partner in a social relationship. Hagiographic stories of saints fasting for a specific purpose generally represented some

81. PBNE 1:39; see also HVSH, 117, 143.
82. HVSH, 186.
83. Ibid., 313.

achievement for their communities within the larger network of monasteries.

Troscud was a practice known to many Indo-European cultures; a similar custom existed as early as the seventh century B.C. in India.[84] The version described in the Irish laws allows an ordinary man to fast against a person of higher social status when all other means of bringing him to justice have failed. Originally, the suitor was prepared to fast until his death on the doorstep of his superior brought shame and pollution to the household. By the eighth century, when scholars had recorded the laws, the archaic practice had become a ritual fast of one day to alert the community to the suitor's claims. The debtor was obliged to counterfast or to accept arbitration of the faster's claims.[85]

Historians have emphasized the differences between the concept of *troscud* and the spiritual fast, *aíne,* but the Irish monks did not distinguish so sharply between the two.[86] Personal spiritual advancement was bound up with social gains for the entire monastic community; spiritual superiority brought political leadership to the monks of early Ireland, as well as more extensive patronage from secular leaders and the rest of the laity. Thus, in the hagiographic context, hospitality contests of feasting and fasting reverberated with connotations of *troscud.* In the *vitae,* monks blatantly practiced both to improve the status of their communities.

Troscud was the weak man's ploy. Monks used a ritual fast against individuals or communities with more power than their own in order to obtain favors or patronage. They also fasted against those who insulted them or did them injustices. Although the subjects of their fasting were occasionally lay people, the monks frequently fasted against other religious professionals and even against God, the ultimate, ubiquitous host of every monastic community. Only when their own kin, clients, and local allies failed to bring monks support and protection did they turn to ritual fasting.

---

84. D. A. Binchy, "Irish History and Irish Law," *Studia Hibernica* 15 (1975), 25–27; Binchy, "A Pre-Christian Survival in Medieval Irish Hagiography," in Dorothy Whitelock et al., eds., *Ireland in Early Medieval Europe* (Cambridge, 1982), 165–78; F. Robinson, "Notes on the Irish Practice of Fasting as a Means of Distraint," in *Putnam Anniversary Volume* (Cedar Rapids, Ia., 1909), 567–83; Whitely Stokes, "Sitting Dharna," *The Academy* 38 (1885), 169.

85. Binchy, "Irish History and Irish Law," 22. For successful cases of *troscud,* see Robinson, "Notes on the Irish Practice of Fasting," 572–73.

86. Binchy was adamant that the existence of two different terms for fasting, one Christian and one derived from Indo-European tradition, proved that their functions and meanings were completely different, suggesting that the literary popularity of monastic fasting could "stem from the folk memory of a distant age when the druids used to employ tactics similar to those of the protesting Brahmins." Binchy, "Irish History and Irish Law," 26–27; cf. Ryan, *Irish Monasticism,* 391.

Several saints fasted against God to obtain more favors for their monasteries than he had bestowed on other communities. One of the most famous incidents of saintly *troscud* was Pátraic's fast against God recorded in the *Vita tripartita*. For forty days Pátraic remained at Cruachán Aigle, refusing all food. God sent an angelic negotiator to the saint, to deny his demands and to order him off his fast, but Pátraic persisted. God sent blackbirds to harass the saint, but Pátraic sang maledictive psalms at them and rang his bell to drive them away. Finally, God instructed the angel to concede Pátraic's demands, beginning with his request to be able personally to save souls. Pátraic bargained hard for extras, like the promise that no Saxons would ever dwell in Ireland. All his demands were granted, and as the hagiographers pointed out, the result was that God admired Pátraic more than any other saint.[87]

The forty-day fast was a creation of the ninth-century hagiographer; earlier lives of the saint contained no bargaining for divine patronage.[88] But the scene was no secular corruption of a spiritual fast by the tradition of *troscud*, as some historians have claimed.[89] The hagiographer placed Pátraic's fast securely in a spiritual context. The writer compared the saint to Moses and assumed that a forty-day fast endowed Pátraic with extraordinary grace. Like all fasting, this *troscud* brought Patraic enhanced spiritual status in the eyes of his patron, God. It also brought an abundance of collective gains to Ard Macha. This was the twofold purpose of Pátraic's *troscud*.

The *Vita tripartita* episode provided the model for similar hagiographic accounts. The saints' demands were calculated to make themselves better patrons of their monks and their lay allies, and to increase the status of their communities in the network of monastic relations.[90] Énda, for example, was provoked by the spirit of monastic competition with one of his monastic guests to fast against God. When Ciarán finally left Ára, Énda watched his own angelic companion depart with his visitor. Énda fasted and prayed until another angel came to discover the cause. Énda demanded his angel back, but the messenger was stern: the angel would remain with Ciarán. Énda would not give up his fast until God compensated his insult with three boons: Those buried in Ára would reach heaven, lay people would call on Énda rather than other saints in times of trouble, and Énda would sit at the right hand of God before other saints

87. VT, 112–30.
88. Bieler, *Patrician Texts*, 152.
89. Binchy, "Irish History and Irish Law," 26.
90. PBNE 1:222–23, 127–28.

on Judgment Day.[91] God had favored Ciarán over Énda, and the latter's only recourse to improved patronage and equal standing was to fast against the deity.

But the targets of most saintly fasts were ordinary men who had insulted the faster or had committed injustices. Sometimes the offenders were lay people. Pátraic, for example, fasted against a slaveowner to obtain the release of mistreated servants.[92] Others fasted outside the forts of kings to force them to give up prisoners, stop extorting dues from clients, or even offer endowments.[93] Mochuda's hagiographer recommended fasting against clients who refused to pay proper dues.[94]

But almost as frequently the saints fasted against each other, often within the context of monastic hospitality, in order to alter their relationships. The effect was to place an even greater obligation on the guest than simple hospitality did; the shame of eating the angry host's food while the host intentionally fasted against him was too great for most guests to bear. Munnu, with one of the nastiest tempers in early Irish monastic society, refused to eat if any of his guests said a disrespectful word to him.[95] Other monks took such insults even more seriously, and provoked even more profound shame in their guests. Ciarán's hagiographer placed great symbolic importance on Saigir's paschal fire, as we have seen; when a visitor from Cluain Moccu Nóis extinguished it, Ciarán predicted with vengeance in his mind that the boy would die the next day for his sacrilege. But when the novice's abbot, Ciarán of Cluain, came to visit, he sat down at the table and announced: "I will not eat now in this place until my boy, who was killed here yesterday, comes to me alive."[96] Ciarán of Cluain had arrived specifically to right the wrong done to his community. The senior Ciarán of Saigir admitted to him, "We know why you have come, and so God will raise that one for us." The boy was revived, everyone ate, and Ciarán of Cluain, called significantly *iunior Kyranus* by the hagiographer, humbly accepted Ciarán senior's blessing before going home. In the weaker position, his only option had been fasting against the more powerful saint, who had suffered an insult but had revenged it with unjust harshness. Ciarán of Cluain took temporary control of the rela-

91. PVSH 2:73–74.
92. VT, 218.
93. PVSH 2:18; VT, 419; Standish O'Grady, ed., *Silva Gadelica* (London, 1892), 1:66; Robinson, "Notes on the Practice of Fasting," 574, 581.
94. PBNE 1:309.
95. HVSH, 209.
96. PVSH 1:231.

tionship until he had shamed his host into righting the wrong; then he reverted to his position of junior.[97]

The shaming technique did not always succeed. Monks on the island of Ára fasted against Saint Énda in an attempt to change their relationships. According to the hagiographer, the monks contended for their own pieces of the island in order to set up independent hermitages; they did not want to form a community, but argued among themselves in order to establish some sort of hierarchy of hermitages. Énda made trouble by demanding an entire half of the island. The others fasted for a few days against God until an angel brought gospels and a reliquary to Énda, proving him first in teaching and ministry. The others accepted the angelic arbitration and acknowledged Énda's higher spiritual status by granting him half of the island.[98]

After fasting, Énda's colleagues had no other means of appeal. Neither did Ciarán of Cluain, or Munnu, or any of the other saints who fasted against each other, against God, or against lay people. In secular life they might take up arms against each other; they might persuade their secular allies to prosecute those who offended their patron saints or trespassed on their property or authority. But if they wanted to maintain intercommunity relations, the monks had to resort to the peaceable rituals of hospitality, particularly feasting and fasting, in order to preserve their status in monastic society and gain reparation for insults and injustices.

In fact, hagiographers were aware that their brothers used the same fasting techniques quite openly to improve their places in the monastic network, even when no provocation had been offered. Ciarán of Saigir supposedly lived only thirty-three years because Ireland's other saints fasted for his death. The others feared, as the commentator on *Félire Óenguso* put it, that "the whole of Ireland would have been his had not that been done."[99] The saintly abbots were worried that Ciarán's community at Saigir would gather all the endowments and donations in Ireland because of their patron's great sanctity. The jealous deed, along with sending Columcille into exile and expelling Mochuda from Rathan, constituted what Ciarán's hagiographer labeled the "three bad stories of the saints of Ireland."[100] Yet at the same time that the other churchmen attacked one of their own, they demonstrated their own solidarity by banding together against Ciarán.

97. Ibid., 229–30.
98. Ibid., 2:68.
99. FO, 204–5.
100. Ibid., 204.

Mochuda's hagiographer provided the most elaborate and revealing story of just and unjust uses of hospitality, and of the religious elite in competitive action against another monk.[101] A dispute between Mochuda and the monks of northern Ireland began to simmer when they visited him at his community. They had all assembled at Mag Léna, near Dermag in Offaly, to fast together in order that God might reveal to them the identity of a murderer. This admirable use of ritual fasting brought the desired results, for the murderer was caught. Mochuda invited the companies from Cluain Iraird, Dermag, and Cluain Moccu Nóis back to his house at Rathan for feasting and entertainment. But at the sight of Rathan, jealousy seized the other monks, "for the number of the monks, the excellence of the monastery, Rahen, for the richness of their food and clothing, and for the excellence of the clerk himself; for he was a man with the grace of God."[102] The hagiographer neglected to mention that regional loyalties added a further point of contention: Unlike all the other monastic leaders assembled at Rathan, Mochuda was not a member of a noble northern family, but a southerner of the Ciarraige Luachra from Munster.[103]

After the visiting monks had stuffed themselves with food they returned to their quarters, only to hear the refection bell ringing to announce a meal. They assumed that they themselves had eaten everything in the settlement, and that nothing could be left for Rathan's monks; thus the bell ringing must be mere boastfulness on their host's part. One of them went into the refectory, claiming to have left his knife in the hall. The spy was astonished when he saw the abundance of food before the monks. Mochuda found him out and cursed him with hunger for himself and his successors as vice-abbots at Cluain Moccu Nóis.

Then the competition became even more serious. Mochuda's guests broke more rules of hospitality by turning on their host and ordering him out of Rathan. "Quit the residence in which you are," they said, "and leave Leth Cuinn [the northern half of Ireland] to Finnian and to Columcille and to Ciarán the carpenter's son."[104] But Mochuda would not allow other monks to promote their communities to the detriment of his own. He refused to budge until kings or bishops, secular authorities within the political order established by monks, forced him out.

101. The fullest and most entertaining account is a twelfth-century or later text in PBNE 1:300–311; the lives of Mochuda give much briefer versions: ibid., 298; PVSH 1:190–94.
102. PBNE 1:301, 2:292.
103. Ibid., 1:291.
104. Ibid., 1:302, 2:292–93.

The northern monks eventually won the conflict, although not before Mochuda had successfully inflicted curses on many of them. Those of the north who pitied Mochuda received his blessing. Those who attacked him suffered loss of their authority, mockery among other monks, disaffection of their congregations, disobedience of their clients, the degeneration of rules for their monks, chaos in their schools, dissension among their elders—all indications of weak and unsupported monastic leadership—along with cold and hunger for their communities, and even hell.

The means by which the monks chose the individual who actually expelled Mochuda revealed the hierarchical relationships among them. First, they cast lots among the major communities of Finnian, Ciarán, and Columcille. Then they cast lots among the monasteries with alliances to Ciarán's settlement at Cluain Moccu Nóis; when the choice fell upon Cell Achaid Drumfata, they cast lots among the various local churches subordinate to that community, and the loser was Cluain Congusa. The *airchinnech* of that church faced the wrath of Mochuda.[105]

Eventually Mochuda settled at the even greater *locus* of Lis Mór, although monastic scholars at Rathan coopted his tradition and kept Mochuda as their patron.[106] But as one poet put the words into Mochuda's mouth,

> We loved Rathan of the saints,
> For we made (there) a noble abode;
> We did not love being chased out of it,
> The change is sad, not joyful.[107]

Mochuda's troubles were clearly the result of monastic competition, but it all began when he invited them home to dinner.

The hagiographers and their brothers were aware of the jealousies that sabotaged relations between communities. Some were critical of the abuse of hospitality and the failures of monastic networks. The twelfth-century author of *Aislinge Meic Conglinne* used a marvelous vocabulary of gluttony, ripe with references to *troscud* and *aíne,* to express his criticism. The problems of the scholar-monk Mac Conglinne began when the monks of Corcach denied him proper hospitality. When Mac Conglinne refused to eat their paltry offerings and instead satirized the monks, they tried to

---

105. Ibid., 1:304.
106. Ibid., 1:313–14.
107. Ibid., 1:313, 2:304, modified translation.

drown him, starve him, and crucify him. They almost succeeded in executing him, except that Mac Conglinne had a miraculous vision of a land of food, where houses were made of bacon and cheese, and forests of carrots and leeks. The monks of Corcach released Mac Conglinne so that he might relate his vision to the king of Munster, who was possessed by a demon of hunger. The king fasted with Mac Conglinne for three nights, not only to exorcise his demon, but so that Mac Conglinne might be protected from the maledictions of the monks of Corcach. Eventually, Mac Conglinne's fasting and vision saved him from the disaster that originated in the monastic politics of food.[108] The author of the tale managed to mock the false asceticism and uncharity of the Corcach monks, as well as the loose morals and gluttony of Mac Conglinne. To the *Aislinge*'s author, neither the manipulations of host nor the countermanipulations of guest were justifiable. He saw that, although useful in controlling the hostility between monastic communities, both fasting and feasting were dangerous tools of monastic competition and sometimes the actual source of conflict. Both guesting and hosting earned his censure.

Ultimately, all monks, whether hosts or guests, knew that they had to preserve the monastic hierarchy. They realized that they were more like each other than they were like their closest kin, their clients, or their secular allies. They shared mentalities, goals, and similar daily experiences. Even though monks exploited relations among their communities in order to improve their own positions within the network, they also joined together to control those inside the network who threatened the network itself, as Mochuda's Rathan threatened the other communities of northern Ireland with dominance. Mochuda caused trouble when he retaliated and cursed Cluain Moccu Nóis for inhospitality, but all the other saints of Ireland worked together to counteract his curse.[109] Monks also used the techniques that they perfected against one another to protect themselves against injustices perpetrated by outsiders. Such a combined effort at ritual manipulation could conquer pagans and heretics, humble the king of Temair, and even kill two thirds of Ireland's population.[110] Indeed, the monks were strongest when they fasted together. They forgot their internal differences when enemies disrupted the sociopolitical order so dear to them, and when they fought as one they were formidable.[111]

108. Kuno Meyer, ed., *Aislinge meic Conglinne* (London, 1892).
109. PBNE 1:180–82.
110. FO, 118; PVSH 2:245–49, 112–13.
111. Monks used other means besides hospitality to cement alliances between themselves and to protect monastic communities. See HVSH, 246, 270, 271, 272, 353; PBNE 1:247; PVSH 2:72.

Despite their recognized need for intercommunity alliances, however, each monastery ultimately had to fend for itself. Every settlement existed, like Clochar and Ard Macha, near enough to other communities for visiting and yet not near enough for familiarity and identity of self-interests.[112] A community relied first on its own members, its clients, and its lay allies. It looked to other communities of its own kind for occasional friendship, for scholarly and religious exchanges, and in times of crisis. But relations among monastic communities remained an uneasy combination of alliances and competition. One *paruchia* was always struggling for dominance over another; one community was always pursuing grievances, seeking restitution for insults, or trying to alter its position in the hierarchy of communities. As the hagiographers showed, no better method served the monks than the rituals of feasting and fasting, which allowed the network to shift a bit here and there and yet remain intact. No monk really needed a sword to fight his brothers, for in the difficult contest between host and guest, the one who controlled his hunger won the battle.

112. VT, 176.

CHAPTER EIGHT

Exile and Pilgrimage

M ONKS SPENT THEIR ENTIRE LIVES LEARNING HOW TO PROTECT themselves and their allies in a world full of dangers. Yet despite— or possibly because of—their unceasing efforts to wall out the world, the most profound expression of monastic spirituality was to sever all social ties and march out of the gates of the sacred enclosure into the wilderness, never looking back. Irishmen became famous for the self-imposed exiles and pilgrimages that took them far from the security of home. The greatest heroes of Irish monasticism were vagrants: Pátraic, Brénainn, Columcille, Columbán. As Saint Columbán pointed out, life itself was a roadway that led to eternity. As long as monks perceived the world beyond the enclosure as hostile to survival, they dreamed of taking that roadway through the desert.

Although famous, the exiles were few; most monks stayed safely at home. Only saints and saintly monks survived voluntary exile. This was because only saints needed no shelter, food, or human companionship. Saints were impervious to the human weaknesses that made ordinary men and women vulnerable to the environment's hostilities. Their vision extended beyond the intimate local landscape to encompass the whole world in a glance. Saints stopped the rain and snow, produced good crops, conquered distance and time by flying in their chariots. They calmed the waves, tamed beasts and brigands, and subdued demons. Armed with such powers, the saints took on the wilderness, with all its physical dangers and its temptations to the soul, and they triumphed. Pátraic left home to convert a foreign nation. Brénainn sailed safely past monsters, demons, and treasures. Columbán and Columcille built prosperous monastic communities in faraway lands.

Although some monks attempted to follow in the footsteps of saintly exiles, not all clerics approved of exile, and a few even frowned upon pilgrimage. The hagiographers betrayed conflicting attitudes toward holy exile, some of them praising it, some criticizing it with almost Benedictine severity as a destabilizing influence. By the ninth century, when the *vitae* were taking shape, changes in the environment and politics of Europe and Britain had already curtailed Irish exile abroad. In Ireland, the population and settlement of the land and the monks' attempt to promote sociopolitical order restricted the search of exiles for solitary refuge. Piety more often manifested itself in pilgrimage, a controlled and temporary kind of exile that benefited the entire community, and thus won general approval, than in permanent wandering.

Holy Exile

Throughout the Middle Ages, particularly from the sixth century through the ninth, Irish monks deliberately left their homes, kinfolk, and allies to seek sanctity in foreign wastes. They devoutly believed that their deaths in the wasteland would demonstrate God's judgment on a sinner, but that their survival would bring spiritual rewards beyond anything they could find at home.

Some historians have attributed the fervor of Irish exiles to genetically inspired wanderlust that drove them to row restlessly away from their rainy island.[1] But the explanation lies more surely in less racist and more complex influences, in particular the development of forced exile as a punishment for the society's worst crimes. Law-abiders condemned criminals to the wilderness for two reasons. First, the legal system and its extralegal supports left no alternative. Because kinship and clientage were so important to the cohesion of communities, the Irish believed that crimes against kin or lord were the most harmful. Although monks and kings worked to impose royal judicial authority upon communities, kin

---

1. Walafrid Strabo, "Vita Galli," in MGH SS. Rer. Merov. 4:336; G. S. M. Walker, ed., *Sancti Columbani Opera* (Dublin, 1970), xvii–xviii; John T. McNeill, *The Celtic Churches* (Chicago, 1974), 156. See Kathleen Hughes's important article "The Changing Theory and Practice of Irish Pilgrimage," *Journal of Ecclesiastical History* 11 (1960), 143–51. Hughes argues that the influence of Anglo-Saxon monks and Carolingian reformers put a stop to Irish pilgrimage abroad, at least as it was practiced by Columbán and others before the ninth century; at home in Ireland, Viking raids ended the monastic practice of voluntary exile on coastal islands off Ireland. She suggests that monks substituted pilgrimage to Rome and voyage tales for permanent exile. However, Hughes neglects the importance of domestic pilgrimage among both the elite and the lower classes.

relationships and lordship still often provided the most effective authority for controlling local crime; thus, the only possible punishment for an offender was to cut him off from the sustaining ties of his allies. A man accused of killing a blood relative or foster relation, betraying his lord, incest, or any other injury to his close allies lost at once his family, patrons, land, legal rights, status, and territorial and tribal affiliations. Second, the wasteland brought its own judgment on men and women who behaved like beasts. God's will was made plain when an outcast succumbed to the weather, wild animals, demons, or enemies in the wild. And if an outcast survived without the protection of society and settlement, he proved himself unfit for society in the first place.[2]

The legal concept of punitary exile, honed by the Christian ideal of rejection of the *saeculum* and by notions of otherworldly journeys, made self-imposed exile popular among the monks.[3] Bad men and good left society for similar reasons; criminals were punished with exile, while religious exiles punished themselves. Criminals were sent away because of their beastly natures and offenses; in the wild, they became the animals that they had imitated in society. But some who called themselves sinners, while neighbors called them saints, chose to follow. Monks left to fight the temptation of animal pleasures, abandoning the support of *familiae* and neighbors and passing through the wilderness on the way to a higher level of existence. Thus the wilderness that debased criminals made monks better than animals, better even than other humans. However, both kinds of exile incurred the distrust of those left behind. Both went where no human should be able to exist; both rejected the civilized protections of a community for a lonelier life.

2. Thomas Charles-Edwards, "The Social Background to Irish *Peregrinatio*," *Celtica* 11 (1976), 43–59, esp. 50.

3. The literature of otherworldly journeys is extensive: A. G. Van Hamel, ed., *Immrama* (Dublin, 1941); H. P. A. Oskamp, ed., *The Voyage of Máel Dúin* (Groningen, 1970); Kuno Meyer, ed. and trans., *The Voyage of Bran Son of Febal*, 2 vols. (London, 1895); Whitely Stokes, ed. and trans., "The Voyage of the Hui Corra," *Revue Celtique* 14 (1893), 22–69; Stokes, ed. and trans., "The Adventure of St. Columba's Clerics," *Revue Celtique* 26 (1905), 130–70; Carl Selmer, ed., *Navigatio Sancti Brendani Abbatis* (Notre Dame, Ind., 1959); HVSH, 56–78; Stokes, *Lismore*, 99–116. For discussions of the voyage literature, see Kenney, *Sources*, 409–11, 447–48, 740–41; Kathleen Hughes, *Early Christian Ireland: An Introduction to the Sources* (London, 1972), 210–16; Alwyn Rees and Brinley Rees, *Celtic Heritage* (London, 1961), 314–25; James Carney, *Studies in Irish Language and Literature* (Dublin, 1955), 276–323; David Dumville, "Echtrae and Immram: Some Problems of Definition," *Ériu* 27 (1976), 73–94; Proinsias Mac Cana, "Mongan mac Fiachna and *Immram Brain*," *Ériu* 23 (1972), 102–42; Mac Cana, "The Prehistory of *Immram Brain*," *Ériu* 25 (1974), 33–52; Mac Cana, "The Sinless Otherworld of *Immram Brain*," *Ériu* 27 (1976), 95–115; Cynthia Bourgeault, "The Monastic Archetype in the Navigatio of St. Brendan," *Monastic Studies* 14 (1983), 109–22.

Not coincidentally, canonists, lawyers, and annalists used some of the same words for a forced exile-by-law and a monk voluntarily seeking exile: in Latin *peregrinus,* in Irish *ailither.*[4] Monastic teachings from the Continent supplied the inspiration, but the fearsome mystery of the Irish wilderness, which helped create the legal and literary traditions of exile, also influenced the Irish expression of piety as exile.

Irish monks, convinced of their sanctity or seeking to test it, won fame for their intrepid missions to Britain and the Continent beyond.[5] Pátraic, a Briton who became the premiere Irish saint, set the first example. He was a reluctant but determined exile from kin and colleagues to the land where he had suffered slavery. Even once he got down to the work of conversion among the Irish he still longed for home, and would have been "only too glad" to see his family in Britain and his fellow clerics in Gaul again. But God had, unfortunately, commanded his exile for the rest of his life.[6] He was "obliged by the Spirit" to reject his kinfolk and gentlemanly social status and become, as he put it, "a slave in Christ to a foreign people for the ineffable glory of the everlasting life which is in Christ Jesus our Lord."[7] Pátraic had learned from a tradition already strong among Christian clergy that rejection of worldly cares and pleasures was a sign of devotion to God. To leave a familiar and secure social context for a strange place, moving like Saint Augustine's pilgrim Christian to those who awaited God's word or to the isolation of the desert, was to enter a higher form of Christian life.[8]

Columbán, born over a century later, fled an Ireland already absorbing Christian ideas and a monastic community settled into the domestic business of scholarship and farming. Columbán did not have Pátraic's doubts about his vocation and the method for pursuing it. According to his hagiographer, who wrote only a generation after the saint's death, Columbán hopped over his mother's grieving, prostrate body at the family threshold and strode off in the direction of Europe.[9] Elaborating on his theme of life-as-highway, the saint later sermonized: "Let us, who are on

---

4. Charles-Edwards, "Social Background to Irish *Peregrinatio,*" 44.
5. Walafrid Strabo in MGH, SS. Rer. Merov. 4:336; Bede, HBE III.3–4, 25.
6. A. B. E. Hood, ed. and trans., *St. Patrick: His Writings and Muirchu's Life* (London, 1978), 31, 50.
7. Ibid., 36, 56, 57.
8. Ibid., 25.
9. MGH, SS. Rer. Merov. 4:69; Dana Carleton Munro, trans., *Life of St. Columban, by the Monk Jonas,* Translations and Reprints from the Original Sources of European History 2 (Philadelphia, 1902), 4.

the way, hasten home; for our whole life is like the journey of a single day. Our first duty is to love nothing here; but let us place our affections above, our desires above, our wisdom above, and above let us seek our home; for the fatherland is there where our Father is. Thus we have no home on earth."[10]

To Columbán's mind, everyone was an alien; the whole world was foreign to a good Christian.[11] But with typical arrogance, the saint conceded that few Christians had the stamina to live as he did, apart from his family, denying himself food, sex, and sleep, taking up temporary residence in a cave, and laboring vigorously in the name of the Lord.[12] Columbán did so gladly. When on the point of being expelled from Gaul for making trouble over King Theuderic's informal liaisons with women and his bastard children, Columbán wrote touchingly to his disciples of how he would be forced to return to Ireland yet longed already to be restored to exile.[13]

Columbán was only one of many. Irish monks and their European followers evangelized in Germany, Flanders, France, and Italy.[14] Columbán's hagiographer, Jonas, wrote that twelve disciples accompanied Columbán from Ireland. Eventually they and others who followed dispersed among his communities at Annegray, Luxeuil, Fontaines, Bobbio, and elsewhere. So many prominent monks in Merovingian Gaul were Irish that hagiographers there blithely assigned an Irish origin to many who did not deserve it.[15] Irishmen had preceded Columbán to Britain and Wales and they succeeded him throughout Europe. Columcille, Fursa, and Gall were among the saintly exiles who founded famous monastic communities outside of Ireland, attracting non-Irish disciples who carried on and

10. Walker, *Sancti Columbani Opera*, 95, 97–99.
11. Ibid., 102; cf. 78.
12. Ibid., 76.
13. Ibid., 34–35.
14. Kenney, *Sources*, 183–209, 486–621. Although this work was comprehensive when it was written, and still is invaluable, some of Kenney's research has been modified by more recent works. See the articles in Heinz Löwe, ed., *Die Iren und Europa im früheren Mittelalter* (Stuttgart, 1982), 1:171–424; Joseph Kelley, "Irish Monks and the See of Peter," *Monastic Studies* 14 (1983), 207–25. Still valuable are Aubrey Gwynn, "Ireland and the Continent in the Eleventh Century," *Irish Historical Studies* 8 (1952/53), 193–216; Tomas Ó Fiaich, "Irish Peregrini on the Continent," *Irish Ecclesiastical Review* 103 (1965), 233–40; Ó Fiaich, *Irish Cultural Influence in Europe, 6th–12th Centuries* (Dublin, 1967); McNeill, *The Celtic Churches*, 155–222. See also H. B. Clarke and M. Brennan, eds., *Columbanus and Merovingian Monasticism* (Oxford, 1981).
15. Kenney, *Sources*, 487.

spread Irish traditions.[16] Their theology and community organization—
or lack of it—made them notorious to Carolingians and English missionaries, prompting severe legislation against *episcopi vagantes* and ordinary
Scotti.[17] Yet several, such as Vergil (Fergil) of Salzburg, Dicuil, Sedulius
Scotus, Marianus Scotus, and Johannes Eriugena, became famous for
scholarship within the formal episcopal and educational structures of the
Empire.[18] The exiles left monasteries, disciples, books, and a lasting impression of a uniquely Irish approach to monastic life behind them.

Irish exiles abroad neither sought nor found isolation. Despite Columbán's fierce determination to reject all worldly ties, despite his abandonment of his poor old mother and his home, even he needed communal
affiliations. He left Ireland with companions; he set up hermitages that
quickly became flourishing settlements of coenobites, attracting visits
from kings and lay pilgrims. He formed affective ties with his monastic
brothers just as monks at home in Ireland did; he wept when they died
and grieved when he left them.[19] He also mingled with, and harassed,
kings, bishops, and popes. His written rules proved a final testament to his
coenobitic ideals, emphasizing the obedience of brothers to one another
and to their superiors, and the necessity of communal labor.[20]

When the exiles left Ireland they cut ties and came out of the sacred
enclosure, but in foreign lands they made new contacts and built new
walls. Scholar-exiles, such as Sedulius and Marianus, built intellectual
networks that stretched across Europe and back to Ireland.[21] Other
Irishmen abroad set up monastic communities composed exclusively of
their fellow émigrés, and offered hospitality to Irish pilgrims en route to

16. Ibid., 206–8; MGH, SS. Rer. Merov. 4:251–80.

17. Kenney, *Sources,* 518; Pierre Riché, "Les irlandais et princes carolingiens aux VIIIᵉ et
IXᵉ siècles," in Löwe, *Iren und Europa,* 2:735–37. See Einhard's slighting reference to Irish
rulers in his life of Charlemagne, ed. Lewis Thorpe (London, 1983), 70; Hughes, "Changing
Theory and Practice of Irish Pilgrimage," 144–46.

18. Kenney, *Sources,* 530–621; Bernhard Bischoff, "Turning-Points in the History of Latin
Exegesis in the Early Irish Church: A.D. 650–800," in M. McNamara, ed., *Biblical Studies: The
Medieval Irish Contribution* (Dublin, 1976), 74–164. Again, see also the articles in Löwe, *Iren
und Europa,* 2:735–940.

19. Munro, "Life of St. Columbán," 17–18, 23–24.

20. Munro, "Life of St. Columbán"; Walker, *Sancti Columbani Opera,* 2–57.

21. Kenney, *Sources,* 530–621. See also Reinhard Düchting, "Sedulius Scottus—ein
'Heilger Drei König mehr' aus dem Abendland," and Anne-Dorothée von den Brincken,
"Marianus Scottus als Universalhistoriker iuxta veritatem evangelii," both in Löwe, *Iren und
Europa,* 2:866–75 and 970–1009.

the famous tombs in Francia and Rome.[22] Irish monasteries continued to supply recruits and monastic communities abroad throughout the Middle Ages; in the thirteenth century, the Abbey of St. James in Ratisbon even kept priories in Ireland from which to draw novices.[23]

The history of pious exile from Ireland was not one of courageous hermits fleeing to the forests and mountains of alien lands, but one of social, political, and cultural networks expanding from Ireland to Slavic territories in the east and Rome in the south. Like outlaws who roamed in bands, monks abroad sought replacements for their forsaken communities. Wherever they went, the Irish monks took their well-developed social models and their intense need to form communities with them.

Pilgrimage

The hagiographers praised the efforts of saints to abandon kin and *patria*, celebrated the voyage of Brénainn and the exile of Columcille, and even manipulated their sacred spaces to find their own temporary solitude from the community. Yet the saints provided the few well-known examples of successful exile; the names of most Irish monks who are famous today for exile and scholarship abroad would have meant little to their contemporaries at home. By relegating exile to stories of ancient saints, the monks could turn it from real practice to abstract ideal. The *vitae* contained a vital debate over the value of exile versus settled coenobitic life that reveals how important the ideal—but not the reality—of exile was to monks in early Ireland.[24]

The possibility of exile contradicted ordinary monastic existence. The monks had always meant their monasteries to be accessible; as we have seen, they settled near the farms of neighbors and the tombs of ancestors. They had a mission to the lay population of Ireland; they existed to pray for other Christians, to heal them, and to bring peace and order. The problematic ideal of withdrawal survived in ecclesiastical and secular literature, but its practice was made difficult by the efforts of communities to

22. Ó Fiaich, "Irish Peregrini on the Continent," 233–40; Joseph P. Fuhrmann, *Irish Medieval Monasteries on the Continent* (Washington, D.C., 1927), 54–69.

23. Fuhrmann, *Irish Medieval Monasteries on the Continent,* 74–111, esp. 103–4; Gwynn, "Ireland and the Continent in the Eleventh Century," 208.

24. HVSH, 81: "Tertius ordo sanctorum. . . . Erant enim presbiteri . . . qui in locis desertis habitabant." Giles Constable has recounted the changing debate over *peregrinatio* and coenobitism in "Monachisme et pèlerinage au Moyen Age," *Revue Historique* 523 (June–September 1977), 3–28.

acquire endowments, to create networks of protective relationships with kinfolk and others, and to impose order on the society surrounding their enclosures. There was no habitable wilderness left for the monks in Ireland. In the eighth and ninth centuries, the *céili dé* were already bemoaning the lack of genuine isolation that characterized even the most ascetic of monastic settlements.[25]

But the hagiographer's criticism of exile stemmed from more than an antagonism toward an unattainable ideal; they genuinely feared exile. According to some writers, exiles caused the disintegration of monastic communities, for they deprived other members of support in the mission to the laity, and left them more vulnerable to the world beyond their fences and clearings. Certainly by the ninth century, if not earlier, members of monastic communities strove to control and restrict the practice of voluntary exile. Some hint of this attempt was already evident in the seventh-century penitentials, several of which decreed that the travels of monks, nuns, and even bishops were subject to the permission of colleagues and superiors.[26] The writers of laws and canons also attempted to restrict monks' mobility, penalizing drifters and rewarding those who promised to return, such as avowed pilgrims.[27]

Even the zealous *céili dé* realized that permanent exile from a coherent community deprived a group of valuable members and brought only questionable good to exiles and those they left behind. Máelruain, the *céile dé* abbot-saint, criticized pilgrims to foreign lands. He even disapproved of anchorites, who journeyed only so far as the local wilderness—he refused to allow a former anchorite into his community because the man had fasted so severely and practiced such heavy penance that he was too weak to do the normal work of a monk. The hermit had made himself unfit for communal life by withdrawing from it in the first place, to devote himself to penitential practices. Máelruain advised him to go back to his hut, but to eat better, to accept visits, and to take donations for distribution among the poor laity.[28] Hearing the story of an anchorite who lived apart from other monks in order to perform seven hundred genuflections a day, the *céile dé* abbot predicted sourly that a time would come when the anchorite would ruin his knees and be unable to practice such excess.[29] The tone of

---

25. Gwynn and Purton, "Monastery of Tallaght," 127–28, 135, 141.
26. Ludwig Bieler, ed., *The Irish Penitentials* (Dublin, 1975), 54, 58, 234–36.
27. Wasserschleben, *Collectio,* 29: "Clericus propriam ecclesiam non relinquat"; 147–50, 151, 152.
28. Gwynn and Purton, "Monastery of Tallaght," 133, 159–60.
29. Ibid., 141.

the entire ninth-century document from which these episodes are taken is one of submission to the moderate and communal rule of the clients of God.[30]

Individual hagiographers captured the arguments for and against exile in their accounts of their heroes' travels. For example, when Mochuda was expelled from Rathan and forced to hit the road in his old age, he wandered from monastery to monastery for a few years. The hagiographer explained the saint's forced exile in sympathetic detail, but he also mentioned that Mochuda's voluntary itinerancy after his expulsion seemed odd to the communities that offered him hospitality. Molua's monks mocked Mochuda. "It's time for this old man to settle down in some monastery," they snickered.[31] Similarly, Cóemgen's hagiographer told how the hermit Garbán ordered the saint home while he wandered in aimless pilgrimage: "It's better to stay piously put in one place than to wander around in your old age," advised the old man, an exile himself but a settled one.[32] Vagrancy in youth was acceptable, if controlled, but the ultimate aim of mature monks was fixed residence in a community of others like himself.

Younger monks needed direction for their pilgrimages. Sometimes, if they were unfit, their elders even prevented them from embarking on spiritual journeys. Colmán Ela wished to emulate his elder colleague, Columcille, and venture farther abroad. His *peregrinatio* almost ended disastrously when a storm broke over his ship in the middle of the sea. Thanks to the omniscience of Columcille, whose prayers saved Colmán and crew from sinking, the travelers reached Í and accepted hospitality there. But Columcille refused to let Colmán join him in exile, lecturing him, according to the ninth-century *vita:* "Brother, do not bother with foreign folks. Do not abandon your own Irish people, but feed them with the word of doctrine and grace which has been given to you. For I was forced to come to this foreign territory. But you I beg to go home, lest that land be empty of the word of God."[33] Columcille's exile was not voluntary, but suggested to him by other Irish clerics as a penalty for bringing about the battle at Cúil Dreimne.[34] To him, the business of

30. Ibid., passim.
31. PVSH 1:176–77.
32. Ibid., 249.
33. HVSH, 213–14; see also 116. See also Bieler, *Irish Penitentials,* 190–91: "de Reliquenda vel Docenda Patria."
34. HVSH, 112–13; cf. PVSH 2:139.

rituals and prayer in Ireland was more important that the soulful search of a monk in exile. Exile was only for sinners like himself.

Some monks tried to rebel against the conservative, stay-at-home direction of angels and abbots. But God himself frequently took a hand, through his angelic messengers and miracles, in keeping a monk from pilgrimage, proving that such a display of piety was sometimes less useful and even less admirable than a domestic mission. The permission of a monk's abbot was also essential for the voluntary exile. Monks of Cluain Eidnech left for Britain via Bennchor without asking leave of Saint Fintan. Soon after, another monk approached the abbot mournfully because he missed one of the departed brothers. He begged to follow the others into exile. But Fintan advised the monk to be joyful, for the very comrade whom he missed would return that day. "His heart could not find peace in exile," explained Fintan, "until he returned."[35]

A monk gained no benefits from his trip if he committed the sins of disobedience and pride by leaving without consent. Adomnán wrote that Cormac ua Liatháin tried repeatedly to sail, like Brénainn, to the "desert in the ocean," where he could exist in utter abstinence; but he was foiled in his fourth attempt by a crew member who had neglected to ask permission of his abbot.[36] The best of motives became mere selfishness if a monk's departure threatened the community's stability. The decision was up to the abbot and to their highest superior.

While monks were rarely allowed to leave their communities in permanent exile unless forced out for their sins, both monks and laics attempted briefer journeys through the wild to important shrines abroad and in Ireland. Pilgrimage was attractive for two reasons: It offered the rewards of exile but brought the wanderer home again; and it allowed the traveler to pick up souvenirs along the way. Few of the saints neglected to make at least one trip to Rome, their favorite pilgrimage destination and shopping spot. Fewer still returned empty-handed. As we have seen, Romans carried on a busy relic trade with the Irish, or so the hagiographers would have us believe. Besides Roman earth for cemeteries, saints brought home consecrated oil and wine, the bones of Peter, Paul, and Thomas, bits of Christ's tomb and the temple at Jerusalem, hair of the Virgin, clothing of the apostles, croziers, books, gospels, vestments, and bells.[37]

But more important, they got "cadhus 7 onóir" (consideration and

---

35. HVSH, 149; see also PBNE 1:42.
36. Adomnán, 222–24.
37. HVSH, 121–22, 226, 405; PVSH 1:88, 218; 2:69–70, 136; PBNE 1:128, 160–61, 201.

honor) from the pope himself, which greatly enhanced their social standing back home.[38] Several saints learned their letters in Roman schools, an enviable achievement, because he who studied in Peter's city was obviously nearer the source of truth and gained a better understanding of it.[39] Others received sacerdotal or episcopal ordination at the hands of the pope.[40] Some hagiographers went even further in claiming pilgrims' honors for their heroes. Ailbe, for instance, begged the pope to ordain him but the pope declined because he recognized Ailbe's greater sanctity. Eventually they worked out a compromise by which the angel Victor, Pátraic's acquaintance, actually performed the ritual.[41]

The trip to Rome itself, without relics or rituals, conferred honor on pilgrims. Máedóc supposedly chose his successors at Druim Lethan from among those who accompanied him to Rome because they had shown themselves more pious than the weak hearts who had stayed at home.[42]

The saints were professional pilgrims, selecting journeys to the most important of shrines in order to prove their spiritual mettle. The only other stops that won repeated mention by hagiographers were Tours and a few Welsh churches. Tours held a place high in Irish affection because of its warrior-healer saint; and the communities of David and other Welshmen played an actual historical role in the interrelations of Irish and British saints.[43] Both were also on the way to Rome.

Domestic destinations, however, drew more Irish pilgrims. Pilgrimage centers at home attracted ordinary monks and lay folk, people without the resources or nerve to venture beyond Ireland. Women did not make Continental journeys. As a saintly old nun explained to Columbán, she would have gone into permanent exile had she been a man, but her gender kept her home.[44] Irish monks spent considerable effort making their own churches popular with women and other pilgrims, as the shrines, decorated tombs, and hagiography demonstrate. Pilgrims valued the monks' protective and healing services, as we have seen; they paid for these with

38. PBNE 1:160–61.
39. PVSH 1:218, 2:38–39.
40. HVSH, 121, 342, 395; PVSH 1:218; 2:38–39, 128; PBNE 1:42, 103.
41. PVSH 1:51–52; see also 70.
42. Ibid., 264.
43. E. G. Bowen, "The Irish Sea in the Age of the Saints," *Studia Celtica* 4 (1969), 56–71; Bowen, "The Geography of Early Monasticism in Ireland," *Studia Celtica* 7 (1972), 30–44; Wendy Davies, *Wales in the Early Middle Ages* (Leicester, 1982), 146–48; McNeill, *The Celtic Churches*, 102–19.
44. MGH, SS. Usum Schol. (1905), 156; cited in Charles-Edwards, "Social Background to Irish *Peregrinatio*," 43.

goods and services that the monks needed and demanded. The annalists listed numerous kings and queens who died as *athláig* in "pilgrimage," that is, in retirement at a famous monastery; in return, no doubt, the royal pilgrim well rewarded his or her hosts and their saint.[45] Royalty could spend years in *peregrinatio* toward the ends of their lives, while ailing farmers took up the staff just long enough to get to a shrine, plead for a cure, and go home again.

Any legitimate pilgrimage had to have a beginning, middle, and end. Journeys to specific destinations for specific purposes brought pilgrims home again. A foray into the wilderness satisfied a pilgrim's desire to escape everyday relationships, conflicts, responsibilities, and status; for the space of the journey he or she could concentrate undistracted on spiritual goals, just as famous hermit-saints did. But such a classless, homeless, liminal state was difficult to assume permanently. Pilgrims longed eventually to return to safety and familiar comforts. Their communities were happy to welcome them back, pleased to have again the absent member's labor and support. The returning pilgrim often gained increased prestige among his comrades. But the best reward was trading the thrill and terror of testing oneself in the wilderness for the minor anxieties of daily life.[46]

Still, even the lesser *peregrinatio* of carefully monitored domestic travel remained suspect to some hagiographers. The very impulse for monks to go on pilgrimage sometimes derived from the Devil. Evil angels always made their unsuccessful attacks on saints on the open road, outside the sacred space of the enclosure.[47] Even such great saints as Cóemgen and Mochuda succumbed to the demons of wanderlust; they attracted these demons to their shoes when they committed minor sins, and indulged in a lot of useless wandering before they discovered and expelled them.[48] Female saints, bound to their nunneries, apparently knew better: as Brigit reminded Brénainn, almost smugly, God deemed her the more pious because she kept her mind on him constantly, whereas Brénainn occasionally let the temptations of travel capture his attention. Samthann, on the other hand, preached that God was accessible from anyplace, Ireland or abroad.[49]

---

45. Mac Airt, *Annals of Inisfallen*, 194–206; AU, 182, 194, 244, 252, et passim; Osborn Bergin, *Irish Bardic Poetry* (Dublin, 1970), 313–14.
46. Victor Turner and Edith Turner, *Image and Pilgrimage in Christian Culture* (New York, 1978), esp. 1–39; McNeill, *Celtic Churches*, 220.
47. Adomnán, 480–81; PVSH 2:117–18.
48. PVSH 2:118, 124–25.
49. PBNE 1:86, 2:260.

If a monk had to turn pilgrim, to seek a cure or a favor, to fulfill a vow, or for less concrete and more purely spiritual motives, domestic destinations were best. Tours or Rome was possible only for kings or saints, and for a few bishops and noblemen. As an old Irish poem advised,

> Going to Rome
> Is lots of effort, little profit.
> You won't find the king you seek there
> Unless you take him along.[50]

By and large, Irish monks followed this sensible advice. A small number ventured over the oceans into exile; a few more passed through the wilderness on their way to the shrines of famous miracle workers, but they always returned again to their own settlements. Most stayed at home among *familiae* and blood kin, clients and tenants, under the loving eyes of their own saintly patrons. They were relatively safe there, inside their consecrated defenses. They knew very well that the perils of the wasteland lurked just beyond their farthest pastures, but they also knew how to endure the severity of the Lord's creation. They built and blessed walls, they made allies, and above all, they prayed to their saints.

50. Whitely Stokes and John Strachan, eds., *Thesaurus Palaeohibernicus* (Cambridge, 1903), 2:296.

Epilogue

THIS BOOK CLOSES AT THE END OF THE TWELFTH CENTURY, JUST after the Normans had arrived in Ireland. Gerald of Wales described Irish monks and their saints then, and had little but disapproval for them: The monks were negligent, overly ascetic, and insincere, the saints simply vindictive. The lay Christians of Ireland were rude and barbarous, as well as ignorant of orthodoxy and orthopraxis.[1] Gerald believed that the monks were to blame for the laity's ignorance of Christianity. Lay folk, relying on monks rather than secular clergy, had not been receiving the instruction and care they needed. As Gerald wrote of Irish bishop-monks: "They are pastors that wish to be fed, and do not wish to feed. . . . They neither preach the word of the Lord to the people, nor tell them of their sins, nor extirpate vices from the flock committed to them, nor instill virtues."[2]

Historians, from Gerald to those of the present, tend to hold the monks responsible for all that they have found wrong with the Christianity of pre-Norman Ireland. Scholars describe how the Irish resisted ecclesiastical reform and speak of the diversity of Irish practice as "decay" and a "disease" to be cured by Continental influence and Norman rule.[3] But the chaos and fragmentation of Irish churches exist only in historiography, not in history. The complex social, economic, and political networks with

---

1. Gerald of Wales, *The History and Topography of Ireland,* trans. John J. O'Meara (London, 1982), 112, 91.

2. Gerald of Wales, *History and Topography,* 112–13.

3. Kenney, *Sources,* 747; John Watt, *The Church and the Two Nations in Medieval Ireland* (Cambridge, 1970), 2–4.

which the monks surrounded themselves were hardly haphazard. The alliances between monastic communities, the intricate symbolic hierarchies of saints so obvious in the *vitae,* the fine maneuvering of abbots and kings, were all part of a highly sophisticated ecclesiastical structure focused on powerful and wealthy monastic settlements. The *vitae* alone attest to the intellectual life of Irish monks, never mind the rest of the great body of Irish learning, artistry, and the scholarly accomplishments of Irish missionaries abroad. And the depth of Christian feeling and the constancy of Christian practice among both monks and laity is manifest in the myriad social ties between them, every one of which was imbued with religious meaning.

So when the irascible Gerald of Wales complained of monastic decadence, he was merely adding his voice to the chorus for reform already strong in twelfth-century Ireland.[4] Reform was, after all, nothing new to the Irish. The *céili dé* had complained of moral degeneracy among clerics in the eighth century. Irish anchorites and pilgrims had carried on the tradition of withdrawal throughout the early Middle Ages. And, as the hagiographers vividly demonstrated, Irish monks had always felt a sharp ambivalence about their participation in secular affairs: they labored to build and maintain their enclosures and their communities, but at the same time praised the saints who abandoned all for the solitude of the wastes.

Previously, the monastic world had adapted to internal reform movements; ideas and customs were altered, but life in the enclosure went on much as before. However, in the mid-eleventh century, more profound change assaulted the sacred enclosures when monastic brothers in France, Germany, and Italy sent home the message of fresh developments on the Continent. The new Benedictines of Cluny had been revitalizing monastic life both spiritually and organizationally. The popes were demanding that monks and priests be celibate, that kings and emperors release their grasp on ecclesiastical offices, that monks withdraw from secular life.[5] And, with a fervor for the desert that the Irish could well appreciate, religious men were once again building simple hermitages far from the houses of the unrighteous. The Irish, who had long been proud of their

4. On the Irish reform, see Kenney, *Sources,* 745–71; Kathleen Hughes, *The Church in Early Irish Society* (London, 1966), 238–74; Watt, *Church and the Two Nations;* John Watt, *The Church in Medieval Ireland* (Dublin, 1972).

5. Aubrey Gwynn, "Irish Monks and the Cluniac Reform," *Studies* 29 (1949), 409–30; Neithard Bulst, "Irisches Mönchtum und cluniazensische Klosterreform," in Heinz Löwe, ed., *Die Iren und Europa im früheren Mittelalter* (Stuttgart, 1982), 958–69.

allegiance to Rome and its bishops, hastened to obey the call for religious renewal.[6] Although the initial impetus for structural reform came from the bishops of Hiberno-Norse urban centers and from the provincial kings of Munster, abbots and bishops across the land were quick to join the movement.[7] In 1044 Irish clerics and kings had called an island-wide reform council; they held at least twenty-seven more provincial and national councils over the next 150 years.[8]

Foreign churchmen were quick to notice the Irish efforts at reform. The new Norman prelates of England took particular interest. They had already sternly reorganized the churches of England. A hundred years before the Norman invasion of Ireland, the archbishops of Canterbury, one after the other, became determined to push Norman-style reform across the Irish Sea. Where Caesar's generals had failed, Lanfranc and his successors succeeded.[9] In 1074 Lanfranc began a correspondence with Toirrdelbach úa Briain, king of Munster, urging him to summon a council of clerical and lay leaders in order to bring the Irish ecclesiastical hierarchy and ecclesiastical law regarding marriage into conformity with Continental practices.[10] Toirrdelbach obeyed. The Uí Briain opened the monastic gates to the Normans just as surely as Diarmait mac Murchadha opened the gates of his royal *ráth*.

During the next two hundred years, native and Norman reformers insisted on nothing less than a complete remodeling of the Irish monastic communities that had developed over six centuries. Instead of the sacred circle of the native enclosure, reformers demanded the cold stone fortresses of Cistercians and Benedictines. They wished to replace the dynasties of politicking abbots with a Continental hierarchy of archbishops, bishops, and parish priests. Abbots and monks were to return to the cloister and leave the ministry to secular clergy. The gates of the monastery must close to the world. Even the monastic texts that document this

6. HVSH, 256; for Irish pilgrimages to Rome in the eleventh century, see Aubrey Gwynn, "Ireland and Rome in the Eleventh Century," IER 57 (1941), 312–32.
7. Kenney, *Sources*, 757–63; Aubrey Gwynn, "The Origins of the See of Dublin," IER 57 (1941), 97–112.
8. Little documentation of conciliar decrees is extant. For the council of Caisel (1101) see "Senchas Síl Bhriain," in Standish O'Grady, ed., *Caithreim Thoirrdealbhaigh* (London, 1928), 174–75. For the councils of Ráth Bresail (1110) and Kells (1152), see Geoffrey Keating, *Forus Feasa ar Éirinn*, ed. P. S. Dineen (London, 1908), 3:298–307, 315–17. For other councils: J. D. Mansi, *Sacrorum Conciliorum . . . Collectio* (Paris, 1901–), 20:951; 21:733; supp. 2, 733; 22:524; N. Coleti, ed., *Sacrosancta Concilia* (Venice, 1728), 12:949, 1081; 13:659.
9. Aubrey Gwynn, "Lanfranc and the Irish Church," IER 57 (1941), 40–55; "Saint Anselm and the Irish Church," IER 59 (1942), 1–14; Watt, *Church and the Two Nations*, 6–10, 217–25.
10. Kenney, *Sources*, 759.

period are unlike earlier records: instead of writing new *vitae* full of marvels and miracles, monks recorded the decrees of reforming synods, while Irish bishops and their Norman colleagues exchanged letters and scholars composed doctrinal tracts.[11]

The native reform movement took a violent turn with the arrival of Norman soldiers in the 1170s. When Gerald sailed with his kinsmen the Fitzgeralds to the Atlantic frontier, he was helping to close a chapter of Irish ecclesiastical history. The Normans took Irish land and lordships, as well as church offices. They visibly altered the Irish landscape, imposing new churches, mottes and towers, and, later, castles. They tried to reorganize the political geography of Ireland; in place of monastic *familiae* and *túatha* bound by alliance and clientage to provincial overkings, they envisioned feudal baronies and bishoprics sworn to the Norman king of England. Yet most of the Normans eventually succumbed, as had the Scandinavian invaders of the ninth and tenth centuries, to the persuasion of local culture. Like the Irish, they came to disregard the will of the Norman monarch; like the Vikings, they participated in Irish feuds and battles, married into Irish families, took Irish names, and learned the language of their adopted home.[12]

The life of Máel-máedóc ua Morgair, known as Saint Malachi, sums up many of the religious and political developments in Ireland on the eve of the Norman invasion.[13] Máel-máedóc was a new kind of saintly hero who appealed to Irish and Normans alike. He was celebrated not for his miracles of protection and resuscitation—although he performed a few—but for his struggle to displace the abbatial dynasty that had controlled Ard Macha for centuries. His *vita* is proof of the changes that he helped to bring about. No product of a prestigious Irish monastery, it was written abroad by a Frenchman hostile to the ancient ways of Irish monks: Bernard of Clairvaux. The great Cistercian composed his life of Malachi the

---

11. Kenney, *Sources,* 745–71; for the tract on structural reform by Gilla-easpuic, bishop of Limerick, see Migne, PL 159:995–1004.

12. For background on the Norman occupation of Ireland and Norman assimilation, see Art Cosgrove, ed., *A New History of Ireland,* vol. 2, *Medieval Ireland, 1169–1534* (Oxford, 1987); Katherine Simms, *From Kings to Warlords: The Changing Political Structure of Gaelic Ireland in the Later Middle Ages* (Woodbridge, Suffolk, 1987), esp. 10–20; A. J. Otway-Ruthven, *A History of Medieval Ireland* (London, 1968); P. W. A. Asplin, *Medieval Ireland, c. 1170–1495: A Bibliography of Secondary Works* (Dublin, 1971).

13. Watt, *Church and the Two Nations,* 19. For editions of Bernard's *vita* of Máel-máedóc: H. J. Lawlor, ed. and trans., *St. Bernard of Clairvaux's Life of St. Malachy of Armagh* (London, 1920); Bernard of Clairvaux, *The Life and Death of Saint Malachy the Irishman,* trans. Robert T. Meyer, Cistercian Fathers ser. 10 (Kalamazoo, Mich., 1978).

Epilogue

Irishman at the request of Irish monks in 1148, soon after Máel-máedóc died at Clairvaux.[14] His sources were different from those of Irish *vitae*; he repeated stories told by Máel-máedóc himself when he visited Clairvaux and by the saint's disciples, left to train as Cistercians in Bernard's monastery. Thus, the agenda of the text is Bernard's, but the emphases are those of the Irish monks.

Bernard's *vita* reveals that Máel-máedóc was very much a product of a typical Irish monastery of the pre-Norman period. The Cistercian admits that "our Malachy was born in Ireland of a barbarous tribe; there he was brought up and educated."[15] Máel-máedóc came of a noble ecclesiastical family. His uncles and brothers were monks, his father an *airdfher leighind* (chief professor) who was also his first tutor.[16] He was both monk and priest, later abbot and bishop. He traveled to Ireland, seeking the hospitality of fellow monks and offering his services as *anmchara* to the king of Munster, Cormac mac Carthaig. When he finally chose his own *locus*, it was the ancient settlement at Bennchor, Comgall's great house of learning, which had been utterly destroyed by repeated Viking raids. His old tutor, the abbot of the church of Peter and Paul at Ard Macha, placed him in charge of the ruined site. His mother's brother owned the lands of Bennchor, but gladly donated his property, himself, and his service to Máel-máedóc and his new community of monks.[17] Thus, Máel-máedóc's family, training, and early career all conformed to the Irish saintly stereotype.

Yet Bernard's life of Malachi also describes a reformer who did not hesitate to abandon old ways and old ties. He refused the properties of Bennchor, taking only the sacred center of the *termonn* where the bones of the saints lay. Although his first church was of polished wooden planks, he later attempted to raise a stone cloister of the sort he had visited in France and England. When he was made bishop of Connor, twenty-five miles distant, Máel-máedóc did not conduct a ceremonial circuit to take dues of his lay neighbors, but instead walked out to preach to them. Like abbots before him, he was a peacemaker, and once he even fasted against an unruly king; but his *vita* shows that when he interfered in politics, he did so never for his own advancement but only as a pastor dedicated to rounding up a disorderly lay flock.[18] He rebuilt churches, reinstituted

14. Watt, *Church and the Two Nations*, 19.
15. Meyer, *Life and Death of Saint Malachy*, 11.
16. Ibid., 15–17; AU, 540, for obituary of Máel-máedóc's father; Watt, *Church and the Two Nations*, 21.
17. Meyer, *Life and Death of Saint Malachy*, 30–31.
18. Ibid., 75–76.

sacraments, and did his best to stamp out clerical concubinage and lay marriage within the forbidden degrees of kinship.

Máel-máedóc's reforms did not come without conflict. Several times his unappreciative and unreformed flock threatened his life.[19] He engaged in two desperate battles during his lifetime: he fought to win the archbishopric of Ard Macha and he worked to bring the Cistercians to Ireland. According to Bernard, the struggle for Ard Macha was so dangerous that Máel-máedóc almost became Ireland's first martyred saint. The reforming bishop Cellach named Máel-máedóc as his successor at Ard Macha, but the Uí Sinaich, who had passed the office to family members for generations, resisted by offering their own candidates. These men actually held the office and its emblem, the Bachall Ísu, for several years, while Máel-máedóc lived outside the walls.[20] Máel-máedóc finally took Ard Macha with the help of his old ally Mac Carthaig and his army. After three years of holding the office and forcing his reforms on the monks of Ard Macha and the surrounding lay community, Máel-máedóc stepped down and returned to the north, to the bishopric of Down.

He also traveled to Rome on business, to beg the pope for *pallia* and official sanctions for Irish reforms. En route, Máel-máedóc met his future crony and admirer Bernard of Clairvaux. So taken was Máel-máedóc with Bernard's order that he returned to Ireland to set up the first Cistercian houses there. Eventually he died on another visit to Clairvaux, surrounded by his Cistercian friends. Unlike the death scenes of the saints of old, no choruses of angels, no balls of fire or floods of light marked his passing; he seemed dead when asleep and asleep when finally dead.[21] No one squabbled over his bones. The Cistercians laid the *peregrinus* Malachi to rest in the cemetery at Clairvaux.

Thus this son of the Irish saints strove to transform the monastic enclosures of Ireland. He snatched Ard Macha from the Uí Sinaich and he brought the Cistercians and Augustinians to Ireland. In the 130 years after the first community of Mellifont was founded in 1142, another thirty-three Cistercian settlements appeared.[22] The Augustinians were equally suc-

---

19. Ibid., 34–35, 42–44.
20. AU, 576; Hughes, *Church in Early Irish Society*, 269–70.
21. Meyer, *Life and Death of Saint Malachy*, 91–92.
22. Watt, *Church in Medieval Ireland*, 41–86; Roger Stalley, *The Cistercian Monasteries of Ireland: An Account of the History, Art, and Architecture of the White Monks in Ireland from 1142 to 1340* (London and New Haven, Conn., 1987), 1; Aubrey Gwynn and R. Neville Hadcock, *Medieval Religious Houses: Ireland (With an Appendix to Early Sites)*, (London, 1970), 114–45.

cessful; sixty-three Augustinian houses flourished in Ireland by 1170.[23] Soon no Irish monastery lacked a Continental rule or affiliation with a foreign order.

Other reformers aided Máel-máedóc by seeking to reform the parish structure and the secular clergy. By 1110, the diocesan structure that exists today was in place. Where previously every significant monastery had hosted a bishop with ritual functions, now bishops held authority over both monasteries and lay communities. The hundreds of Irish bishops were reduced to forty-eight, along with two archbishops and a papal legate.[24] Both reforming abbots and the new bishops went to work on the Christian praxis of the laity. "This is a filthy people, wallowing in vice," wrote Gerald; but already in the mid-eleventh century, according to Bernard, the Irish had begun to participate in the sacraments, pay their tithes, and avoid the traditional practices of polygamy and divorce.[25]

These reforms struck at the heart of the old monastic organization. The new spirituality that informed religious renewal demanded a separation of lay people from their ecclesiastical professionals, at the same time that it enriched the religious life of the laity. The networks that bound monks to their neighbors were an obstacle to reformers: the political alliances, the parish functions of the monks, their close ties to blood kin, all distracted the monks from their proper business of prayer. From now on, the hermit's flight from the *saeculum* was to be every monk's goal, not just a saintly ideal.

Thus, to a certain extent, Irish monasticism, ecclesiastical organization, and orthopraxis changed as the reforms of the eleventh and twelfth centuries succeeded. But, to a larger extent, the monks and lay Christians of Ireland lived as they had for centuries. No doubt Máel-máedóc was able to accomplish his reforms partly because he came from a famous ecclesiastical family and had trained in the foremost monastic school in Ireland, Ard Macha. The Cistercians flourished because, like the old monastic pioneers, they set up their houses in the wastelands but near enough other settlements for social, economic, and political interaction; and because both Irish kings and Norman lords saw in the abbeys a chance to extend their

---

23. Watt, *Church and the Two Nations*, 26–27; Gwynn and Hadcock, *Medieval Religious Houses*, 146–200.
24. Watt, *Church and the Two Nations*, 15.
25. Gerald of Wales, *History and Topography of Ireland*, 106; Meyer, *Life and Death of Saint Malachy*, 34–35.

territorial control. By 1170, four of five provincial kings patronized Cistercian settlements even as they continued to support all their old monastic allies.[26]

In fact, Cistercian communities, like those of other Continental orders, recruited so many Irish monks that they quickly went native. The French monks who came to set up Mellifont left in a huff because they could not endure the barbarity of Irish language and custom.[27] Irish abbots soon returned to their independent ways and refused to attend the required annual general meetings of Cistercian abbots at Cîteaux; it was just too much trouble.[28] Even the rectangular stone cloisters of the Cistercians were unpopular. "Scotti sumus non galli," the monks of Ard Macha had complained to Máel-máedóc when he suggested the first one be built.[29] When the Cistercian Visitor, Stephen of Lexington, came to Ireland in 1227, he found Cistercian brothers living in traditional wattled huts outside their stone cloisters (Fig. 15).[30]

Eventually Irish monasteries became segregated from Anglo-Irish houses. Backed by the papal bull *Laudabiliter* (1155), which granted Ireland to Henry II, the Norman lords of Ireland imposed their own clerics on the ecclesiastical hierarchy. As Norman warriors claimed Irish lordships, so French-speaking abbots and bishops replaced those who knew only *Goídelc*.[31] But the great *familiae* of the monastic elite lingered on as semireligious officials well into the seventeenth century. In the Inquisitional records of the Stewart occupation, abbatial families appear, still holding former monastic estates, still collecting rents and dues, although no longer performing blessings and healings in return.[32]

Inevitably the old saints suffered some small loss of power and prestige, but they remained the spiritual protectors of an earlier age. In the new monasteries, Peter, Paul, and the Virgin reigned; in the more established communities, Brigit, Pátraic, and Ciarán had to compete for the allegiance

26. Stalley, *Cistercian Monasteries of Ireland*, 13–16.
27. Ibid., 15.
28. Ibid.
29. Meyer, *Life and Death of Saint Malachy*, 77n.
30. Stephen of Lexington, *Letters from Ireland, 1228–1229*, trans. Barry W. O'Dwyer, Cistercian Fathers ser. 28 (Kalamazoo, Mich., 1982), 44; cited in Stalley, *Cistercian Monasteries of Ireland*, 9.
31. Stanley, *Cistercian Monasteries of Ireland*, 16; Watt, *Church and the Two Nations*, 31–84, esp. 45–46, 48–51. See also Proinsias Mac Cana, "The Rise of the Later Schools of *Fílidheacht*," *Ériu* 25 (1984), 126–46.
32. *Inquisition in Officio Rotulorum Cancellariae Hiberniae*, vol. 2 (Dublin, 1829), p. xxxi and passim.

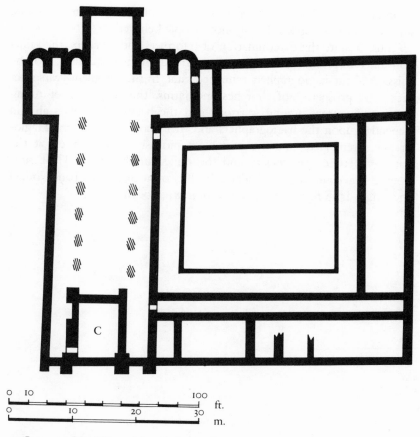

C

15. Layout of Mellifont. After Françoise Henry, *Irish Art in the Early Romanesque Period (1020–1170 A.D.)* (Ithaca, 1970).

and the donations of Irish Christians. But foreign and native clergy continued to usher the faithful into the presence of the Irish saints. Norman hagiographers rushed to borrow Irish texts, to copy them and to learn about the festivals and shrines of the holy men and women with the names they could not pronounce.[33] Indeed, a few new Irish saints appeared in the post-Norman period to aid the old. Besides Máel-máedóc ua Morgair there was Lorcán ua Tuathail, whose heart, caged in iron, still draws pilgrims to Dublin's Christchurch Cathedral. To this day the little

33. Kenney, *Sources,* 16–26.

country shrines of Irish saints attract offerings of pennies, plastic flowers, and the discarded spectacles of once myopic believers.

Thus, despite the determination of reformers and invaders, the saints continued to preside over the hearts and minds of the Irish. Thus, too, the mission of the hagiographers remained vital. In the turbulent years after 1200, the prosperity of churches and farms, the endurance of ruling houses, the peace among warriors, and the health of invalids all still depended upon the hagiographers and their monastic brothers. Hagiographers remained, like the porters of monastic communities, at the gateway between lay society and the milieu of the saints. Their *vitae* opened heaven to earth and linked this life to the next; their hands joined the Anglo-Irish future to the *insula sanctorum* of the past.

APPENDIX A

Place Names

The following is a list in Irish and English of places mentioned in the text:

Achad Fobuir	Aghagower
Achad Aball	Aghowle
Ára	Inishmore
Ard Ferta	Ardfert
Ard Ileán	High Island
Ard Macha	Armagh
Ard Mór	Inishmore
Ard Pátraic	Ardpatrick
Ard Stratha	Ardstraw
Baile Muirne	Ballyvourney
Bennchor	Bangor
Birra	Birr
Cell Achaid Drumfata	Killeigh
Cell Da Lua	Killaloe
Cell Dara	Kildare
Cell Íte	Killeedy
Cell Śléibe	Killevy
Cenannas	Kells
Cenn Éitig	Kinnitty
Cluain Brónaig	Clonbroney
Cluain Eidnech	Clonenagh
Cluain Eois	Clones
Cluain Ferta Brénainn	Clonfert
Cluain Iraird	Clonard
Cluain Moccu Nóis	Clonmacnois

Corcach	Cork
Daim Inis	Devenish
Daim Liac	Duleek
Doire	Derry
Druim Lethan	Drumlane
Dub Ileán	Duvillaun
Dún Bleisce	Doon
Dún Lethlgas	Downpatrick
Durmag	Durrow
Ferna Mór	Ferns
Fobar	Fore
Fochard	Faughart
Glenn Dá Locha	Glendalough
Í	Iona
Imlech	Emly
Inis Cáin Dego	Inishkeen
Inis Chathaig	Scattery Island
Inis Cheltra	Inishcaltra
Inis Muiredaig	Inishmurray
Lann Ela	Lynally
Liath Mór	Liathmore/ Leamokevoge
Lis Mór	Lismore
Lothra	Lorrha
Mag Bile	Moville
Mag Eo	Mayo
Mainistir Buite	Monasterboice
Nóendruimm	Nendrum
Poll Ruadáin	Pollrone
Riasc	Reask
Ros mBendchuir	Ross Managher
Ros Cré	Roscrea
Ros Inbir	Rossinver
Saigir	Seirkieran
Scelec Mhichíl	Skellig Michael
Slemain	Slane
Snám Luthair	Slanore
Sord	Swords
Tamlachta	Tallaght
Tech Moling	Timoling/ St. Mullins
Tech Munnu	Taghmon
Temair	Tara
Tempul Crónáin	Temple Cronan
Tír Dá Glas	Terryglass

APPENDIX B

Saints' Names

The following is a list in Irish, Latin, and English of some Irish saints' names. (Latin names are in italics, English names in parentheses.) Included are nicknames and variants of Irish names. The list is not meant to be comprehensive; it is intended merely to help the reader find a particular saint in a variety of primary or secondary sources. For a full list of Irish saints' names see Pádraig Ó Riain, *Corpus Genealogiarum Hiberniae* (Dublin, 1985), 225–66.

Áed, Áedán, Máedóc
Bairre, Bairrfind, Findbarr
Baíthíne, Báetán, Mobáe
Beinén, *Benignus*
Brénainn, *Brendanus, Brandanus* (Brendan)
Buite, *Boecius*
Brigit, *Brigida*
Cainnech, *Cannichus, Kennichus* (Canice)
Ciarán, *Kyranus, Queranus* (Kieran)
Cóemgen, *Caemgenus, Cayminius, Kyminus* (Kevin)
Colmán, Mocholmóc
Colum, Columb, Columcille, *Columba*
Columbán, *Columbanus*
Comgall, Mochoma, *Comgellus*
Cumaín, Cuimmíne
Daig, Dego, *Dagaeus*
Énna, Énda, Éinne, Énán, Ménóc, Moénóc, *Endeus*
Finnian, Findbarr, *Vinnianus*
Flann, Flannán

Fursu (Fursey)
Gobbán, Mogobbóc
Ibar, Ymar, *Ymarus*
Íte, Míte, *Yta*
Mochóemóc, Cóemán, Cóemóc, Cóemgen
Mocholla, Mochuille, Mocholmóc
Mochua, Crónán, Cuan
Mochuda, Mochuta, Carthach
Molaisse, Lasrán, Laisrén, *Lasreanus*
Moling, Dairchell, Tairchell
Molua, Lugaid, Dolua, *Lugidus*
Monenna, Moninne, Darerca, Sárbile
Munnu, Fintan
Pátraic, *Patricius* (Patrick)

Selected Bibliography

Primary Sources

Anderson, A. O., and M. O. Anderson, eds. *Adomnan's Life of Columba*. London, 1961.

Bede, the Venerable. *The History of the English Church and People (Historia Ecclesiastica gentis Anglorum)*. Trans. Leo Sherley-Price. London, 1955, rpt. 1982.

Bernard, J. H., and R. Atkinson, eds. *The Irish Liber Hymnorum*. Henry Bradshaw Society, vols. 13, 14. London, 1898.

Bernard of Clairvaux. *The Life and Death of Saint Malachy the Irishman*. Trans. Robert T. Meyer, Cistercian Fathers ser. 10. Kalamazoo, Mich., 1978.

Best, R. I., et al., eds. *The Book of Leinster*. 6 vols. Dublin, 1954–1983.

Bieler, Ludwig, ed. *The Irish Penitentials*. Dublin, 1975.

———, ed. *Patrician Texts in the Book of Armagh*. Dublin, 1979.

Binchy, D. A. "Bretha Crólige." *Ériu* 12 (1934–38), 1–77.

———. "Bretha Déin Chécht." *Ériu* 20 (1966), 1–66.

———. "Saint Patrick's First Synod." *Studia Hibernica* 8 (1968), 49–59.

———, ed. *Corpus Iuris Hibernici*. 6 vols. Dublin, 1978.

———, ed. *Críth Gablach*. Dublin, 1941.

Carney, James, ed. "A Maccucáin, Sruith in Tíag." *Celtica* 15 (1983), 25–41.

Cogitosus, *Vita Brigidae*. In Migne, PL 72:775–90.

Connolly, S., and J.-M. Picard, trans. "Cogitosus: Life of Saint Brigit." JRSAI 117 (1987), 5–27.

Esposito, M., ed. "Conchubrani vita sanctae Monennae." PRIA 12 C (1910), 202–51.

Fraser, J., P. Grosjean, and J. G. O'Keeffe, eds. *Irish Texts*. Fasc. I–V. London, 1931–33.

Gerald of Wales. *The History and Topography of Ireland*. Trans. John J. O'Meara. London, 1982.

Gwynn, E. J., ed. "The Rule of Tallaght." *Hermathena* 44, second suppl. vol. Dublin and London, 1927.

Gwynn, E. J., and W. J. Purton, eds. "The Monastery of Tallaght." PRIA 29 C (1911), 115–79.

Hancock, W. N., et al., eds. *The Ancient Laws of Ireland.* 6 vols. Dublin and London, 1865–1901.

Heaney, Seamus, trans. *Sweeney Astray.* London, 1984.

Heist, W. W., ed. *Vitae sanctorum Hiberniae.* Subsidia Hagiographica 28. Brussels, 1965.

Herren, Michael, ed. *Hisperica Famina: I. The A-text.* Toronto, 1974.

Hood, A. B. E., ed. and trans. *St. Patrick: His Writings and Muirchu's Life.* London, 1978.

Hull, V. "Cáin Domnaig." *Ériu* 20 (1966), 151–77.

Jonas. *Vita Sancti Columbani.* MGH SS. Rer. Merov. 4 (1902), 64–108.

Kinsella, Thomas, trans. *The Táin.* Dublin, 1969, and Oxford, 1977.

Knott, Eleanor, ed. *Togail Bruidne Da Derga.* Dublin, 1975.

Mac Airt, Seán, ed. *The Annals of Inisfallen.* Dublin, 1951.

—— and Gearóid Mac Niocaill, eds., *The Annals of Ulster (to A.D. 1131).* Dublin, 1983.

Mac Eclaise. "The Rule of St. Carthage." IER 27 (1910), 495–517.

Mac Eoin, Gearóid. "A Life of Cumaine Fota." *Béaloideas* 39–41 (1971–73), 192–205.

Mac Niocaill, Gearóid. "Tír Cumaile." *Ériu* 22 (1971), 81–86.

Meyer, Kuno. "Siebenteiluug [*sic*] aller geistlichen und weltlichen Rangstufen." ZCP 5 (1905), 498–99.

——, ed. *Aislinge meic Conglinne.* London, 1892.

——, ed. *Betha Colmáin maic Luacháin.* Todd Lecture ser. 8. Dublin, 1911.

——, ed. *Cáin Adamnáin: An Old Irish Treatise on the Law of Adamnán.* Oxford, 1905.

——, ed. *The Voyage of Bran Son of Febal.* 2 vols. London, 1895.

Mulchrone, Katherine, ed. *Bethu Phátraic. The Tripartite Life of Patrick.* Dublin, 1964.

Munro, Dana Carleton, trans. *Life of St. Columban, by the Monk Jonas.* Translations and Reprints from the Original Sources of European History 2. Philadelphia, 1902.

Murphy, Gerard. *Early Irish Lyrics.* Oxford, 1956.

Ó hAodha, Donncha, ed. *Bethu Brigte.* Dublin, 1978.

Ó Coileáin, Seán, ed. and trans. "Ceisneamh Inghine Ghuil." From Houghton Library MS 3. Translation in the collection of the Robinson Library, Harvard University, 1970.

O'Donovan, John, ed. *The Annals of the Kingdom of Ireland by the Four Masters.* Dublin, 1848–51.

O'Grady, Standish. *Silva Gadelica.* 2 vols. London, 1892.

O'Keeffe, J. G., ed. *Buile Suibhne (The Frenzy of Sweeney). Being the Adventures of Suibhne Geilt.* London, 1910.

——, ed. "Cáin Domnaig." *Ériu* 2 (1905), 189–214.

——, ed. "Colman mac Duach and Guaire." *Ériu* 1 (1904), 44–48.

——, ed. "Mac Dá Cherda and Cummaine Foda." *Ériu* 5 (1911), 18–44.

——, ed. "The Rule of Patrick." *Ériu* 1 (1904), 216–24.

O'Neill, Joseph, ed. "The Rule of Ailbe of Emly," *Ériu* 3 (1907), 92–115.

Ó Riain, Pádraig, ed. *Corpus Genealogiarum Sanctorum Hiberniae*. Dublin, 1985.

Oskamp, H. P. A., ed. *The Voyage of Máel Dúin*. Groningen, 1970.

Plummer, Charles, ed. *Bethada Náem nÉrenn*. 2 vols. Oxford, 1922.

——, ed. *Irish Litanies*. Henry Bradshaw Society, vol. 62. London, 1925.

——, ed. *Miscellanea hagiographica Hibernica*. Subsidia Hagiographica 15. Brussels, 1925.

——, ed. *Vitae sanctorum Hiberniae*. 2 vols. Oxford, 1910.

——, trans. "Cáin Éimíne Báin." *Ériu* 4 (1910), 39–46.

Poppe, E. "A Middle Irish Poem on Éimíne's Bell." *Celtica* 17 (1985), 59–72.

Selmer, C., ed. *Navigatio Sancti Brendani Abbatis*. Notre Dame, Ind., 1959.

Stokes, Whitely. "The Adventure of St. Columba's Clerics." *Revue Celtique* 26 (1905), 130–70.

——. "The Birth and Life of St. Moling." *Revue Celtique* 26 (1906), 257–312.

——, ed. *Félire Óengusso Céli Dé*. Henry Bradshaw Society, vol. 29. London, 1905.

——, ed. *Lives of the Saints from the Book of Lismore*. Oxford, 1890.

——, ed. *The Tripartite Life of Patrick and Other Documents Relating to the Saint*. London, 1887.

——, ed. and trans. "The Voyage of the Hui Corra." *Revue Celtique* 14 (1893), 22–69.

Strachan, John. "An Old Irish Metrical Rule." *Ériu* 1 (1904), 191–208.

—— and J. G. O'Keeffe, eds. *Táin Bó Cúailnge from the Yellow Book of Lecan*. Dublin, rpt. 1967.

Ulster Society for Medieval Latin Studies, ed. "The Life of Saint Monenna by Conchubranus." I, *Seanchas Ard Mhacha* 9 (1979), 250–73; II, 10 (1980–81), 117–40; 10 (1982), 426–53.

Van Hamel, A. G., ed. *Immrama*. Dublin, 1941.

Walker, G. S. M., ed. *Sancti Columbani Opera*. Dublin, 1957.

Wasserschleben, H., ed. *Die irische Kanonensammlung*. Leipzig, 1885.

Secondary Sources

Aalen, F. H. A. *Man and the Landscape in Ireland*. London and New York, 1978.

Aldridge, R. B. "Notes on Children's Burial Grounds in Mayo." JRSAI 99 (1969), 83–87.

Baker, Alan R. H., and Robin Butler, eds. *Studies of Field Systems in the British Isles*. Cambridge, 1973.

Baker, Derek, ed. *The Church in Town and Countryside*. London, 1979.

Barnes, J. A. "Social Networks." *Addison-Wesley Modules in Anthropology* 26 (1972), 1–29.

Barrett, Gillian. "Problem of Spatial and Temporal Continuity of Rural Settlement in Ireland, 400 to 1169." *Journal of Historical Geography* 8 (1982), 245–60.

——. "The Reconstruction of Proto-historic Landscapes Using Aerial Photography: Case Studies in County Louth." *Journal of the County Louth Archaeological and Historical Society* 20 (1983), 215–36.

Barry, J. "The Appointment of Coarb and Erenagh." IER 93 (1960), 361–65.

——. "The Coarb in Medieval Times." IER 59 (1958), 24–35.

——. "The Distinction between Coarb and Erenagh." IER 104 (1960), 90–95.

——. "The Duties of Coarb and Erenagh." IER 104 (1960), 211–18.

——. "The Erenagh in the Monastic Irish Church." IER 59 (1958), 424–32.

——. "The Status of Coarbs and Erenaghs." IER 94 (1960), 147–53.

Bateson, J. D. "Further finds of Roman Material from Ireland." PRIA 76 C (1974), 171–80.

Berlière, U. "La familia dans les monastères bénédictines du Moyen Age." *Académie Royale du Belgique* 29 (Brussels, 1931).

——. "Le nombre des moines dans les anciens monastères." *Revue bénédictine* 41 (1929), 231–61; 42 (1930), 19–42.

Bethell, D. L. T. "The Originality of the Early Irish Church." JRSAI III (1981), 36–49.

Bieler, Ludwig. "The Celtic Hagiographer." *Studia Patristica* 5 (1962). Also in *Texte und untersuchungen zu Geschichte der altchristlichen Literatur* 80 (1959), 243–65.

——. "Christianity in Ireland during the 5th and 6th Centuries: A Survey and Evaluation of the Sources." IER 101 (1964), 162–67.

——. "The Christianization of the Insular Celts during the Sub-Roman Period and Its Repercussions on the Continent." *Celtica* 8 (1968), 112–25.

——. "Hagiography and Romance in Medieval Ireland." *Medievalia et Humanistica* n.s. 6 (1975), 13–24.

Binchy, D. A. *Celtic and Anglo-Saxon Kingship.* Oxford, 1970.

——. "Irish History and Irish Law." *Studia Hibernica* 15 (1975), 7–36; 16 (1976), 7–45.

——. "St. Patrick and His Biographers, Ancient and Modern," *Studia Hibernica* 2 (1962), 7–173.

——. "Sick-Maintenance in Irish Law," *Ériu* 12 (1934–38), 78–134.

Bitel, L. "Women's Monastic Enclosures in Early Ireland: A Study of Female Spirituality and Male Monastic Mentalities." *Journal of Medieval History* 12 (1986), 15–36.

Bossy, John, ed. *Disputes and Settlements: Law and Human Relations in the West.* Cambridge, 1983.

Bourgeault, Cynthia. "The Monastic Archetype in the Navigatio of St. Brendan." *Monastic Studies* 14 (1983), 109–22.

Bowen, E. G. "The Geography of Early Monasticism in Ireland." *Studia Celtica* 7 (1972), 30–44.

——. "The Irish Sea in the Age of the Saints." *Studia Celtica* 4 (1969), 56–71.

——. *Saints, Seaways, and Settlements in the Celtic Lands.* Cardiff, 1969.

Bowen, H. C., and P. J. Fowler, eds. *Early Land Allotment in the British Isles.* Oxford, 1978.

Breatnach, Liam. "Canon Law and Secular Law in Early Christian Ireland: The Significance of Bretha Nemed." *Peritia* 3 (1984), 439–59.

Brown, Peter. *The Cult of the Saints: Its Rise and Function in Latin Christianity.* Chicago, 1981.

——. The Rise and Function of the Holy Man in Late Antiquity." *Journal of Roman Studies* 61 (1971), 80–101.

Buchanan, R. H., et al., eds. *Man and His Habitat: Essays Presented to Emyr Estyn Evans.* London, 1971.

Burn, A. R. "Holy Men on Islands." *Glasgow Archaeological Journal* 1 (1969), 2–5.

Bynum, Caroline. *Holy Feast and Holy Fast: The Religious Significance of Food to Medieval Women.* Berkeley and Los Angeles, 1982.

Byrne, Francis John. *Irish Kings and High-Kings.* London, 1973.

——. "'Senchas': The Nature of Gaelic Historical Tradition." *Historical Studies* 9. Belfast, 1974.

——. "Seventh-Century Documents." IER 108 (1967), 164–82.

Carney, James. *Studies in Irish Language and Literature.* Dublin, 1955.

Case, H. J., et al. "Land Use in Goodland Townland, Co. Antrim, from Neolithic Times until Today." JRSAI 99 (1969), 39–53.

Centro Italiana di Studi Sull' Alto Medioevo. *Le Chiese nei regni dell 'Europa occidentalle.* Spoleto, 1960.

Charles-Edwards, Thomas. "The Social Background to Irish *Peregrinatio.*" *Celtica* 11 (1976), 43–59.

Clarke, H. B., and M. Brennan, ed. *Columbanus and Merovingian Monasticism.* Oxford, 1981.

Constable, Giles. "Monachisme et pèlerinage au Moyen Age." *Revue Historique* 523 (June–September 1977), 3–28.

Corish, Patrick. *The Christian Mission.* Dublin, 1972.

——. "The Pastoral Mission in the Early Irish Church." *Léachtaí Choluim Cille 1971: II. Stair* (1971), 14–25.

Crozier, Isabel R., and Lily C. Rea. "Bullauns and Other Basin-Stones." UJA 3 (1940), 104–14.

Culleton, E. B., and G. Mitchell. "Soil Erosion Following Deforestation in the Early Christian Period in South Wexford." JRSAI 106 (1976), 120–23.

Cuppage, Judith, et al., eds. *Archaeological Survey of the Dingle Peninsula.* Ballyferriter, 1986.

Dark, K. R. "Celtic Monastic Archaeology 5th to 8th Centuries." *Monastic Studies* 14 (1983), 17–30.

Davies, O. "Contributions to the Study of Crannogs." UJA 8 (1945), 14–30.

Davies, Wendy. "Clerics as Rulers: Some Implications of the Terminology of Ecclesiastical Authority in Early Medieval Ireland." In *Latin and the Vernacular Languages in Early Medieval Europe,* ed. N. P. Brooks, 81–98. Leicester, 1982.

—— and Paul Fouracre, eds. *The Settlement of Disputes in Early Medieval Europe.* Cambridge, 1986.

Davy, Marie-Magdeleine. "Le thème du désert dans le monachisme chrétien." In *Le désert et la quête,*ed. Stella Corbin and Jean-Louis Vieillard-Baron, 45–70. Cahiers de l'Université Saint Jean de Jerusalem 8. Paris, 1982.

Delaruelle, E. "Le travail dans les règles monastiques occidentales, 4ᶜ–9ᶜ siècles." *Journal de psychologie normale et pathologique* 41 (1968), 51–62.

de Paor, Liam. *The Peoples of Ireland*. South Bend, Ind., 1986.

——. "Saint Mac Creiche of Liscannor." *Ériu* 30 (1979), 93–121.

——. "A Survey of Sceilg Mhichíl." JRSAI 85 (1955), 174–87.

Dillon, Myles. *Early Irish Literature*. Chicago, 1948.

Doherty, Charles. "Exchange and Trade in Early Medieval Ireland." JRSAI 110 (1980), 67–89.

——. "The Historical Value of the Medieval Lives of Máedóc of Ferns." 2 vols. Master's thesis, University College, Dublin, 1971.

——. "Monastic Towns in Early Medieval Ireland." In *The Comparative History of Urban Origins in Non-Roman Europe,* ed. A. B. Clarke and A. Simms, 45–75. Oxford, 1984.

——. "Some Aspects of Hagiography as a Source for Irish Economic History," *Peritia* 1 (1982), 300–328.

Drury, H. C. "The Rush Light and Its Associates." JRSAI 55 (1925), 99–111.

Duignan, Michael. "Irish Agriculture in Early Historic Times." JRSAI 74 (1944), 124–45.

Dumville, David. "Echtrae and Immram: Some Problems of Definition." *Ériu* 27 (1976), 73–94.

Eliade, Mircea. *Cosmos and History*. New York, 1959; rpt. 1970.

Evans, E. E. *Irish Folk-Ways*. London and Boston, 1957; rpt. 1976.

——. *The Personality of Ireland: Habitat, Heritage, and History,* Cambridge, 1973.

——. *Prehistoric and Early Christian Ireland: A Guide*. London, 1966.

Fanning, Thomas. "Excavation of an Early Christian Cemetery and Settlement at Reask, Co. Kerry." PRIA 81 C (1981), 67–172.

Fichtenau, Heinrich. *Lebensordungen des 10. Jahrhunderts*. 2 vols. Stuttgart, 1984.

Firey, Ann. "Cross-Examining the Witness: Recent Research in Celtic Monastic History," *Monastic Studies* 14 (1983), 31–51.

Firth, R. "Verbal and Bodily Rituals of Greeting and Parting." In *Interpretation of Ritual,* ed. Jean La Fontaine, 1–38. London, 1972.

Fleetwood, John F. *The History of Medicine in Ireland*. Dublin, 1957; rpt. 1983.

Ford, Patrick, ed. *Celtic Folklore and Christianity*. Santa Barbara, Calif., 1975.

Foster, George, and Barbara G. Anderson, eds. *Medical Anthropology*. New York, 1978.

Fuhrmann, Joseph P. *Irish Medieval Monasteries on the Continent*. Washington, D.C., 1927.

Gaiffier, B. de "Hagiographie et historiographie." *Subsidia Hagiographica* 61 (1977), 139–66.

——. "Mentalité de l'hagiographie médiévale." *Analecta Bollandiana* 86 (1968), 391–99.

——. "Les revendications de biens dans quelques documents hagiographiques." *Analecta Bollandiana* 50 (1932), 123–28.

Gardiner, M. J., and P. Ryan. "A New Generalised Soil Map of Ireland and Its Land-Use Interpretation." *Irish Journal of Agricultural Research* 9 (1969), 95–109.

Geary, Patrick J. *Furta Sacra: Thefts of Relics in the Central Middle Ages.* Princeton, N.J., 1978.

——. "Vivre en conflit dans une France sans état: Typologie des mécanismes de règlement des conflits (1050–1200)." *Annales, E.S.C.* 41 (September–October 1986), 1107–34.

Geertz, Clifford. "Religion as a Cultural System." In *The Interpretation of Cultures,* 87–125. New York, 1973.

Goody, Jack. *Cooking, Cuisine, and Class.* Cambridge, 1982.

——. *The Devlopment of the Family and Marriage in Europe.* Cambridge, 1983.

Gougaud, L. "Étude sur les loricae et sur les prières qui s'en rapprochent." *Bulletin d'ancienne littérature et d'archaéologie chrétiennes* 1 (1911), 265–81; 2 (1912), 33–41, 101–27.

Graham, J. "Anglo-Norman Settlement in Meath." PRIA 75 C (1975), 233–44.

Graus, František. *Volk, Herrscher und Heiliger im Reich der Merowinger: Studien zur Hagiographie der Merowingerzeit.* Prague, 1965.

Grosjean, Paul. "Édition et commentaire du Catalogus sanctorum Hiberniae." *Analecta Bollandiana* 73 (1955), 197–213, 289–322.

——. "Notes d'hagiographie celtiques." *Analecta Bollandiana,* 1943–1963.

Gwynn, Aubrey. "Ireland and the Continent in the Eleventh Century." *Irish Historical Studies* 8 (1952/53), 193–216.

Gwynn, Aubrey, and R. Neville Hadcock. *Medieval Religious Houses: Ireland (With an Appendix to Early Sites).* London, 1970.

Hamlin, Ann. "The Archaeology of Early Christianity in the North of Ireland." 3 vols. Master's thesis, Queen's University, Belfast, 1976.

Hamlin, Ann, and Claire Foley. "A Women's Graveyard at Carrickmore, Co. Tyrone, and the Separate Burial of Women." UJA 46 (1983), 41–46.

Heist, W. W. "Hagiography, Chiefly Celtic, and Recent Developments in Folklore." In *Hagiographie, cultures, et société, IVᵉ–XIIᵉ siècles: Actes du colloque organisé à Centre de recherches sur l'antiquité tardive et le haut moyen age,* 121–42. Paris, 1981.

——. "Irish Saints' Lives, Romance, and Cultural History." *Medievalia et Humanistica* n.s. 6 (1975), 25–40.

Henry, Françoise. "Early Irish Monastic Beehive Huts and Dry-Stone Houses in the Neighbourhood of Cahirciveen and Waterville." PRIA 58 C (1957), 45–166.

——. *Irish Art during the Viking Invasions.* London, 1967.

——. *Irish Art to 800.* London, 1965.

——. "Remains of the Early Christian Period on Inishkea North, Co. Mayo." JRSAI 95 (1945), 128–55.

Herity, Michael. "The Building and Layout of Early Irish Monasteries before the Year 1000." *Monastic Studies* 14 (1983), 247–84.

——. "The High Island Hermitage." *Irish University Review* 7 (1977), 52–69.

——. "Prehistoric Fields in Ireland." *Irish University Review* (1971), 258–65.

——. "A Survey of the Royal Site of Cruachain in Connacht." JRSAI 113 (1983), 121–42.

Herlihy, David. *Medieval Households*. Cambridge, Mass., 1985.

Hogan, E. I., ed. *Onomasticon Goedelicum locorum et tribuum Hiberniae et Scotiae*. Dublin, 1910.

Horden, Peregrine. "Saints and Doctors in the Early Byzantine Empire: The Case of Theodore of Sykeon." In *The Church and Healing*, ed. W. J. Sheils, 1–13. London, 1982.

Hughes, Kathleen. "The Changing Theory and Practise of Irish Pilgrimage." *Journal of Ecclesiastical History* 11 (1960), 143–51.

——. *The Church in Early Irish Society*. London, 1966.

——. "The Cult of St. Finnian of Clonard from the Eighth to the Eleventh Century," *Irish Historical Studies* 9 (1954–55), 13–27.

——. "The Distribution of Irish Scriptoria and Centres of Learning from 730 to 1111." In *Studies in the Early British Church*, ed. Nora Chadwick, 243–72. Cambridge, 1958.

——. *Early Christian Ireland: An Introduction to the Sources*. London, 1973.

——. "The Historical Value of the Lives of St. Finnian of Clonard." *English Historical Review* 272 (July 1954), 353–72.

——. "Some Aspects of Irish Influence on Early English Private Prayer." *Studia Celtica* 5 (1970), 48–61.

—— and Ann Hamlin. *Celtic Monasticism: The Modern Traveller to the Early Irish Church*. New York, 1977.

Hurley, Vincent. "Additions to the Map of Monastic Ireland: The Southwest," JCHAS 85 (1980), 52–65.

James, Edward. "Bede and the Tonsure Question." *Peritia* 3 (1984), 85–94.

Jones, M. E. "Climate, Nutrition, and Disease: An Hypothesis." In *The End of Roman Britain*, ed. P. J. Casey, 231–50. Oxford, 1979.

Kelleher, John V. "Early Irish History and Pseudo-History." *Studia Hibernica* 3 (1963), 113–27.

——. "The Pre-Norman Irish Genealogies." *Irish Historical Studies* 16 (1968), 138–53.

——. "The Táin and the Annals." *Ériu* 22 (1971), 107–29.

Kelly, Fergus. *A Guide to Early Irish Law*. Dublin, 1988.

Kenney, James F. *Sources for the Early History of Ireland*. Vol. 1, Ecclesiastical. New York, 1929; rpt. Dublin, 1979.

Kleinman, Arthur. *Patients and Healers in the Context of Culture*. Berkeley and Los Angeles, 1980.

Lacy, Brian, et al., eds. *Archaeological Survey of County Donegal*. Dublin, 1983.

Laing, Lloyd, ed. *Studies in Celtic Survival*. Oxford, 1977.

Lawlor, H. C. *The Monastery of Saint Mochaoi of Nendrum*. Belfast, 1925.

Leask, Harold G. *Irish Churches and Monastic Buildings*. Vol. 1, *The First Phases and the Romanesque*. Dundalk, 1955; 2d ed. 1977.

Lesne, Emile. *Histoire de la propriété écclesiastique en France*. 6 vols. Paris, 1943.

Little, Lester K. "La morphologie des malédictions monastiques." *Annales, E.S.C.* 34 (1979), 43–60.

Löwe, Heinrich, ed. *Die Iren und Europa im früheren Mittelalter*. 2 vols. Stuttgart, 1982.

Lucas, A. T. "Irish Food before the Potato." *Gwerin* (1960), 8–43.

———. "Irish-Norse Relations: Time for a Reappraisal?" JCHAS 71 (1966), 62–75.

———. "The Plundering and Burning of Churches in Ireland, 7th to 16th Century." In *North Munster Studies,* ed. Etienne Rynne, 172–229. Limerick, 1967.

———. "The Sacred Trees of Ireland." JCHAS 68 (1963), 16–54.

Lynch, Ann. *Man and Environment in Southwest Ireland, 4000 B.C.–A.D. 800.* Oxford, 1981.

Lynn, C. J. "Early Christian Period Domestic Structures: A Change from Round to Rectangular Plans?" *Irish Archaeological Research Forum* 5 (1978), 29–45.

———. "Early Christian Period Site in Ballybrolly, Co. Armagh." UJA 46 (1983), 47–51.

———. "The Medieval Ringfort—An Archeological Chimera?" *Irish Archaeological Research Forum* 2 (1975), 29–36.

MacAlister, R. A. S. *Ancient Ireland.* London, 1935.

———. "The Ancient Road in the Bog of Allen." JRSAI 62 (1932), 137–41.

Mac Cana, Proinsias. "Mongan Mac Fiachna and *Immram Brain.*" *Ériu* 23 (1972), 102–42.

———. "The Prehistory of *Immram Brain.*" *Ériu* 25 (1974), 33–52.

———. "The Sinless Otherworld of *Immram Brain.*" *Ériu* 27 (1976), 95–115.

McCone, Kim. "Brigit in the Seventh Century: A Saint with Three Lives?" *Peritia* 1 (1982), 107–45.

———. "Clones and Her Neighbors in the Early Period: Hints from Some Airgialla Saints' Lives." *Clogher Record* 11 (1984), 305–25.

———. "An Introduction to Early Irish Saints' Lives." *Maynooth Review* 11 (1984), 26–59.

MacDonald, Aidan. "Aspects of the Monastery and Monastic Life in Adomnán's Life of Columba." *Peritia* 3 (1984), 271–302.

Mac Eoin, Gearóid. "The Invocation of Nature in the Loricae." *Studia Hibernica* 2 (1962), 212–17.

McNeill, John T. *The Celtic Churches.* Chicago, 1974.

Manning, C. "Early Christian Enclosures of Killederdadram, in Lackenavorna, Co. Tipperary." PRIA 84 C (1984), 237–80.

Mitchell, Frank. *The Irish Landscape.* London, 1976.

Mitchell, J. "Social Networks." *Annual Review of Anthropology* (1974), 279–99.

Moody, T. W., F. X. Martin, and F. J. Byrne, eds. *The New History of Ireland.* Oxford, 1976–. Vol. 9, *Maps, Genealogies, Lists.*

Morris, J. "The Dates of the Celtic Saints." *Journal of Theological Studies* 17 (1966), 341–91.

Nees, Lawrence. "The Colophon Drawing in the Book of Mulling." CMCS 5 (1983), 67–91.

Ní Chatháin, Proinséas, and Michael Richter, eds. *Ireland and Europe.* Stuttgart, 1984.

Ní Donnchadha, Máirín. "The Guarantor List of Cáin Adamnáin, 697." *Peritia* 1 (1982), 178–215.

Norman, E. R., and J. K. S. St. Joseph. *The Early Development of Irish Society.* Cambridge, 1964.

Ó Briain, Felim. "The Expansion of Christianity to 1200: An Historiographical Study." *Irish Historical Studies* 3 (1942–43), 241–66; 4 (1944–45), 131–63.

——. "Irish Hagiography: Historiography and Method." In *Measgra i gCuimhne Mhíchíl Uí Chléirigh,* ed. S. O'Brien, 119–31. Dublin, 1944.

——. "Miracles in the lives of the Irish Saints." *Irish Ecclesiastical Record* 66 (1945), 331–42.

——. "Saga Themes in Irish Hagiography." In *Féilsgríbhinn Torna,* ed. Séamus Pender, 25–40. Cork, 1947.

O'Brien, D. M. "A List of Some Archaeological Sites on the Berehaven Peninsula." JCHAS 75 (1979), 12–25.

O'Connell, M. "The Developmental History of Scragh Bog, Co. Westmeath, and the Vegetational History of Its Hinterland." *New Phytologist* 85 (1980), 301–19.

O'Connor, F. J. "Solar Eclipses Visible in Ireland between A.D. 400 and A.D. 1000." PRIA 56 A (1952), 61–72.

Ó Corráin, Donnchadh. "Dál Cais—Church and Dynasty." *Ériu* 24 (1973), 52–63.

——. *Ireland before the Normans.* Dublin, 1972.

——. "Nationality and Kingship in Pre-Norman Ireland." In *Nationality and the Pursuit of Independence,* ed. T. W. Moody. *Historical Studies* 11. Belfast, 1978.

——. ed. *Irish Antiquity.* Cork, 1980.

Ó Corráin, Donnchadh, Liam Breatnach, and Aidan Breen. "The Laws of the Irish." *Peritia* 3 (1984), 382–438.

O'Dwyer, P. *Céli Dé.* Dublin, 1981.

Ó Fiaich, Tomas. "The Church of Armagh under Lay Control." *Seanchas Ard Mhacha* 5 (1969), 75–127.

——. "Irish Peregrini on the Continent." *Irish Ecclesiastical Review* 103 (1965), 233–40.

O'Kelly, M. J. "Church Island near Valencia, Co. Kerry." PRIA 59 C (1958), 57–136.

——. "An Island Settlement at Beginish." PRIA 57 C (1956), 159–94.

——. "Monastic Sites in the West of Ireland." *Scottish Archaeological Forum* 5 (1973), 1–16.

Olmsted, G. S. "A Contemporary View of Irish Hill-Top Enclosures," *Études celtiques* 16 (1979), 171–86.

O'Neill Hencken, H. "Balinderry Crannog, No. 2." PRIA 47 C (1941–42), 1–76.

Ó Riain, Pádraig. "Battle-Site and Territorial Extent in Early Ireland." ZCP 33 (1974), 67–80.

——. "Boundary Association in Early Irish Society." *Studia Celtica* 7 (1972), 12–29.

——. "Cainnech Alias Columcille, Patron of Ossory." In *Folia Gadelica,* ed. Pádraig de Brun, et al., 20–35. Cork, 1983.

——. "The Composition of the Irish Section of the Calendar of Saints." *Dinnseanchas* 6 (1975), 77–92.

——. "St. Findbarr: A Study in the Cult." JCHAS 72 (1976), 63–82.

——. "Towards a Methodology in Early Irish Hagiography." *Peritia* 1 (1982), 146–59.

——. "Traces of Lug in Early Irish Hagiographical Tradition." ZCP 36 (1977), 138–56.

Otway-Ruthven, J. "The Organization of Irish Agriculture in the Middle Ages." JRSAI 81 (1951), 1–13.

Pearce, S. M., ed. *The Early Church in Western Britain and Ireland*. Oxford, 1982.

Poulin, Jean-Claude. *L'idéal de sainteté dans l'Aquitaine carolingienne d'après les sources hagiographiques, 750–950*. Quebec, 1975.

Power, Patrick, ed. *Críchad an Chaoilli*. Cork, 1932.

Praeger, R. Lloyd. *The Irish Landscape*. Cork, 1953.

Prinz, F. "Aristocracy and Christianity in Merovingian Gaul." In *Gesellschaft-Kultur-Literatur: Beitrage Liutpold Wallach gewidmet*, ed. K. Bosl. Stuttgart, 1975.

——. *Frühes Mönchtum im Frankenreich: Kultur und Gesellschaft in Gallien, den Rheinlanden und Bayern am Beispiel der monastischen Entwicklung (4. bis. 8. Jahrhundert)*. Munich and Vienna, 1965.

Proudfoot, V. B. "The Economy of the Irish Rath." *Medieval Archaeology* 5 (1961), 106–15.

——. "Further Excavations at Shaneen Park, Belfast. Ballyaghagan Townland, Co. Antrim." UJA 21 (1958), 18–38.

Raftis, James A. "Western Monasticism and Economic Organization." *Comparative Studies in Society and History* 3 (1961), 452–69.

Rahtz, Philip. "Monasteries as Settlements." *Scottish Archaeological Forum* 5 (1973), 125–35.

Reece, Richard. "Recent Work on Iona." *Scottish Archaeological Forum* 5 (1973), 36–46.

Rees, Alwyn, and Brinley Rees. *Celtic Heritage*. London, 1961.

Reeves-Smyth, Terence, and Fred Hamond, eds. *Landscape Archaeology in Ireland*. Oxford, 1983.

Renfrew, Colin. *Approaches to Social Archaeology*. Southampton, 1984.

Robinson, F. "Notes on the Irish Practice of Fasting as a Means of Distraint." In *Putnam Anniversary Volume*, 567–83. Cedar Rapids, Ia., 1909.

Rohan, P. K. *The Climate of Ireland*. Dublin, 1975.

Rousselle, Aline. "Abstinence et continence dans les monastères de Gaule Méridionale à la fin de l'antiquité et au début du Moyen Age: Étude d'un régime alimentaire et de sa fonction." In *Hommages à André Dupont*, 239–54. Montpellier, 1974.

——. "Du sanctuaire au thaumaturge: Le guérison en Gaule en IVe siècle." *Annales, E.S.C.* 31 (1976), 1085–1107.

Royal Commission on the Ancient and Historical Monuments of Scotland. *Argyll*. Vol. 4, *Iona*. Edinburgh, 1982.

Ryan, John. *Irish Monasticism: Origins and Early Development*. Dublin, 1931.

——, ed. *Féil-sgríbhinn Eóin mhic Néill*. Dublin, 1940.

Seiber, J. *Early Byzantine Urban Saints*. Oxford, 1977.

Sharpe, Richard. "Hiberno-Latin *Laicus*, Irish *Láech* and the Devil's Men." *Ériu* 30 (1979), 75–92.

——. "Some Problems Concerning the Organization of the Church in Early Medieval Ireland." *Peritia* 3 (1984), 230–70.

——. "Vitae S. Brigidae: The Oldest Texts." *Peritia* 1 (1982), 81–106.

Sheehy, Maurice. "The Collectio Canonum Hibernicum—A Celtic Phenomenon." In *Die Iren und Europa im früheren Mittlealter,* ed. Heinrich Löwe, 1:525–35. Stuttgart, 1982.

Sigal, Pierre-André. *L'homme et le miracle dans la France médiévale (XIᵉ–XIIᵉ siècle).* Paris, 1985.

Simms, Katherine. "Guesting and Feasting in Gaelic Ireland." JRSAI 108 (1978), 67–100.

Smyth, A. P. *Celtic Leinster.* Blackrock, 1982.

Somerville, Boyle. "'The Fort' on Knock Drum, West Carberry, County Cork." JRSAI 61 (1931), 1–14.

Stalley, Roger. *The Cistercian Monasteries of Ireland: An Account of the History, Art and Architecture of the White Monks in Ireland from 1142 to 1540.* London and New Haven, Conn., 1987.

Stancliffe, Clare. *St. Martin and His Hagiographer: History and Miracle in Sulpicius Severus.* Oxford, 1983.

Swan, Leo. "The Hill of Tara, Co. Meath: The Evidence of Aerial Photography." JRSAI 108 (1978), 51–66.

——. "The Recognition and Recovery of Ecclesiastical Enclosures by Aerial Observation and Air Photography." 3 vols. Master's thesis, University College, Dublin, 1971.

Tambiah, Stanley. "The Magical Power of Words." *Man* 3 (1968), 175–208.

——. *A Performative Approach to Ritual.* Oxford, 1979.

Thomas, Charles. *Christianity in Roman Britain to A.D. 500.* London, 1981; rpt. 1985.

——. *The Early Christian Archaeology of North Britain.* Oxford, 1971.

Thrall, F. W. "Clerical Sea Pilgrimages and Immrama." In *The Manly Anniversary Studies in Language and Literature.* Chicago, 1923.

Thurneysen, Rudolf. "Zur Nomentypus abret. to-woedoc air do-dimoc." ZCP 19 (1933), 354–67.

Toumey, C. P. "Raths and Clachans: The Homogeneity of Early Irish Society." *Éire-Ireland* 15 (1980), 86–105.

Turner, Victor, *Dramas, Fields, and Metaphors.* Ithaca, N.Y., 1974.

——. *The Ritual Process.* Ithaca, N.Y., 1969.

Turner, Victor, and Edith Turner. *Image and Pilgrimage in Christian Culture.* New York, 1978.

Ullmann, Walter. "Public Welfare and Social Legislation in the Early Medieval Councils." *Studies in Church History* 7 (1971), 1–39.

Vauchez, André. *La sainteté en occident aux dernières siècles du moyen age.* Paris, 1981.

Wailes, Bernard. "Irish Royal Sites in History and Archaeology." CMCS 3 (1982), 1–29.

Walsh, Paul. "The Monastic Settlement on Rathlin O'Birne Island, County Donegal." JRSAI 113 (1983), 53–66.

Ward, Benedicta. *Miracles and the Medieval Mind.* London. 1982.

Warner, R. B. "Some Observations on Exotic Material in Ireland." PRIA 76 C (1976), 267–92.

Waterman, D. M. "A Marshland Habitation Site near Larne, Co. Antrim." UJA 34 (1971), 65–76.

——. "A Neolithic and Dark Age Site at Langford Lodge, Co. Antrim." UJA 26 (1963), 43–78.

Watt, John. *The Church and the Two Nations in Medieval Ireland.* Cambridge, 1970.

Wemple, Suzanne. *Women in Frankish Society: Marriage and the Cloister, 500 to 900.* Philadelphia, 1981.

White, Stephen. "Feuding and Peace-making in the Touraine around the Year 1100." *Traditio* 42 (1986), 195–263.

Wollasch, J. "Parenté noble et monachisme réformateur." *Revue Historique* 535 (June–September 1980), 3–24.

Young, B. K. "Exemple aristocratique et mode funéraire dans la Gaule mérovingienne." *Annales, E.S.C.* 41 (1986), 379–407.

Subject Index

Abbots and abbesses, 89–90, 97–98, 138–40, 166, 239–40; affective relations of, 90–92; as political mediators, 150–52

Agriculture, 23–27

Airchinnech, 139–41

Angels, 32, 55, 62, 121, 131, 132, 206, 212, 215, 231, 232

Animals: domestic, 23, 33–34, 134; wild, 32–33, 55

Anmcharae, 92–94

Athláig, 108–9, 170, 212, 233

Bachall, 61, 150–51, 158

Bachall Ísu, 153, 240

Baptism, 73

Bíli, 44–45

Bishops, 141, 241

Blessing, 63, 125, 132, 156

Boundaries, 34, 58–66, 82. See also Fords

Bullauns, 51, 186

Burial, 127

Cáin Adamnáin, 163–65

Cána and *cúarta*, 163–66, 186, 192

Céili dé, 92–93, 126, 142, 229–30

Celibacy, 105, 126

Cemeteries and shrines, 50–51, 66–70, 185

Children, 106–8, 179–80

Churches, 70–73, 239

Clients and clientage: base, 118–19; extra-legal, 169–70, 187–89; free, 117–18; monastic, 115–28

Climate, 7, 19–20, 26

Confession, 92–93, 126

Confessor. See Monastic officers

Consecration of space, 61–63

Crafts and craftsmen, 129–30, 135

Crosses, 51, 52, 64–66, 78

Cursing, 124, 152–55, 165, 184, 219

Demons and devils, 32, 180–81, 206, 232

Diet, 109, 175, 208–10

Donations and endowments, 40–42, 98, 134, 158, 188–90. See also Rents and dues

Druids, 45, 169, 187. See also Pagans and paganism

Dues. See Rent and dues

Ecclesiastical reform, 236–41. See also Céili dé

Enclosures: external walls (*vallum*), 58–63; layout, 61–62, 74–76, 80–82, 201–2, 243; sacred centers, 66–79. See also Boundaries; Sacred space

Exile: Christian, 224–26; European, 226–28; legal, 223–224

Exorcism, 181, 206

Familiae. See Monastic families

Family. See Kinship and kinfolk

Fasting, 191, 210–11; *aíne*, 213–14; *troscud*, 213–17

Feasting, 203, 207–9

Fords, 45–46

Fosterage. See Kinship and kinfolk

Index of Proper
Names and Places

Index